PASSCHENDAELE

PEN & SWORD MILITARY CLASSICS

We hope you enjoy your Pen and Sword Military Classic. The series is designed to give readers quality military history at affordable prices. Pen and Sword Classics are available from all good bookshops. If you would like to keep in touch with further developments in the series,

Telephone: **01226 734555**,
email: **enquiries@pen-and-sword.co.uk**,
or visit our website at **www.pen-and-sword.co.uk**.

PASSCHENDAELE

The Story Behind the Tragic Victory of 1917

Philip Warner

PEN & SWORD MILITARY CLASSICS

First published in Great Britain in 1987 by Sidgwick & Jackson Limited
Published in this format in 2005 by
Pen & Sword Military Classics
An imprint of
Pen & Sword Books Ltd
47 Church Street
Barnsley
South Yorkshire
S70 2AS

ISBN 1 84415 305 3

Printed and bound in England
By CPI UK

Pen & Sword Books Ltd incorporates the Imprints of Pen & Sword Aviation,
Pen & Sword Maritime, Pen & Sword Military, Wharncliffe Local history, Pen & Sword Select,
Pen & Sword Military Classics and Leo Cooper.

For a complete list of Pen & Sword titles please contact
PEN & SWORD BOOKS LIMITED
47 Church Street, Barnsley, South Yorkshire, S70 2AS, England
E-mail: enquiries@pen-and-sword.co.uk
Website: www.pen-and-sword.co.uk

CONTENTS

Acknowledgements vii
List of Illustrations ix

1	It Must Come to a Fight	1
2	The Cockpit of Europe	15
3	The Preliminary Rounds	20
4	The Mines at Messines	32
5	Everywhere Successful	53
6	Did We Really Send Men to Fight in This?	66
7	See You Again in Hell	96
8	The Difficulties Were Greatly Underestimated	130
9	The Focus of a Spider's Web	169
10	The Supporters	191
11	The Other Side of the Hill	220
12	The View from the Trenches	239
13	Hindsight	252
14	Visiting the Battlefield Today	255

Select Bibliography 260
Index 263

ACKNOWLEDGEMENTS

I am deeply grateful to many people for their generous assistance to me while I was writing this book.

Mr Roderick Suddaby, Keeper of the Documents at the Imperial War Museum, greatly facilitated my research and drew my attention to many letters and diaries which have proved invaluable. Lord Blake very kindly gave me permission to quote from his book *The Private Diaries of Sir Douglas Haig 1914–19.* Mr J. W. Hunt, Mr M. H. Wright and the ever-helpful staff of the library at the Royal Military Academy, Sandhurst, gave me expert guidance on sources. Mr Leo Cooper has not merely given me essential advice but has also allowed me the free use of material of which he holds the copyright. Mr John Terraine, whose knowledge of the First World War is encyclopaedic, has tempered my judgements. Lieutenant-Colonel Alan Shepperd has always been available to give me the answers to difficult military questions. Mrs Desmond Allhusen very kindly provided all the information I requested about the late Major Desmond Allhusen's career. Mr Stephen Lushington allowed me to quote from his father's book, *The Gambardier*, and provided the further details I asked for. Mrs W. H. Lambert kindly supplied me with information about her father, the late Brigadier-General F. A. Maxwell VC, CSI, DSO, and allowed me to quote material of which she holds the copyright.

The executors of Dr Norman Gladden generously allowed me to quote freely from *Ypres 1917.* Siegfried Sassoon's poem 'The Troops' is quoted by kind permission of Mr George Sassoon. Mr Bruce Haigh, whom I met in Ypres, gave me very helpful advice about Australian source material.

The following publishers kindly gave me permission to quote from books for which they hold or control the copyright:

Methuen and Co. Ltd for Hugh Quigley, *Passchendaele and the Somme.*

William Heinemann Ltd for H. Dearden, *Medicine and Duty.*

Leo Cooper for E. C. Vaughan, *Some Desperate Glory*.

Century Hutchinson Publications Ltd for D. E. Hickey, *Rolling into Action*.

J. M. Dent and Sons Ltd for Huntly Gordon, *The Unreturning Army*.

Cassell and Co. Ltd. for B. H. Liddell-Hart, *History of the First World War*.

Every possible effort has been made to trace holders of any existing copyrights. If an existing copyright has inadvertently been overlooked, the claimant is requested to contact the author.

LIST OF ILLUSTRATIONS

Thomas, Haig, Joffre and Lloyd George.
Crown Prince Rupprecht of Bavaria.
Hindenburg, the Kaiser and Ludendorff.
German blockhouse in the remains of Remus Wood.
This was once Kemmel Château.
Gun crew at Pilckem Ridge.
Norton Griffiths, the mining expert.
Allied sappers using a geophone to detect counter-mining.
Germans counter-mining.
View from inside the Spanbroekmolen crater.
A Mark IV tank, 12 October 1917.
Soldiers at Zonnebeke, October 1917.
Duckboards over the mud at Pilckem.
Stretcher-bearers at Pilckem Ridge.
A trench in the Ypres Salient, October 1917.
A typical Bairnsfather cartoon.
Ypres in 1914.
Ypres after the bombardment.
The choir of Ypres Cathedral in 1914.
The choir in 1917, reduced to rubble.
The medieval Cloth Hall of Ypres in 1914.
The Cloth Hall in ruins, seen from the cathedral.
All that remained of Hooge in 1917.
Passchendaele village, November 1917.
Passchendaele today.
Pastureland near Sanctuary Wood seven years after the battle.

The following maps of the battlefield are taken from a 1920s French source and a note on place names may be helpful.

Côte = hill; *B.* = *Bois* = wood; *F., Fe.* or *Fme.* = *Ferme* = Farm; *Etg.* or *Etang* = pond; *Chau.* = château; *Rte.* = *Route* = road

The British offensive of 7 June against Messines Ridge.

The front line before the Allies' offensive of 31 July.

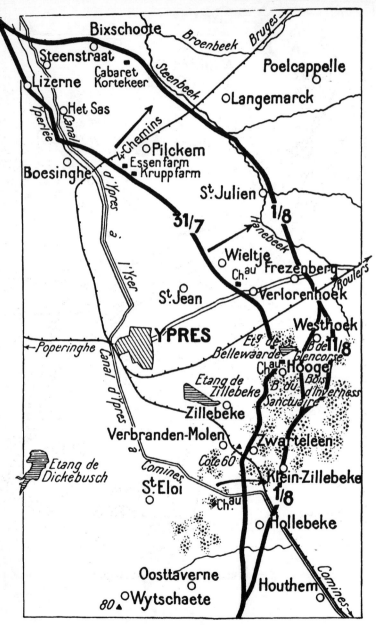

First stage of the Allies' advance: 31 July – 11 August.

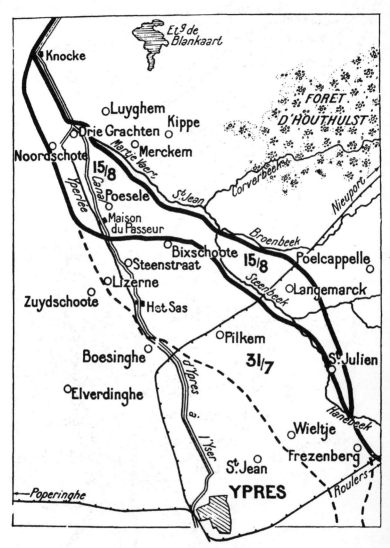

Second stage: the attack of 15 August.

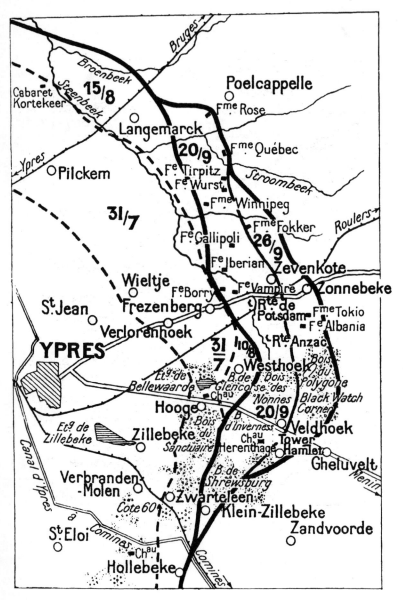

Third stage: the British advance of 20–26 September.

Fourth stage: 4 October.

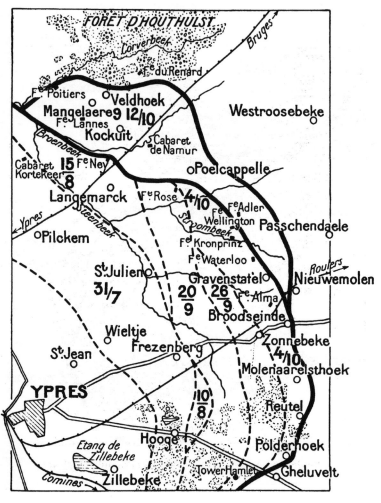

Fifth stage: the British approach Passchendaele.

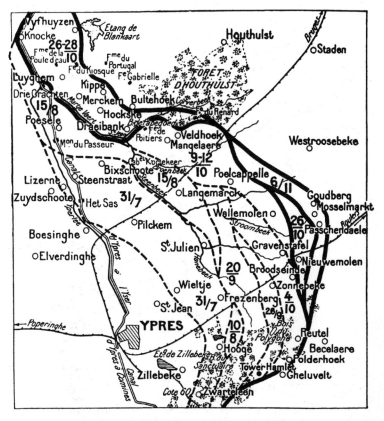

Sixth stage: by 6 November Ypres was completely cleared.

1

It Must Come to a Fight

Passchendaele is a small Belgian village, but it is also the name given to one of the most gruelling, bloody and bizarre battles of the First World War. The village itself was eventually captured by the Canadian 2nd Division, but before that happened approximately half a million men – British, French, Canadians, Australians, New Zealanders and, by no means least, Germans – had become casualties.[1] It is not merely the number of deaths which makes that battle in the autumn of 1917 unique in the history of warfare – it is the almost unimaginable horror of the circumstances. That men could survive such an experience and remain sane is, perhaps, even more astonishing than the death toll. On the Allied side 90,000 men were reported 'missing', which on this occasion was an official acknowledgement that they had been blown to unrecognizable fragments, drowned or suffocated in liquid mud. Usually the remains of a body can be identified by the tag worn on a cord round every soldier's neck. There are two discs: one red, one green. Each is marked with the name, religion and number of the soldier. When he is killed, one disc is taken and sent to records, while the other stays with the body so that it may be identified when that body is later reinterred in a war cemetery. This is the way in which 'missing' men, previously thought to have been killed, are identified. But at Passchendaele there was no trace of either bodies or ID tags of thousand upon thousand.

The Germans thought that Passchendaele was their worst battle of the war – worse, in fact, than Verdun, and Verdun was bad enough. Kuhl, the German historian and a former Chief of the German General Staff, wrote:

The sufferings, privations and exertions which the sol-

1

diers had to bear were inexpressible. Terrible was the spiritual burden on the lonely man in the shell hole, and terrible the strain on the nerves during the bombardments which continued day and night. The 'Hell of Verdun' was exceeded by Flanders. The Battle of Flanders [the German name for Passchendaele] has been called 'The greatest martyrdom of the World War'.

No division could last more than a fortnight in this hell. Then it had to be relieved by new troops. Looking back it seems that what was borne here was superhuman. With respect and thankfulness the German people will always remember the heroes of Flanders.

There is a reason behind every battle, however illogical in retrospect that reason may seem. The Battle of Passchendaele was inevitable in the strategic and tactical context of the First World War. It was not, however, an isolated battle, nor even the last of a series of battles. It took place in an area which in the past had known other bloody conflicts, an area whose geographical situation made battles for key points amost unavoidable, but what made Passchendaele so appalling was that it was fought when the weather made it almost – but not quite – impossible. If those who directed it had known the conditions in which Passchendaele would be fought, it is unlikely – though one cannot be certain of this – that they would have embarked on it. It is said that Kiggell, Haig's Chief of Staff, wept when he eventually reached the mere edge of the battlefield, and exclaimed, 'Did we really send men to fight in this?'

Seventy years later the events which eventually led to Passchendaele have become clearer, and the battle's origins can be seen to go back a long way. They are also the origins of the First World War, and it is necessary to examine them in order to grasp the feelings of frustration on both sides which made the battle take the course it did. Those events started with Bismarck's successful campaign for the transformation of Germany, under Prussian leadership, from a collection of independent states into a modern industrial power, complete with colonies to provide both raw materials and outlets for manufactured goods. It had begun with

Prussia's war against Denmark, which was won within three months in 1864. Prussia fought another tidy little war with Austria in 1866, all finished within six weeks; and a slightly longer one with France in 1870, but that too was over in six months. However these, Bismarck and his successors realized, were only interim wars. France, caught in a weak moment, had been defeated, but it had learnt its lesson and would not be so easily dealt with next time. There remained Russia and, of course, Great Britain. Russia blocked German expansion to the east, while France and Britain prevented any movement into the Mediterranean region.

By 1914 Germany had made considerable progress with the formation of a colonial empire, but it was obvious that she had come into the field late and had only acquired the less desirable colonies, the territories which other countries felt they could spare. The rich prizes, like India, West Africa, Indo-China and the East Indies, were firmly in British, French or Dutch hands. Even Belgium, with the best part of the Congo in her grasp, was in a better position than Germany. Efforts to gain a foothold in the Mediterranean were blocked in Morocco in 1911,[2] even though Germany did gain a few thousand miles of virtually useless territory in the Congo in compensation. But before this occurred Germany had decided that the only way to challenge her rivals was by building an impressive navy. British policy at the time was to maintain a navy equal to any two others in the world, so the German task would not be easy. Attempts had been made at the Hague conferences[3] to limit the arms race, which was an obvious danger to peace, but the conferences achieved nothing concrete and could only try to humanize war when it began. From this came agreements not to bomb unfortified towns, and that prisoners-of-war would be treated with some consideration: they were not invariably observed.

Even so, the Great Powers might have continued for years without coming to blows had there not been a detonator in what was known as 'the Balkans'. The term 'Balkans' has now slipped into disuse, but in the early part of the twentieth century it often cropped up in conversation as symbolizing the potential dangers which arise when a strategically important area is occupied by a number of small, highly antagonistic, unstable states. Those states were Greece, Turkey, Bulgaria, Albania, Romania, Serbia and

Bosnia-Herzegovina, the last two of which are now incorporated into Yugoslavia. Most of these small states had been broken away from the decaying Turkish Empire in the previous century, and one, Serbia, had ambitions to build a 'Greater Serbia'. Russia liked to pose as the patron of small Slav states such as Serbia which were struggling to establish their independence, but in fact her motives were less benevolent than calculating: she hoped to use such states in her attempt to obtain access to the Mediterranean. However, after the 1908 'Young Turk' Revolution and the deposition of the Sultan Abdul Hamid the Turkish Empire temporarily stopped crumbling and its new, more efficient government was not likely to look kindly on Russian attempts to expand in this area. A somewhat nervous spectator of all this was Austria-Hungary, an ancient, also crumbling, empire which sprawled across southern Europe with a multitude of different peoples under its uncertain control. Among its indigestible elements were a number of Serbs which Serbia itself hoped to use in its plans for expansion. However, in 1908 Austria-Hungary had frustrated Serbian ambitions by calmly annexing the states of Bosnia and Herzegovina, immediately to the north of Serbia. In 1912 and 1913 there were two minor wars in the Balkans, the outcome of which was that Turkey was almost driven out of Europe but acquired a new friend in Germany and began receiving German arms and German officers. Russia viewed with satisfaction the fact that its potential allies had increased their influence, while Austria-Hungary was now seriously alarmed by the progress of aggressive small powers, such as Serbia, which could help further to undermine the ramshackle Austro-Hungarian Empire.

On 28 June 1914 the Austrian Archduke Francis Ferdinand, who was heir to the Austrian throne, chose to visit Sarajevo, the Bosnian capital. Ironically the Archduke was a liberal and had he succeeded he might well have made many concessions to the Slavs in the Austrian Empire. Unfortunately 28 June was St Vitus' Day, a Serbian national holiday, and that alone would have been sufficient to cause trouble. A bomb thrown at his car[4] missed, but he was shot later, almost by chance, by a nineteen-year-old Bosnian who was soon discovered to be a member of the Black Hand, a Serbian secret society. There was, however, no reason to suppose that the Serbian government was implicated.

4

Nevertheless, it suited Austria to assume that Serbia was involved, and the Austrian Government decided that this was an appropriate moment to settle with the Serbs once and for all. First, however, it ascertained that it had adequate backing from Germany. It then made ten demands on Serbia in the form of an ultimatum, all to be conceded within forty-eight hours. The Serbs promptly agreed to all but two (which were referred to The Hague Tribunal for arbitration), but this did not satisfy Austria. Within a month, against German advice, Austria invaded Serbia. Germany hoped the war would be limited to Serbia, but events were now moving fast. Russia felt bound to support Serbia and began to mobilize her vast army. This move alarmed Germany, who sent the Russians an ultimatum demanding that their mobilization should stop. The ultimatum was ignored, so on 1 August 1914 Germany declared war on Russia.

Germany had already asked France what action it was likely to take in the circumstances, but France had refused to answer the question. France had a defensive alliance with Russia, so when Germany declared war on the latter France had no option but to support its ally. France mobilized on 1 August, and two days later Germany declared war on France also.

None of these moves had committed Britain. Indeed, Britain was not interested in the Balkans apart from a standard policy of opposing any move by Russia which might bring that country nearer to the Mediterranean. In fact, Britain had an inclination to support Austria, as that country's very existence was a check to Russian expansion westwards. After some three centuries of varying degrees of hostility towards France, however, Britain now had an entente with her former enemy. An entente fell short of being an alliance, but was an agreed friendly relationship. As such it would not commit a country to war, but as Russia was also a signatory to this entente Britain could hardly stand idly by if her two principal friends were destroyed by belligerent Germany, Austria and Turkey, as seemed a possibility. Furthermore, the growing strength of the German Navy was not a threat to be ignored and might require military measures.

These intangibles were resolved in a manner which no one expected and involved the country where the longest and bitterest battles of the war would be fought – Belgium. It all stemmed from a treaty which was nearly a hundred years old. In 1831, following a revolt against the predominant north, Belgium had secured its independence from Holland with whom Napoleon had united it into the kingdom of the Netherlands. Belgium's status was finally recognized by the Great Powers in the Treaty of London of 1839, by which Britain, France, Austria, Russia and Prussia all recognized the new state's independence and guaranteed to protect it against any attack on its territory or possessions. Luxembourg was granted similar guarantees. On 31 July 1914 the Foreign Secretary, Sir Edward, later Lord, Grey asked both Germany and France for guarantees that, if the war spread, Belgian neutrality would be respected. France gave the required assurance without hesitation, but Germany refused to do so on the dubious grounds that if she did she might unwittingly reveal some of her military plans. Two days later German troops swept into Luxembourg. Strictly speaking, this alone should have brought Britain into conflict with Germany. However, it was Germany's next act, which was to demand free passage of troops through Belgium (for which an indemnity would be paid), which tipped the scales. Belgium refused the German request and appealed to Britain for support. On 4 August, ignoring Belgian protests, German troops invaded Belgium and as a result Britain declared war on Germany. In the event, the German attack on Belgium and France was mounted with such vigour that there was little that could be done at first except to try to delay it. To hold it at the frontier was clearly impossible, but in one vital area it was held, and that area was around Ypres. Ypres had therefore assumed more than a simple military importance: it had become a symbol of Belgian resistance to tyranny and of British support for her ally. Retaining a piece of Belgian territory demonstrated to the world that Britain stood by her treaty obligations, and that its word was its bond. Unfortunately, in the military sense this was a disastrous policy, which cost thousands of lives. Holding Ypres meant holding a salient – a tongue of territory extending into the enemy positions and therefore vulnerable to attack on three sides. Even worse for the British was the fact that the salient was mostly on flat or hollow land, all of which was overlooked by enemy positions on the surrounding hills. Even Ypres itself was under constant observation and was steadily pounded to rubble by well-positioned German guns.

But that is not the whole story either. Knowing as they did the risk (they saw it as no more) of bringing Britain into the war, there must clearly have been a compelling reason for the Germans to involve Belgium. That reason was a strategy which had embedded itself deep into German military thought. Known as the Schlieffen Plan, it was ambitious, daring and totally unscrupulous; it was also new and enormous in concept. Those last two factors might have made Germany hesitate to implement the Schlieffen Plan had there been any sensible alternative.

As long ago as 1902 Italy, which with Austria formed Bismarck's Triple Alliance, had decided that an entente with France was preferable: her former allies called it 'desertion'. Germany also had considerable doubts about the value of its remaining ally, Austria, many of whose regiments contained Slavs whose behaviour could not be predicted if they were sent to fight fellow Slavs on the Russian Front. Slav solidarity had suddenly become a force to be reckoned with, not something merely to be observed with detached interest. Turkey might prove to be an enemy rather than a friend: already there were indications that the Allies were trying to bring Turkey in on their side, as indeed they were doing, more successfully, with Italy.

Germany, although well armed and well organized, had now got itself into a difficult position. It had lost one ally, retained one of dubious value and involved itself in a war on two fronts – a strategic nightmare. The countries which Germany was fighting had greater resources, in terms of both material and manpower, than it had itself. If Germany was to win this war it must win quickly, even though that meant taking even greater risks. And the Schlieffen Plan, on which Germany relied to produce a quick, devastating victory over France, was undoubtedly a risk. If it succeeded, France would be out of the war within a few weeks; its friends and allies would be too surprised and stunned to help her. Russia would then be pleased to accept a humiliating peace. Britain would be untouched, but would no doubt be easier to deal with once it had seen the might and skill which Germany could unleash.

But there was a twofold risk. The first problem was that Britain would pay attention to that century-old treaty, 'the scrap of paper' as the Kaiser called it, and actually go to war to help Belgium.

This, the Germans felt, could probably be discounted. The second was more serious. Would the plan work when it was used?

Count von Schlieffen had been Chief of the German General Staff from 1891 to 1907. He died in 1913, so he never saw his plan put into operation and fail. If anyone had predicted that the principal result of his military thinking would be the slaughter of hundreds of thousands of soldiers, of which over half would be German, in the morass of Passchendaele, he would have dismissed the idea in a second. Von Schlieffen applied ruthless logic to military matters, which were his only interest. It was said that once, in Austria, an exceptionally beautiful view was pointed out to him. He paused, thought for a moment, and then said. 'The river is too narrow for an obstacle, and there is insufficient cover for troops on those slopes.'

In 1893, when Russia and France had signed a Dual Alliance – a course to which they had been driven by the aggressive policies first of Bismarck, then of Kaiser Wilhelm II – Schlieffen immediately saw the new alliance not as a natural response to Germany's Triple Alliance, but as a move requiring Germany to devise a strategy to win a quick war. War, he felt, was inevitable. France, he well knew, burned to wipe out the disgrace of its defeat by Germany in 1871 and at the same time to recover the lost province of Alsace-Lorraine, including the cities of Metz and Strasbourg. He knew, too, that the French were prepared for another aggressive move from Germany, probably instigated by the belligerent Kaiser, and had therefore heavily fortified their frontier from Verdun to Belfort, near Switzerland. They had not, however, fortified their frontiers opposite Belgium and Luxembourg, for these countries, they knew, had a guaranteed neutrality. But Schlieffen's planning took no account of neutrality except in relation to the opportunities it presented.

Schlieffen's predecessors in German military planning, Helmuth and Moltke, had also considered the dangerous possibility of having to fight a war on both Eastern and Western Fronts but had reasoned that, if that situation occurred, Russia should be eliminated first, then France. Schlieffen decided that Russia would mobilize so slowly and inefficiently that it offered no immediate threat, though subsequently that country might take longer to subdue than his predecessors had imagined.[5] Schlieffen's plan,

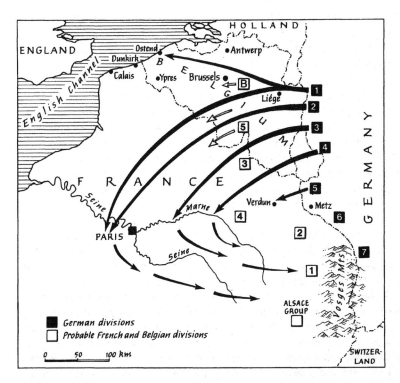

Schlieffen's original concept was to have five German armies pivoting on
Metz (the hinge of the opening door). British involvement was not
originally considered likely. In the event the British took the area opposite
the German 3rd Army. The Germans abandoned their drive to the
Channel ports and curved in to the east of Paris. The plan to envelop the
French armies and trap them in the south of the region was foiled by the
French counter-attack on the Marne. The failure of the Schlieffen Plan led
to the 'Race to the Sea', in which both sides dug trenches from the Belgian
coast to Switzerland. The line ran just east of Ypres. Schlieffen had said:
'Keep the right wing strong', but Moltke had instead strengthened the
centre. Gaps developed between the German 1st and 2nd Armies, both of
which had outrun their supply columns.

9

originally drafted in 1895, was modified and perfected each year until Schlieffen retired in 1905. His final plan allotted a mere ten divisions to the Eastern Front and a mere eight to control the French where they were strongest. The bulk of the German Army, fifty-three divisions, was to be disposed on the right wing and was to pivot on Metz like a wheel. This swinging force was to sweep through Belgium and northern France so that its extreme right would actually pass west and south of Paris. The maneouvre would first outflank the French, then push an overwhelming force up behind them and trap the main French Army against Lorraine and the Swiss frontier (see map on p. 9). Schlieffen thought that violating Belgian neutrality would probably bring Britain in, but too late to affect the outcome in Europe. It is said that his dying words were: 'It must come to a fight. Keep the right wing strong.'

But, as Tennyson neatly put it, 'Authority forgets a dying king', and even faster does it forget the views of a retired or dead officer, however eminent he may have been in his day. Schlieffen's successor, the younger Moltke, had no inhibitions about violating Belgian neutrality, but of the nine new divisions he raised only one went to the right wing; the rest went to the left. He also shortened the sweep of the right wing.

In the event, much went wrong with Schlieffen's plan. The Belgians, although taken by surprise, put up a much stronger resistance than the Germans had anticipated. Instead of obeying orders, several of the German Army commanders decided to use their own misguided initiative: Bülow and Kluck closed up and formulated a private strategy. The vast sweep of the 'swinging door' caused the Germans on the right to outrun their supplies (there was no bread issue for four days), and made their commanders extremely nervous that gaps would develop along the Front through which enemy forces would get in behind them. The British force at Mons and the French force at Charleroi halted the German onslaught for a time and caused the wing to straighten and lose its original objective. Instead of encircling the Allies in northern France and at the same time capturing the Channel ports which were within reach, the Germans now concentrated on reaching Paris. At this moment Marshal Joffre saw his opportunity to attack the now disorganized German Army on its flank along the Marne. This was the famous occasion on which he used Paris taxi-cabs to convey reinforcements to the Front: it must have been an impressive sight, but not one for the faint-hearted. Moltke, having proved himself a pale shadow of his great ancestor, was now dismissed and replaced by Falkenhayn. Surveying the wreck of the original plan, Falkenhayn decided that his best move would be to seize the nearest Channel ports, notably Dunkirk, Calais and Boulogne; Ostend and Zeebrugge were already in German hands. Now the weight of the attack fell on the British, who had been rapidly moved up from the Aisne to the sector on the extreme left. Here, reinforced by some French and Belgians, they began that long, slogging series of battles which would eventually lead to Passchendaele.

At this stage, October 1914, the war was still young and anything might happen. Commanders on both sides considered the possibility of lightning thrusts and adroit outflanking movements. But, as the defence of Ypres was doggedly continued through the months of October and November, both the Germans and the Allies settled down to consolidating a defensive system of trenches which extended from the Channel in the north to the Swiss frontier in the south, a distance of some 400 miles. In general the defensive pattern was satisfactory to both sides: where it was not, local attacks were made to capture valuable features. At intervals there would be larger offensives when one side or the other would try to break through. The French broke through at Artois in April 1915, gained three miles and were then driven back to their original positions, having lost 400,000 men. In September they tried again, in Champagne, with an equally disappointing result. The British tried a breakthrough on the Somme in 1916; four months later they had captured seven miles at a cost of 450,000 casualties, many of them occurring in the first few hours. The Germans were equally devoid of subtlety in their approach to the problem. In February 1916 they had tried to capture Verdun, preceding their attack with the heaviest bombardment ever known in war. They won some territory, but lost it again in heavy French counter-attacks. Verdun was more than a strongpoint in the French defensive system: it was a symbol of France's determination not to be conquered. When Pétain said: '*Ils ne passeront pas*', he meant it, and every Frenchman supported him. In one week the Germans lost 120,000 men. But the strain on the French had left them exhausted and disorganized. Morale was affected. This was particularly unfortunate for the

British, who had already taken over more than their share of the line and in addition been disappointed when the French contribution to the Battle of the Somme shrank from the original forty divisions to a mere sixteen, of which only five attacked on 1 July. But there was worse to come.

In retrospect it seems almost incredible that the British and Empire forces were able to fight and endure as they did. Soldiers and officers up to the rank of colonel doggedly battled against the Germans without time or opportunity to think of what they were being asked to do. The masters of their destiny, the senior commanders, seldom came near the battlefield; they were never seen by the fighting soldier, who could only hope that those remote figures, few of whom he knew by name, really knew what they were doing and that it was all for the best. Patriotism, regimental discipline and a wish not to let down his comrades kept him going. He did not know that the tactics of Joffre, Rawlinson and Haig were more likely to bring him a swift death than an early victory. Even if the Somme offensive had been successful, it would merely have created another dangerous salient, a site for endless bloodletting, a counterpart to Ypres.

By 1916 the French had lost their faith in Joffre, who had undoubtedly saved them in the Battle of the Marne in 1914 but now appeared to have run out of ideas. In December 1916 he was replaced by Nivelle, a younger man who had a clear idea about how to break through the German line and end the deadlock of trench warfare. But whatever chance Nivelle's plans might have had of succeeding was effectively removed when the Germans found them in the belongings of some prisoners they captured. But while the Germans knew Nivelle's plans, he remained quite unaware of the fact that they had prepared a new defensive line a few miles further back, which they called the Siegfried Line and the Allies called the Hindenburg Line. When, in April 1917, Nivelle attacked along a fifty-mile front, he found, after easy initial successes, that he was facing an apparently impregnable defensive system. Fifteen thousand French troops were killed, and a further 60,000 wounded. Nothing significant had been gained. It was the end of Nivelle. In May 1917 he was replaced by Pétain, who had Foch as his Chief of Staff. But by this time the French Army had had enough of being hurled against barbed wire and impregnable defences. Mutiny broke out on 3 May and spread quickly. So many men simply deserted that whole sections of trench were left unguarded. Pétain's first task, therefore, was to restore morale and fighting ability. He did so by touring the Front, visiting almost every division. The mutiny was quelled within a month; twenty-three ringleaders were shot and a further hundred deported. But while all this was going on, the full weight of responsibility for holding the Germans fell on the British. The British Army now had sixty-four divisions in France, its highest number so far, but the pressure on them was enormous. The Bolshevik Revolution was gaining impetus and, as a result, Russia was drifting out of the war. In consequence the Germans were able to take troops from their Eastern Front and despatch them to the West.

Haig's reaction to the British Army's problem of keeping the Germans occupied while the French recovered and until the Americans put in an appearance was to launch the Passchendaele offensive. In any other terrain but that around Ypres Haig's idea might perhaps have had something to recommend it, although considering the greater German resources of manpower even that might be debatable. But Haig was a cavalry officer and, although he had learnt some bitter lessons in the Boer War and earlier in this one, he still held a deep conviction that a swift thrust, or series of thrusts, would find a weak point in the enemy line, break through it and sweep forward to overwhelming victory. Haig, of course, was by no means the only cavalry officer in a senior position in the First World War, and at his councils he would see nods of assent to this sort of suggestion even though hundreds of thousands of bodies already testified to the bankruptcy of such ideas. Second only to the belief that a swift, cavalry-type attack could achieve a break-through was the conviction that artillery could pound the opposing defences to rubble and clear gaps which the infantry could stream through. But the inability of shells to destroy barbed wire and concrete defences had already been demonstrated on many occasions in this war, notably on the Somme and at Laon. Nevertheless, the British had the guns and, for the moment, the ammunition, and that was how it would begin. In subsequent wars generals have come to realize that an artillery bombardment can sometimes make an advance more difficult than it would otherwise have been. Roads and towns blocked with the rubble of shattered houses and vehicles pose a problem worse than any which might have been encountered had they been left intact. It was a lesson which was learnt very fully by the Allies as they advanced towards Berlin in the Second World War. But the obstacles created by the preliminary bombardment on the German positions around Ypres were far worse than ruined buildings and wrecked transport. To understand how great was this folly it is necessary to turn to Ypres itself.

Notes

1 'Casualties' is the general term for killed, wounded and missing. In most wars those killed outright comprise one-third of the total. In Flanders the majority of the 'missing' were also dead. 'Wounded' included sufferers from the effects of poison gas; many wounded died later, and others were permanently incapacitated.
2 In 1911 Germany sent a gunboat, the *Panther*, to Agadir on the Moroccan Atlantic coast, as a protest against the probable French annexation of Morocco. Following lengthy negotiations Germany agreed to a French protectorate over Morocco in return for 100,000 square miles of French Congo.
3 The Hague conferences had begun in 1899 on the initiative of Tsar Nicholas II of Russia, with delegates from twenty-seven states. The first conference broke down, but the armaments race during the following years became so alarming and financially damaging to everyone that a second conference was convened in 1907. Attempts to limit armaments were soon found to be hopelessly impracticable, but certain conventions were agreed for the apparently inevitable next war. They included not bombing unfortified towns, and provided for the humane treatment of prisoners of war.
4 The car is now in the Heeresgeschichtliches (Military) Museum in Vienna.
5 This, of course, was a theory which Hitler, many years later, found to be correct.

2

The Cockpit of Europe

Ypres was no stranger to warfare. This part of the Netherlands, known as Flanders, had been invaded by Julius Caesar in 57 BC and subjected to Roman rule after a long and bloody campaign. Some five hundred years later, when Roman power was ebbing, it was conquered by the Franks. This period saw the beginnings of the polarization of Belgium into the two linguistic and ethnic groups which characterize it today, and which creates the contrast between names obviously of French origin – Liège, Namur – and those which will be encountered later – Zonnebeke, Gheluvelt and, of course, Passchendaele. When Charlemagne reigned as Holy Roman Emperor, between AD 800 and 814, he held Belgium in high esteem, partly perhaps because it was close to his favourite palace at Aachen; as a result the area remained stable, but after he died his grandsons fought over his lands, eventually partitioning them between them. In the ninth and tenth centuries Flanders was invaded and pillaged by raiding Vikings, but this did not cause the country to disintegrate; instead there emerged a dynasty of extremely powerful Counts of Flanders, the first of whom, Baldwin Iron Arm, turned Ghent into a fortress. His son, another Baldwin, built the walls of Bruges and Ypres, and one of his descendants, Matilda, married William the Conqueror, the first Norman king of England. This period of strong autocratic rule gave Flanders a degree of stability which enabled it to develop by the twelfth century a prosperous economy founded on cloth. Wool was imported from England (leading to a valuable export trade in East Anglia) and woven and marketed in Ghent, Bruges and Ypres. Belgium had many factors in its favour. It was close to three international rivers, the Rhine, the Scheldt and the Meuse; it also had good ports on the coast, a tradition of skilled craftsmanship and a good road system. As the cities prospered they were able to obtain privileges for themselves, and became virtually states within states. Liège became a centre of ironworking and weapon manufacture, Bruges a focus for banking and finance, and Ypres grew so prosperous that it was able to build the huge and magnificent Cloth Hall which, though destroyed in 1914–18, has now been rebuilt as a reminder of the town's former commercial glory. At the time when the original Hall was built, in 1214, Ypres had a population of 200,000.

Inevitably, the prosperity and independent status of Flanders aroused jealousy and envy in its neighbours, notably France. However, France's attempt to reassert itself in what had once been a French province did not achieve ready success. On 11 July 1302 the cream of the French Army was slaughtered near Kortrijk in an engagement which became known as the Battle of the Golden Spurs. It was a triumph of courage and determination by the Belgians, but they had little time to savour it. In spite of spirited attempts to fight back, resistance was gradually crushed during the next eighty years, and the population of Ypres fell dramatically to a mere 40,000, a figure which by the sixteenth century had shrunk to 3000.[1]

The fourteenth and fifteenth centuries saw sporadic revolts, and 'peacekeeping' expeditions by the French, followed by conflicts between Austria and France over who should control the region. Ypres and its neighbours were frequently besieged by German mercenaries. Stability and prosperity returned when Charles V became Holy Roman Emperor, and Flemish merchants and seamen began to take Belgian products all over the world. Mercator, who was born in Rupelmonde and educated at Louvain, produced maps of the world in the mid-sixteenth century; perhaps not surprisingly, on his projections Flanders appears at the centre of the civilized world.

However, although Charles had been born in Ghent and had much affection for his Flemish subjects, this did not extend to being over-indulgent towards them. He tried to stamp out Calvinism, the local form of Protestantism, and allowed thousands to be tortured and executed by the Spanish Inquisition. And before he died a growing feeling of resentment against the ruling elite had arisen among the new, prosperous merchant class. Not the least of the merchants' complaints was an ever-increasing tax burden to finance Charles's wars.

After Charles's death, however, his reign seemed in retrospect the epitome of benevolence, for his successor, Philip II of Spain, who married England's Mary Tudor, encouraged the Inquisition to greater efforts. Inevitably revolts occurred, and Philip despatched the Duke of Alva to restore order. Alva's cruelties alienated both Calvinists and Catholics, but his taxation offended even more. He introduced a value added tax but with no system of refunds: the result was first stagnation of industry, then nationwide revolt. One by one the great towns were besieged by Alva's soldiers, and when they fell – usually through starvation – the survivors were executed in their thousands. Two years later the Spanish troops mutinied and began an orgy of pillage and murder, the notorious Spanish Fury. Belgium has certainly seen more than its share of the horrors of war.

Eventually, in the late sixteenth century, the southern districts surrendered to Spanish demands. The north and the cities such as Ypres battled on; these independent areas became known as the United Provinces. It is remarkable to think that this period of unrest, persecution and danger was also the great age of Dutch painting, when Rubens, Van Dyck and many lesser, but still famous, artists flourished. Flemish towns now became part of what was about to constitute the powerful Dutch Republic – but not an important part, for Dutch power was concentrated on the navy and on overseas trade. Holland soon controlled the northern approaches to what had recently been the Spanish Netherlands, and France began making encroachments in the south.

However, after the Glorious Revolution of 1688, when William of Orange accepted the English crown, the fortunes of Britain and the United Provinces became closely allied. This, as every student of British military history knows, helped to make the Low Countries the cockpit of Europe. Louis XIV's uncontrollable ambition to be master of Europe led to a series of wars, mostly involving Marlborough, some of whose famous victories were achieved in the Low Countries. At the end of a number of bloody battles the ravaged countryside was handed over to Austria, whose claim to suzerainty was better than anyone else's – as it had originally been part of the Hapsburg domains, in 1598 Philip II of Spain gave it to his daughter as a dowry when she married the Archduke Albert of Austria. But by now the inhabitants of this region, who were beginning to call themselves Belgians after the original pre-Christian tribe which had settled in the area, were starting to nurture ideas about independence. Soon they were in rebellion against their Austrian overlords, but it did them no good. First they were suppressed by the Austrians themselves, then both fell under the control of the French revolutionary armies after 1789.

The next few years were among Belgium's worst. The country was torn between those who supported the principles of the French Revolution and those who opposed them, and Belgian regiments fought on both sides in the campaigns which followed. Appropriately, Belgium provided the setting for the Battle of Waterloo, which ended the seemingly interminable Napoleonic Wars. But the great victory did little for the Belgians. In the subsequent peace treaty they found themselves merged into the kingdom of the Netherlands, of which William of Orange, who was strongly pro-Dutch, became king as William I.

Not surprisingly, there was soon rioting, particularly as there seemed to be little tolerance for Catholics, and Dutch speakers appeared to be favoured more than their French-speaking counterparts. An enquiry revealed that the civil service had a Dutch majority of ten to one and the War Office of thirty to one. In 1831 the inevitable revolt occurred. William tried to crush the rebel Belgians, but his Dutch soldiers were defeated. A provisional Belgian Government was formed and national independence was proclaimed.

Other countries which had connections and interests in Belgium now became involved. The French hoped to place a nominee of theirs on the Belgian throne, and were prepared to back him with 50,000 troops. However, at the London Conference of 1831 it was eventually decided that the new king should be Prince Leopold of Saxe-Coburg, the uncle of Queen Victoria (who had not, as yet, succeeded to the British throne). William objected strongly to this appointment and refused to relinquish Antwerp. However, the French were prepared to support Prince Leopold, who soon married into the French royal family and dealt firmly with William: he was ejected from Antwerp after an assault and a blockade of Dutch ports.

Even then, Belgium was far from stable. William made periodic attempts to reimpose his authority before he finally accepted defeat in 1839, when a further London Conference issued an agreement signed by Austria, Britain, Prussia, France and Russia, stating that the independence and neutrality of Belgium was guaranteed by them. This was the 'scrap of paper', as the German Kaiser scornfully described it in 1914, when he was reminded that Britain had a written, as well as a moral, obligation to assist Belgium if that country's neutrality was violated.

For the Belgians the next seventy-five years were the most stable and happy in their existence. The country was soon experiencing the benefits of an industrial revolution and expanded into a prosperous colonial power. Ironically, it was now the turn of the Flemish speakers to feel aggrieved, for they felt that all the best posts in industry and government services at home were going to the French speakers; overseas, in the new colony in the Congo, the situation was even worse. Not until after the First World War did that pendulum begin to swing back.

But never in their worst nightmare could the Belgians have imagined the events of 1914–18 taking place in their country, which was almost totally overrun by the invaders.

This brief account of Belgian history has revealed two main themes. One is that Belgium has seen more continuous warfare, persecution and disruption than most countries, and the other that over the years Belgium has on many occasions looked on Britain as a friend and ally against oppressors. The great prosperity of the wool trade, and of Ypres in particular, was built up on firm Anglo–Belgian co-operation; relief from Spanish tyranny followed the English defeat of the Spanish Armada; French ambitions to absorb the country were frustrated first by Marlborough, then by Wellington; and finally Britain was the leading figure in securing Belgian independence from Dutch domination. Small wonder that to this day there is an underlying feeling of goodwill between the Belgians and the British, even though neither realize how far back into history that affinity reaches.

Note

1 It is now 35,000.

3

The Preliminary Rounds

Officially Passchendaele is known as Third Ypres – the third Battle of Ypres. In order to understand it, it is important to look both at its predecessors and at the countryside in which it was fought.

The town of Ypres stands at the western end of a low-lying plain surrounded on all sides by low, wooded hills. The plain is intersected by canals which are part of a complex drainage system. Even on the slopes, drainage systems are necessary or the rains will collect and make the ground waterlogged. Most of the canals, of which the Yser is the most important, flow diagonally across the plain from south-east to north-west. In addition there are a number of streams flowing in the same direction, and three substantial stretches of water known as ponds: the Dickebusch, Zillebeke and Bellewaarde. The effect of this on ground which is virtually at sea level is that, once the drainage pattern is disturbed, either by natural forces such as unduly heavy rain, or by man's interference, the whole area is transformed into a morass. This is not so obvious today, when the surface looks stable again, but, as the troops in 1914–18 quickly discovered, this area was quite different from anywhere else on the Front. In other sectors men might have difficulty in hacking their way through chalk or even rock; here it was easy enough to remove the loose, muddy surface, but all that was then left was a pool of water, not a trench or a dugout. On the slopes of the hills – when they were reached – it would be possible to dig proper trenches and dugouts, even to make concrete blockhouses, but first those hills had to be gained, and the only way to them was over a plain consisting of liquid mud varied only by deep, water-filled shell craters.

In such a terrain the slightest piece of rising ground or cover is of inestimable value. At the start of the Ypres battles there were farms

20

set on little knolls of higher ground – but still low-lying – and woods, of which Houthulst Forest was the largest. In the course of the fighting most of the woods were blown to fragments, and what are now once again Sanctuary, Polygon, Glencorse and Herenthage were reduced to a few shattered tree stumps. Today, in parts where the trenches have been preserved – and Sanctuary Wood is one of the most extensive – remains of trees can be seen as they were left in 1918. The so-called 'hills' would scarcely be noticeable as such were it not for their history. Most of them are gentle slopes leading up to ridges. The notorious Hill 60 was given that name because it rises to a mere 60 metres (195 feet) above sea level. Low though those wooded slopes were, they were sufficient to dominate the waterlogged plain below and even to give observation into Ypres itself. These are therefore the places where the fighting concentrated and where the graves now lie thickest.

The Ypres battles had begun on 15 October 1914. At that time the Belgians had taken up a position on the Yser Canal. (Ypres lies on a tributary of the Yser, known as the Yperlee.) Immediately next to them on their right were the French and then next to them was the British I Corps, which had just come from fighting on the Aisne. I Corps had been ordered to occupy Menin, but were halted some three miles short of their objective. As further German troops came up to increase the pressure on the somewhat weary Corps it fell back to Gheluvelt. Next to it came IV Corps, holding the central sector, between Zonnebeke and Zondervoorde, after which came Allenby's cavalry and then III Corps covering Armentières.

The brunt of the heavy German attack was borne by 7th Division, no stranger to bitter fighting. The Germans lost heavily at Langemarck, where 1500 men were killed; this subsequently became the site of a large German cemetery. On more than one occasion the Germans broke through the line, but each time they were contained, though at appalling cost to 7th Division. Seventh were relieved by 1st Division, who were immediately repulsed by a German attack but subsequently managed to claw back the lost ground. The struggle had now become more than a normal battle but was taking on the character of other actions in this war, such as Verdun, where a line was held more for its value to prestige and morale than for military advantage. German efforts were encouraged by the Kaiser, who came to this sector and repeatedly urged his troops that Ypres must be taken at all costs. Ten days after their initial attacks the Germans made a final desperate effort to break through at Gheluvelt. Stunned by the unexpectedly heavy bombardment and relentless infantry attacks, 1st Division was forced back into what were still woods behind Gheluvelt, a mere four miles from Ypres itself.

Hooge Château, which had somewhat unwisely been selected for the headquarters of both 1st and 2nd Divisions, now came under shellfire, resulting in both the divisional commanders being wounded, one fatally, and six of their staff being killed. (The Château was to disappear completely in the following years.) Although unaware of their success at Hooge, the Germans increased their efforts, regardless of cost. As whole battalions of British troops were gradually annihilated, it seemed that the line must soon give and Ypres be lost. Allenby was holding off the advance of two entire German Corps which were trying to get to this sector, and the French, who had problems of their own, were doing what they could to help. But the gap in the British line was there.

Suddenly it was closed, and by one British battalion. The 2nd Worcesters had been in support at Polygon Wood but, called into the vital sector by Brigadier-General Fitzclarence, VC (killed a few days later), surged into Gheluvelt and took it at the point of the bayonet. Had this extraordinary feat not happened, nobody would have believed it possible. But it was more than enough for the Germans to have an attack on their flank at the very moment they thought they were through to victory; they broke off the action and counted their losses. But they were by no means defeated: in the confused fighting which followed they occupied Hollebeke, Messines and Wytschaete. The last of these was retaken two days later, but soon fell once more into German hands.

The stage was now set for the prolonged artillery battles of the following years, with the Germans in possession of all the best positions and observation points. It was not yet the end of the infantry battles, however, for on 11 November the Germans launched their best units into a final desperate attempt to break through the line at Gheluvelt again. They seemed indifferent to losses but eventually were checked and driven back. By the end of the following week the weather had become so bad that the

German High Command decided to postpone further operations in this sector until the following spring, when they hoped to have a surprise for the Allies.

This had been First Ypres. The 'butcher's bill', as soldiers cynically call it, was 50,000 British casualties, about 20,000 French and Belgian, and 150,000 German. The Germans, as the attackers, irrespective of whether they were determined to press forward regardless of loss, would expect to have twice as many casualties as the defenders. In fact they had done better than they knew. They had destroyed many of the best and most experienced regiments of the British Army, men who could only be replaced by volunteers and conscripts. Courageous and dedicated though the latter were, there was no immediate substitute for the training and experience of the regulars; most of the newcomers were put in the line with nominal training and were by definition inexperienced. The value of the regular soldier was that he had practised his skills, such as markmanship and fieldcraft, so often that they had become automatic: his replacement had usually undergone such a short period of training that he had to think what he was doing before he did it. If the newcomer survived, he became battle-hardened. Many did, and fought superbly. In the conditions of Passchendaele normal experience counted for little, but nearly three years of trench warfare would take place before that began. Troops who had been serving in the front line were usually incensed to find that during their 'rest' periods they were given training by officers and NCOs, sometimes their own, but often others with little or no familiarity with battle. The soldiers believed that the aim of this particular exercise was to make them so disgusted with behind-the-line routine, drill parades, riding instruction, saluting, guard duties and so on that they would regard their return to the trenches with relief. There is no doubt an element of truth in the belief that life out of the trenches was deliberately made difficult, and that some of those serving in rear areas took pleasure in making it so, but the original purpose was to improve skills which had become neglected in the trenches but which one day could well be needed.

Trench warfare in the Ypres sector during the winter of 1914–15 was so unpleasant that the troops serving there felt that whatever happened in the following spring and summer could only be better. Even those trenches which had been dug earlier in what seemed slightly drier conditions now filled up with water, and in some it was waist deep. Sickness rates soared and the ominous expression 'trench foot' was widely used. Normal sickness which would take a man off duty was ignored: if a man said he was too ill to continue he would receive a sympathetic hearing from the doctor but have to carry on none the less. 'Trench foot', with its unpleasant and intensely painful symptoms of swelling, discoloration, ulcers, blisters, loss of toenails and gangrene, was said to be both avoidable and curable. It could be avoided by keeping the feet dry, and always wearing dry socks and boots; curing it required six to ten weeks' rest. No special instructions were issued about taking these precautions when standing in three feet of filthy, freezing water.

But at last spring came. It was warmer, slightly drier, and a symbol of hope. Summer, it was felt, might be quite tolerable even though the death and destruction would continue unabated.

At the beginning of the third week of April 1915 it became obvious that any optimism about the future was premature. An unexpected and particularly heavy bombardment sent a stream of shells into Ypres, which so far had escaped lightly. But the Germans were determined either to capture Ypres or make it a desert. The irony was that in the early days of the war they had made a reconnaissance of Ypres with a cavalry patrol, which had been followed by 20,000 Germans marching through the town as Falkenhayn adjusted the deployment of the German Army to the situation which followed the failure of the Schlieffen Plan. In the following four years they suffered some 300,000 casualties trying to get back into the town.

In this new bombardment the Cloth Hall was hit several times and the future outlook for the town looked ominous. The local people, who had stayed on in Ypres thinking they were relatively well protected, soon changed their minds and departed hastily. The Allies had expected some form of spring offensive and were not particularly disturbed. But there was worse to come.

On the early evening of the 22nd, to the north-west of the town the salient was held by French troops, many of whom were Algerians. South-east were two brigades of Canadians and on their right were the British 28th and 27th Divisions. At 5 p.m. in the sector it seemed like a peaceful spring evening until suddenly the Germans opened up a tremendous bombardment. The British troops noticed to their surprise a greenish yellow fog over the French positions: it did not disperse like normal gunsmoke, but drifted westwards. Suddenly a desperate stream of French and Algerian soldiers began rushing back into the area behind: they were choking and coughing, and some pointed their fingers towards their throats. The French guns, which had been replying to the German bombardment, suddenly stopped. A few gun teams had managed to limber up and move to the rear. In the general panic and confusion it was hard for anyone to get clear. This was the first, but by no means the last, use of poison gas – in this case chlorine – on the Western Front. It came as a complete surprise, even though the Allies had learnt from prisoners that the Germans possessed this weapon and intended to use it. A deserter had talked about stacks of cylinders in the German trenches and, although his report was confirmed by prisoners, the French Corps commander simply refused to believe what his intelligence officers told him. Even the details of how the gas was to be used failed to impress.

But this was not the only instance in this war – and others – when senior commanders refused to believe intelligence reports. On occasions they were right, for some of the intelligence officers were naïve and too lacking in experience to make a proper evaluation of either their sources or the information they produced. Even if a prisoner was trying to be genuinely helpful to his captors, it was probable that much of his report was based on rumour and hearsay. However when a number of prisoners, all from different units, are telling the same story, it is a very stupid and bigoted commander who ignores it. But so deeply ingrained was prejudice against clever linguists, who were thought to be amateur soldiers advising professionals what to do, that vital information was either ignored, or considered and rejected. The idea that information gained at the risk of a man's life is eagerly received and acted on by politicians and senior commanders belongs to the world of fiction rather than that of fact.

Suddenly there was a gap of four miles in the lines protecting Ypres, and coincidentally that gap was four miles from Ypres. The Germans could hardly believe their success: they came through the gap, advanced two miles, then stopped. They were not confident that their own very crude gasmasks, made of tow soaked with oxygen, would give more than short-term protection. Some spirited resistance by a few small groups of Canadians also helped to deter their further advance. That night and the following day the Canadians and certain British units forced the Germans back, though only temporarily. At 4 a.m. on the 24th the Germans launched another gas attack, this time on the Canadians. The Canadians had no gasmasks, of course, and could only protect themselves by covering their noses and mouths with handkerchiefs or bandages soaked in their own urine. But, helped by two Yorkshire Territorial battalions, they pushed the Germans back.

It was hoped that, after these efforts to stabilize the situation, the French would be able to mount a substantial counter-attack to retake the ground lost in the first German attack, but Joffre unfortunately was less interested in this than in his planned offensive at Arras. On 1 May the British Commander-in-Chief, Sir John French, reluctantly came to the conclusion that Foch, the overall Commander-in-Chief, had no intention of mounting a large counter-attack in the Ypres sector but instead was withdrawing troops for use in Joffre's offensive at Arras. At this point it would have been sensible to withdraw the whole Allied line to the Yser Canal, which runs at the outskirts of Ypres, but this was felt to be politically undesirable as it meant surrendering more Belgian territory and reducing that historic town to a mere point in the front line. In the event, Ypres might just as well have been in the front line, for it was soon to be reduced to piles of rubble by shellfire, but as long as it was actually behind the line it had a certain symbolic value.

The trench line was pulled back to form a straighter but still bulging line, some three miles from Ypres. This was a worse position than the original salient for it surrendered over half the former area, which would subsequently have to be won back at appalling cost. Ypres was now within easy range and observation for the Germans. The worst part of all was that, while the British were waiting for support from the French, they had done remark-ably well in recovering some of the lost territory. Unfortunately however, without support they were unable to hold most of this against German forces of twice their number, and in trying to do so their casualties mounted to some 60,000, twice those of the enemy. The attitude of the British to their French allies, whose negligence had let in the first German success and who had then failed to support the British and Canadians, was understandably bitter. Foch, of course, was not really interested in Belgium and its predicament: there were Germans on French soil too, and he felt that his standing with his countrymen would be better if he concentrated on those. This was folly of a high degree, for the strategic value of the Ypres sector was enormous. If the Germans broke through there they would gain the Channel ports, deny the Allies supplies and be able to turn the entire Allied line.

By the end of May the new positions were being consolidated by both sides. Names which would later symbolize the grimmest aspects of this war were beginning to take on their reputations. The Menin Road led to Hooge, a battlefield whose horrors and miseries have never been surpassed. But before it reached Hooge it came to Hellfire Corner, which was the junction of the Menin Road with the Potijze–Zillebeke Road. Nearby was the Ypres–Roulers railway crossing. The Germans knew the range of Hellfire Corner to a yard and hammered it with shells day and night. Any movement immediately attracted a shell, so every reinforcement which went up or down the line, every supply or ambulance wagon, encountered German fire. Camouflage screens were erected along the sides to try to hide the size and number of the forces moving along the road, but achieved only limited success. It was impossible not to use the road, for no vehicle, horse or man could get through the waterlogged ground on either side.

Eight hundred yards from Hellfire Corner was Birr Crossroads. Like most of the places on the military maps of the period, this otherwise anonymous point had been given a title by troops who distinguished themselves there. This one was given its name by the Leinster Regiment, which also christened the nearby buildings Leinster Farm: their regimental depot was at Birr in Ireland. There were many similar christenings – Lancer Farm, Dragoon Farm, Shrapnel Corner, Dormy Farm, Paradise Alley, Stirling Castle, Bitter Wood, Shrewsbury Forest, Bass Wood, Clapham Junction, Inverness Copse, Railway Wood, Tower Hamlets, Wimbledon, Abraham Heights, Calgary Grange, Dash Crossing, Daring Cross, Tricky Farm, Ugly Wood and Ugly Farm. Some names were ironic, half-humorous, and made light of something which was hideous: Daring Cross earned its name from the number of soldiers who met their death there. There was great nostalgia in the names, many of which recalled home towns in Australia, Canada, England, Scotland, Wales and Ireland. Once a name was given, it quickly became official; no attempt was made by relieving units to change it once it was well known.

During that summer of 1915 the casualties continued, the numbers periodically surging upwards on both sides. The Château at Hooge gradually disappeared (it has now been rebuilt). Here the enemy was very close, but even closer were the dead of both sides, under their feet, half buried in the sides of trenches, lying in the slimy water in the shell holes, and constantly disturbed by shelling and digging. Even for the dead there was no peaceful resting place. There were battles around Hooge in April 1915: the Château stood on slightly higher ground and the area was heavily garrisoned by German troops. The position was mined by British troops and when it was blown up a huge crater was left. It became known as the Witches' Cauldron, and as bodies fell or were flung into the water which soon filled it, the crater became indescribable. Worse was to come. In July the Germans had had a temporary success with a new weapon, the *Flammenwerfer* or flame-thrower. The Rifle Brigade and the 60th Rifles caught the brunt of it. They were driven back but, shortly afterwards, rallied and made a counter-attack to recover lost ground. One of those killed in this counter-attack was Lieutenant Gilbert Talbot; he is buried in the Sanctuary Wood Cemetery. A rest centre with an unobtrusive religious basis established in Poperinghe, six and a half miles behind Ypres, was named Talbot House in his memory. It soon, however, became known as Toc H, Toc being the phonetic term for 'T' at this time. The first warden of the centre was the Reverend Philip Clayton, always known as 'Tubby'. At the top of the building was a room used as a chapel: here a lamp was lit when services were held. Toc H, which was situated in the Rue de l'Hôpital (now Gasthuisstraat), was everyman's club and had a notice over the door which said: 'Abandon rank all ye who enter here.' At least half a million soldiers visited this little haven of peace and sanity.[1]

All through the summer and winter of 1915 the two armies remained locked in a desperate struggle in the salient. Periodically one side or the other would mount a local attack to gain some small feature, but most of these were abortive. Casualties continued steadily from the effects of sniping, shellfire and machine guns.

In June 1916 a heavy German attack at Corps strength was launched in the Sanctuary Wood/Maple Copse area, where the trenches were held by Canadians. It forced its way into the front line trenches but could get no further. As the Canadians doggedly held on against the torrent of Germans, losses mounted rapidly on both sides, but after eleven days the Canadians mounted a night counter-attack and regained all their lost ground. Among the many Canadian units to distinguish themselves were Princess Patricia's Canadian Light Infantry, known as the Patricias: one company held off the German attack on Sanctuary Wood for eighteen hours. Another unit which the Germans had cause to remember was the Canadian Mounted Rifles, which had been converted to infantry a few months earlier. The final attack was a triumph of co-ordination: a 218-gun force, made up of Canadian, British, Indian and South African artillery units, shielded the infantry with a creeping barrage as they moved forward through the mud. Among the prizes won in that counter-attack were Mount Sorrel, Armagh Wood, Observatory Ridge, Sanctuary Wood and Hills 61 and 62.[2]

Although it was impossible to dig proper trenches in the surface of the ground in the Ypres Salient, it was nevertheless possible to mine it. To do so required extraordinary skill on the part of the Engineers. The soil structure consists of a layer of sand or sandy loam, below which is a layer of half-liquid sand and clay; below that is a deep seam of blue clay. Mining had been begun by both sides early in the war, but until 1917 most of it had been done through the second layer. This process involved scooping out the liquid mess and revetting the sides of the tunnel so that it did not collapse. In this way the Hooge Crater had been made and, more importantly, Hill 60 had fallen into Allied hands.

Hill 60, although insignificant as a hill, was nevertheless of vital importance as an observation and artillery post. It was not a natural feature but simply a large heap of soil and rubble from the nearby railway cutting on the rail link between Ypres and Comines, an important rail junction. It was captured by the Germans from the French in December 1914, but in 1915, when this sector became a British responsibility, it was considered essential that Hill 60 should be retaken.

As any surface approach to the hill would be observed in its entirety by the Germans, and dealt with accordingly, the British

High Command decided that mining was the only effective way to regain this feature. Consequently 171 Tunnelling Company, Royal Engineers, was set to work. Three galleries were driven into the hill, not without considerable difficulty. Military mining is, of course, a practice which has been in existence for several thousand years.[3] In pre-Christian times miners were detected by putting bowls of water on the ground and observing whether the water moved as a result of vibrations below. In the conditions of the Western Front there was already too much vibration from gunfire, so mining was detected mainly by listening devices, called geophones, underground. Deception played a part too: occasionally a shaft was directed to a certain area in order to divert the counter-miners' attention from some much more important work.

Six mines were exploded on the evening of 17 April. The middle of the hill was blasted upwards, and equipment and bodies were flung in all directions. In case there should be many survivors, the mines were followed by a short but heavy bombardment. Finally 13th Infantry Brigade went forward, occupied the summit and dug in.

But the Germans did not give up lightly. They first poured a torrent of shells on to the British soldiers trying to dig in on the hilltop, then sent in their infantry. The 13th Brigade had now been reinforced, and a continuous close-quarter battle, using rifle, grenade and bayonet, raged on the summit. After forty-eight hours of failing to take the hill by attacks, the Germans turned once more to artillery. But still the British clung on. Among the newcomers were the 9th (Queen Victoria) Rifles, a London Territorial unit which fought like veterans; one of its officers, Lieutenant G.H. Woolley, was awarded a VC. By this time there were some five thousand bodies, a mixture of British and German, lying on the hill. At last it seemed that the Germans had had enough. As their artillery came under fierce Allied bombardment, it gradually withdrew: their exhausted infantry followed. For the moment the hill was in British hands.

But further north the Germans were now using poison gas, and on 5 May it was Hill 60's turn. Evil-looking clouds of gas came sliding over the hill in the early morning. The defending British infantry had no protection at all, but refused to give way. When the Germans attacked, the defenders were unable to resist and Hill 60 fell into German hands once more. And there it stayed for the next two years.

Six months after the April explosions a further set of tunnels was begun by 175 Tunnelling Company, RE. The following April, 3rd Canadian Tunnelling Company took over, and in November 1916 1st Australian Tunnelling Company relieved the Canadians. In June 1917 these deep-laid mines blew the top of the hill to pieces and the ground was occupied by Allied troops.[4]

Notes

1 It is still there today (although it was once hit by a German shell) and is open to visitors.
2 Today there is a Canadian memorial on Hill 62 and a line of Canadian maples on either side of the road leading up to it. On the ground round the memorial the visitor will find indicators showing where Hill 62 lay in relation to the other villages and features in the area.
3 Previous centuries offer numerous examples of counter-miners breaking into mine galleries and often fighting pitched battles in them. When Henry V was besieging Melun in 1420, miners and counter-miners met so often that they created a large underground chamber in which they fought: more fighting went on underground than above it, and even Henry himself took part. And St Andrews Castle in Scotland contains a mine and counter-mine dating from slightly later.
4 Today Hill 60 remains very much in its original state, as a memorial to those who died there; they include many who were trapped in collapsed galleries in the hill itself.

4

The Mines at Messines

In 1917 there were three good reasons for putting pressure on the Germans in the Ypres sector. The first was the need to divert German attention away from the French weakness; the second was the need to widen the salient and capture, if at all possible, some of the ridges from which the Germans were able to pick off the defenders at will; the third was the necessity, it was thought, to prevent an atmosphere of stalemate. Senior commanders are always alert to the dangers of troops losing their 'offensive spirit' through being kept too long in static lines; often this leads to quite unnecessary local attacks which cause losses of manpower for gains of little tactical significance. There is also a military maxim that one should always reinforce success, never failure. Success had certainly been the story of the mining operations at Hill 60 and Hooge.

The Messines Ridge seemed an area which would be vulnerable to operations of this nature, and in fact as early as spring 1915 a tentative start had been made. However, it was not till September of that year that the full plan was made by an engineering contractor with considerable military experience. Major J. Norton Griffiths, MP, proposed that instead of mining through the subsoil the shafts should go much deeper, some 60 to 90 feet below the surface, right through the blue clay. As this clay was stable, much longer galleries could be made: one, in fact, was 720 yards long. At a depth of 90 feet or even lower as they tunnelled to their final objectives, there was very little chance of the miners being detected by the enemy; if they were discovered at all it was much more likely to be through the German aviators (or spies) seeing piles of blue clay outside. In order to make sure this did not occur, the blue clay which had been extracted was either taken right away and hidden in the woods behind, or packed underneath the trench parapets. Yet in spite of this, in April 1917 a German raiding party came across a small heap of blue clay and took back a sample. Fortunately for the success of the Messines project, however, this discovery was dismissed as being merely an isolated experiment of no particular importance.

Norton Griffiths had the backing of an astute Engineer-in-Chief, Brigadier-General G.H. Fowke, who began implementing the Messines plan months before it was officially approved. The mine shafts were disguised by being labelled as 'deep wells', for their continuation was as likely to be interrupted by officialdom on the Allied side as by offensive action from the Germans. After the plan had been approved, six deep tunnels began to edge forward under the German positions. In the earlier stages an attempt was made to use mechanical diggers of the type used when the London Underground was being constructed (also through blue clay); however they were soon abandoned because they got bogged down in the heavy ground, and were replaced by relays of miners with picks. The tunnellers were British, Canadian and Australian, and the scale of their operation was immense. They constructed 5000 yards of underground tunnels, six feet high by three feet wide, and enough accommodation to sleep 6000 men and shelter 10,000. There were numerous deep dugouts for brigade or battalion headquarters, should these be needed, and a number of machine gun and observation posts on the surface to protect the operations below. The workings had to be fitted with noiseless water pumps, air conditioning (also silent) and rescue equipment in case of accidents which might be either natural or caused by heavy German bombardments. In addition the Germans were always liable to use *camouflets* – explosive charges specially designed to damage the sub-strata while leaving the surface undisturbed; these could cause galleries to collapse, often burying miners and mine together. However, the Germans had less success with countermining than might have been anticipated: the Allies, of course, used *camouflets* against German counter-mines.

Because it was thought that the mines would be only partly successful in crushing German resistance, a vast collection of artillery was brought into position to follow up the effect of the mines; it totalled 2266 guns and howitzers, in addition to the artillery already in use. Transporting the ammunition, a total of 144,000 tons, was a huge and dangerous task. Meanwhile the Royal Flying Corps photographed the German defences daily. A slight setback was the information (gained from prisoners and captured documents) that the new German tactic was to withdraw as many troops as possible from the front line, replacing manpower with strongpoints and machine gun posts. The second line of defence would be twice as strong and would be ready to launch a devastating counter-attack if the Allies penetrated the forward defences; it would also be beyond the range of the existing mines. Owing to the nature of the ground, which could sometimes be like a quicksand, the Germans built surface strongpoints of ferro-concrete; the gravel for the concrete was of very high quality and came by barge through Holland from the Rhine. In consequence these shelters were immensely strong and could withstand a direct hit – even though their occupants would be none the better for the experience. The strongpoints were called pillboxes because they looked like the flat white boxes in which chemists used to dispense pills at that period; it was also said that their loopholes made them look like post office pillar boxes – at a distance.[1]

In the preliminary bombardment, from 26 May to 6 June, three and a half million shells were fired on to the German positions. British Mark IV tanks, 28-tonners with a speed of two to three and a half miles per hour, and a variety of 6-pounders and Lewis guns moved up to their start lines. The noise of their clanking progress was masked by the Royal Flying Corps flying at low levels over the German front line. Zero hour was fixed for 3.10 a.m. on the 7th. At 3 a.m. the Front was so quiet it was said that nightingales could be heard singing; the survival of birds on the battlefield was one of the mysteries and miracles of the war. In the unnatural stillness the assault divisions stood waiting in the trenches, bayonets fixed.

At 3.10 exactly all nineteen mines went up in an explosion so loud that it caused panic in Lille, fifteen miles away, and was even heard in London. Nineteen volcanoes seemed to have erupted almost simultaneously (there was in fact a gap of eighteen seconds between the first and the last) as over a million pounds of ammonal tore apart carefully constructed defences from which the Germans had been dominating the Allied lines for the past two years. And as the pillars of smoke billowed upwards into the sky, the Allied artillery followed it by an unrelenting assault on all known German artillery positions behind the ridge. Nine Allied infantry divisions, a total of well over 100,000 men – British, Australians, New Zealanders, Irish and Welsh – swarmed forward. There was little opposition: most of the German defenders were too stunned and dazed to react; the main obstacles to the Allies were German shellfire from well behind the Messines position, using a mixture of high explosive and gas shells, and the huge craters which the mines had left. But the attackers still needed to be careful: the Germans were likely to recover quickly and, in addition to the expected counter-attack by troops hastily assembled from the rear and other areas, there was a danger that the places now being over-run would contain a number of soldiers who had escaped the shock of the explosion and could now be emerging from deep dugouts *behind* the attacking Allied troops. Though patches of strong resistance were encountered at some points, everything had gone so well up to now – the mines had exploded on time, the effect on the Germans had been even greater than expected, and fewer than half the British tanks had broken down – that the Allied troops risked under-rating the demoralized enemy. But the enemy was not too demoralized to use machine guns on the British soldiers, who made excellent targets as they began to dig in on top of the newly captured ridge.

However General Plumer, commanding 2nd Army, was not likely to let this prize slip from his grasp. He was one of the shrewdest generals of the war, a fact which became even more obvious as he directed his troops to occupy the vital points. A new line was established by 14 June. Over 7000 prisoners had been taken and large quantities of German arms captured. The German official history gave their casualty figures as 23,000, but this did not include the lightly wounded. Second Army casualty figures were 24,562, over half of which were in the Anzac Corps. The tragedy of the situation was that in the early stages immediately after the explosion, when the ridge was captured, Allied casualties had been very light: they had increased sharply as the troops moved ahead to consolidate the position and the Germans mounted a series of desperate counter-attacks.

Although nineteen huge mines had been exploded, two others of the same size and several lesser ones were not detonated. This was because these two larger mines had been set further forward than was needed for the capture of the ridge.[2] Four smaller mines south-east of Ploegsteert Wood were not exploded because the German position was over-run before they were needed.[3]

A full account of the Messines operation appears in *War Underground* by Alexander Barrie, published in 1961. Barrie was in time to interview a good selection of those most closely concerned. He records that Norton Griffiths had commanded the Scouts in the Matabeleland–Mashonaland War and again in the Boer War. Even before the First World War broke out he was advertising for recruits for an irregular regiment. Nationality did not matter, but experience did. Five hundred were quickly enrolled, and it was christened the Colonial Corps.

Kitchener, who had just been made Secretary of State for War, disapproved of irregular units and even Territorials. However, Norton Griffiths had known Kitchener in South Africa and Egypt and eventually persuaded him to accept this 'private army' as part of the official forces: it therefore became 2nd King Edward's Horse. Norton Griffiths travelled everywhere in a 2½-ton chocolate and black landaulette Rolls Royce, equipped with silk blinds, luxurious upholstery and a large table. He gave up much time to recruiting meetings, but also kept an eye on the progress of the contracts he had arranged. One of these was for tunnelling under Manchester to make a drainage system, and as he watched the Moles, as the men called themselves, he wondered whether their skills could be applied to military engineering.

Their skill was 'clay-kicking' or 'working on the cross'. They sat in the tunnels, supported at an angle of 45° by a wooden cross at their backs. They hacked out the clay with a light spade and passed it back with their feet for disposal behind, working very fast. On 15 December he wrote to the War Office, where his letter was acknowledged, noted and filed. No more would have been heard of it had the Germans not then blown up portions of the Allied line near Festubert. The Royal Engineers did their best to countermine, but had too many other commitments and too few men.

In mid-February 1915 Kitchener suddenly sent for Norton Griffiths and asked his advice, as a tunnelling contractor, about the best course of action to take over the success of the German mines. Norton Griffiths said: 'Clay-kickers,' and promptly sat on the floor and demonstrated the technique. 'Good,' said Kitchener. 'Recruit ten thousand.' Norton Griffiths was then sent off to see Brigadier-General Fowke. Both men were large, exuberant, like playful bulls, and they liked each other from the start. There were not, of course, ten thousand experienced clay-kickers in the country, but two hundred were soon found, some already in their sixties but capable of hard work just the same. No one gave his age as much over thirty, however white his hair and toothless his gums. Military etiquette was not their strongest point.

But theirs was not an unbroken success story. At Hill 60 German counter-miners, snipers and artillery fire caused large numbers of casualties and many problems. Norton Griffiths visited other units to recruit experienced tunnellers who were being employed on other duties. His visits were not popular with the officers concerned, so he always carried a few cases of excellent port for presenting to those most indignant. The arrival of miners in a fairly quiet sector was often unwelcome, for it could mean counter-mining and other retaliatory action by the Germans, a process which often caused losses to outweigh gains. Tunnelling officers who announced they were about to start mining grew accustomed to being treated like outcasts: one junior officer, Barrie recalled, responded by telling an immaculate brigadier that he looked 'like a bloody tart at a wedding'. But during the first half of the war the Germans were achieving better results from their mining than were the Allies; and men died from carbon monoxide gas which had collected in underground pockets, from explosions, collapsing tunnels and flooding.

Early listening devices had been crude and inefficient. Some were too weak: others were over-sensitive and recorded too much. Eventually the geophone solved the problem. It had been developed at the Sorbonne and consisted of two wooden discs faced with mica and filled with mercury. A stethoscope was plugged in behind.[4]

Mines were not used again by the Allies after Messines, but no one seems able to explain why such a valuable and perfected device should suddenly have been abandoned. Complaints had, of course, been made that after an explosion the Germans – particularly the Bavarians – were quicker at occupying and defending craters than the Allies were, and that one effect of the explosions was to make the way for advancing infantry extremely difficult. It appears that it was easier and quicker to allow men to be mown down by machine guns in thousands than to wait a little longer, take more trouble and save lives.

In retrospect it seems inconceivable that the Messines successes were not properly exploited and that six weeks were allowed to slip away before the next attack. From the excellent position at Messines Allied troops should have been able to advance on to the Passchendaele–Staden Ridge. This would have avoided the appalling difficulties of advancing over the plain up to the Passchendaele Ridge, as eventually occurred at terrible cost. Instead, the main assault was to be made by 5th Army under General Gough, who was given a task which he did not feel was sensible. Haig believed that the German Army was nearing the point of collapse and, the more it could be drawn into the Flanders sector and further weakened, the sooner would the war end successfully for the Allies. He felt that the Germans' resolution was wavering after many setbacks, including the failure of their Austrian ally to carry out its tasks, and not least the fact that American troops would soon become available to the Allies in large numbers. (They entered the war on 6 April 1917.) The British War Cabinet did not share Haig's optimism and was by no means sure that his new offensive should be sanctioned, even though it realized that German pressure must be diverted from the French sectors. He complained that the War Cabinet was not trusting the judgement of the commander on the spot. In view of the ignorance of Haig and his staff of the terrain over which the new offensive was to be launched, his reference to being 'on the spot' seems ironic at the very least.

The main offensive by 5th Army was to be supplemented by the transfer of divisions from 2nd Army, 3rd Army and certain other areas. A French Corps would give support on the left. With these came artillery, tanks and aircraft. The total air strength now amounted to 406 aircraft and eighteen kite balloon sections. Haig did not envisage a long campaign, but explained to the War Cabinet that he might occasionally be held up. Once the ridges were in his possession he thought that further advances would quickly become practicable. Although it was realized that the original drainage system had been destroyed, leaving the low-lying land in swampy condition, it was thought that adequate supplies of road-making material were available. Other sectors, such as Ploegsteert and Givenchy, were considered to be wetter than Ypres, and considerable success had been achieved by using sandbags in those areas. Reports from the Ypres battlefield indicated that it was not invariably swampy; some parts were liquid mud, like cream cheese, but others were firm enough to allow a trench to be dug in them. But, as the battle progressed, shellfire transformed the whole area into a vast, evil-smelling swamp, full of quicksands into which men, horses and guns could disappear quickly and leave no trace.

Gough was not entirely happy with the timetable he was given. The first day's objective was to be limited to a mile, after which there would be a period of consolidation lasting two days. Subsequent timings and objectives were equally unsatisfactory and it seemed highly unlikely that he would be able to follow Haig's instructions to capture Passchendaele Ridge, advance to Roulers and then continue to Ostend. Gough felt that he had insufficient troops for such an ambitious plan and that in any case Plumer should have been put in charge, not himself, for Plumer had two years' experience of the area while he himself had none. The date of the offensive was fixed for 25 July and it was assumed that the Passchendaele Ridge would be captured within four days; in the event it took four months.

Haig's optimism now seems impossible to understand. Up till this point he had had considerable support from Lloyd George, who had become Prime Minister in late 1916. Both men believed that, if a massive attack was now made on the German line in Flanders, resistance would crumble and the Allies could make a decisive breakthrough. But Lloyd George saw this as possible only if the French gave it their full support. Once Lloyd George realized that the French were either unable or unwilling to make a full contribution, he began to have considerable doubts about the policy of sending Haig the troops he was asking for; instead he tried to restrain the Commander-in-Chief from sacrificing more men in doubtful enterprises. Lloyd George's views on Haig were shared by other members of the Cabinet. However, when Haig was summoned to attend a Cabinet meeting he convinced them that he could defeat the Germans with British forces alone. This was welcome news to the Admiralty, which had persuaded itself that unless the Channel ports were taken from the Germans the Navy would no longer be able to cope with the U-boat menace. Haig's confidence that he could solve the Admiralty's problems with a land attack gained him its support. What Haig did not disclose was that his professed ability to beat the Germans without French support was based upon intelligence surveys which had assumed that the Russians would still be tying down large numbers of Germans on the Eastern Front; that, of course, was no longer true. As the Revolution gained impetus the Russian armies were disintegrating.

In spite of the enormous casualties which seemed inevitable as a result of his tactics, Haig has his supporters as well as his detractors. In *The Donkeys* by Alan Clark he is severely criticized, as are many of his military colleagues. Clark's title comes from a passage in Falkenhayn's *Memoirs* which quotes General Ludendorff as saying: 'The English soldiers fight like lions,' to which his Army colleague Hoffman replied, 'True. But don't we know they are lions led by donkeys.'

Haig was the youngest of nine surviving children of a prosperous whisky distiller, related to a distinguished Scottish family. Somewhat surprisingly, the boy was sent to school at Clifton College, Bristol, where 'he made no special mark in work or games'. Clifton seems an odd choice for the son of a prosperous Edinburgh tradesman. It had been founded a mere thirteen years earlier, had, as yet, acquired no special distinction, had financial troubles and was a long way from Scotland; however its headmaster, the Rev. John Percival, was a man of exceptional ability whose reputation had travelled far. From Clifton Haig went to Brasenose College, Oxford which, like some other colleges, did not have an entrance examination. At the end of three years at Oxford – reading for a pass, not an honours, degree – he failed to obtain a degree at all because he had missed a term's residence through illness. He could, of course, have made up the term by staying in residence another eight weeks. A pass degree is not a serious qualification at all: in those days it was based on a simple syllabus which made no demands on the intellect other than that the candidates should remember to attend a few lectures and complete nine terms of residence. Following Oxford, Haig entered Sandhurst, for which he was excused the entrance examination by virtue of having been at Oxford! One of his biographers wrote: 'There [at Sandhurst] he concentrated almost exclusively on work. He was not distracted by his companions who were mostly straight from school and three years younger than he. As a result he made few friends but he passed out first and was awarded the Anson Memorial Sword as Senior Under Officer.' In fact he does not appear on any list as having passed out first and the Anson Memorial Sword (now abolished) was not an award for that achievement.

He was commissioned into the 7th Hussars, played polo well, but in 1893 failed the examination to pass into the staff college. Three years later, however, he sidestepped this major obstacle by obtaining a nomination from the Commander-in-Chief of the Army, the elderly and often unpredictable Duke of Cambridge. Haig had set his mind on attaining military advancement, but his early career shows little trace of the ability which might have justified it. However, Haig knew there was usually more than one path to the top of the mountain and that some ways might be easier than others.

His progress thenceforward was smooth. With the influence of Sir Evelyn Wood, VC, Haig obtained a commission in the Egyptian Army. He was present at the Battle of the Atbara and Omdurman. Soon after this he was serving as Chief Staff Officer to General (later Sir John) French, who was commanding that cavalry in the Boer War. Subsequently he became ADC to King Edward VII. From then onwards his career proceeded even more smoothly, and one influential appointment followed another. Those who knew him well in the Army had less confidence in his military ability than in his ability to secure high appointments. In spite of the fact that the Boer War had shown how limited was the usefulness of cavalry in modern warfare, most of the senior officers at the start of the First World War had, like Haig, a cavalry background and outlook. The best of them was undoubtedly Allenby, who was able to conduct an efficient cavalry campaign in Palestine in 1917.

Although Haig knew what had happened to cavalry in the Boer War when faced with barbed wire or well-positioned riflemen, he did not lose faith in this arm. After his term as Inspector General of Cavalry in India, between 1903 and 1906, he published a book entitled *Cavalry Studies: Strategical and Tactical* in which he wrote:

The role of the cavalry on the battlefield will always go

on increasing because
1. The extended nature of the modern battlefield means that there will be a greater choice of cover to favour the concealed approach of cavalry.
2. The increased range and killing power of modern guns, and the greater length of time during which the battle will last will augment the moral exhaustion, will affect men's nerves more and produce greater demoralisation amongst the troops. These factors contribute to provoke panic and to render troops (short service soldiers nowadays) ripe for attacks by cavalry.
3. The longer the range and killing power of modern arms the more important will rapidity of movement become because it lessens the relative time of exposure to danger in favour of the cavalry.
4. The introduction of the small-bore rifle, the bullet from which has little stopping power against a horse.

He was forty-six when he wrote this. Nine years later he would be holding the highest military appointment in the British Expeditionary Force with the power of life and death – usually death – over millions. It must have been difficult for even the most intelligent officer to cope with his responsibilities when he found himself in command of vast forces and new weapons, but it seems to have presented no problems to Haig. He was the type of officer whom the Germans considered the most dangerous to his own side: unintelligent, industrious and ambitious. To him, strategy was a simple matter: you attacked until the enemy had no more troops left. The problem of whether you might run out of cannon fodder before the enemy did was not really a problem at all. The Allies had the British, Canadians, Australians and New Zealanders, together with their French allies and their Russian allies. It was a war of attrition and the Allies would win. It was not the way the cavalry would have preferred to do it, but if it went on long enough it would work. And what better way to die than fighting for one's country in a great war in the full enthusiasm of youth?

Haig died in 1928 at the age of sixty-seven. But he had not been alone in his convictions. There were other Allied generals of the same opinion and as many, if not more, on the other side.

In his *History of the First World War* B.H. Liddell Hart wrote:

> The real source of the offensive, more potent than any of the arguments with which he buttressed his case, seems to have been Haig's optimistic belief that he could defeat the German armies single-handed – in Flanders. In large measure it was to be a battle fought for British prestige. If such a single-handed design had little support in the history of war, the geography of Flanders offered still less. A plan that was founded on faith rather than on reason, both plan and faith were to be sunk in the mud of Flanders.
>
> Haig adopted the plan in face of formidable facts. His meteorological advisers had collated weather statistics, based on 'the records of eighty years', which showed that he could not hope for more than a fortnight, or at the best three weeks, of fine weather.
>
> Worse still, the Ypres offensive was doomed before it began – by its own destruction of the intricate drainage system in this part of Flanders. The legend had been fostered that these ill-famed 'swamps of Passchendaele' were a piece of ill-luck due to the heavy rain, a natural and therefore unavoidable hindrance that could not be foreseen. In reality, before the battle began, a memorandum was sent by Tank Corps Headquarters to General Headquarters pointing out that if the Ypres area and its drainage were destroyed by bombardment the battlefield would become a swamp. This memorandum was the result of information from the Belgian 'Ponts et Chaussées' and local investigation – the facts had indeed been brought to light by the engineers in 1915, but apparently forgotten. The area had been reclaimed from marshland by centuries of labour and in consequence the farmers of the district were under penalty to keep their dykes clear. Land used for pasture was such because it was subject to flooding and too wet for cultivation.

According to the official history, *Military Operations in France and Belgium 1917*, Haig was anxious for the offensive to begin as soon as possible because his Intelligence Section had told him that a period of wet weather began in early August. Whether the postponement of the offensive from 25 July to 31 July made any real difference seems debatable. A number of reasons were given for the delay. The Commander of the French 1st Army, General Anthoine, had said that an offensive beginning on the 25th would not give him sufficient time for his artillery preparations (it was considered important for French morale that they should take a leading role in this new operation which was certain to be a success), and diversionary attacks in other sectors also needed setting up. The success of the Messines attack was now seen as a hindrance to the Passchendaele offensive; it had been carried out prematurely in order to divert German attention from the French but, as it had not been followed up, it had warned the Germans to make special preparations on the Passchendaele front as that was obviously where the next blow would fall. The Germans knew very well what was coming. The second half of July had produced the most vigorous air battles seen so far: the battle above Polygon Wood on 26 July involved ninety fighters. Very gradually the Royal Flying Corps established superiority, with the result that most battles took place above the German lines; this was all the more creditable because one of the best fighter squadrons had been sent back to England following two heavy German raids on London, in the fires of which 162 people had been killed and 432 wounded.

If Haig was confident of the outcome of the offensive, so too were the Germans. Crown Prince Rupprecht, the Army Group Commander, and General Sixt von Arnim, Commander of the 4th Army which would be holding the sector, both felt that their numbers and dispositions were adequate for any emergency.

The preliminary bombardment, which has been criticized for making the terrain both impossible and impassable, might well have destroyed any battlefield, let alone one as frail as this. It began on 22 July and employed over three thousand guns. It was calculated that four and three quarter tons of shells were thrown at every yard of the Front. The bombardment lasted ten days, and ended at 3.50 a.m. on 31 July. Then it turned into a creeping barrage moving forward at 100 yards every four minutes, a pace geared to that of the advancing infantry whom it was designed to protect. Low clouds, some 500 to 800 feet up, prevented aerial observation of the battlefield. At zero hour, twelve divisions advanced on an eleven-mile front in torrential rain. The weather, which had been expected to remain fine until early August at least, had not fulfilled expectations. The rain continued day after day.

In order to prevent the Germans seeing exactly what was intended for them, zero hour had been fixed for nearly an hour before dawn. The effect of the relentless barrage had been to make the Germans keep their heads down. As the creeping barrage moved backwards into the German lines, the advancing troops marked their direction by using the light of thermite and oil bombs, neither of which encouraged German morale. Within the first hour, 800 yards was gained; the best progress was made on the left where Bixschoote, St Julien, and the Steenbeek and Pilckem Ridges were all captured. Matters were less satisfactory along the Menin Road. All the tactical moves had been rehearsed on a two-acre model in the rear area, and battalion officers down to the rank of company commander had been sent in rotation for instruction in what was expected of them when the day came. A considerable part of this preliminary briefing had dealt with the problem of ruined villages and farmhouses whose innocuous-looking walls had been lined with concrete and loopholed for machine guns. These were attacked by a combination of outflanking movements and concentrated fire from trench mortars, rifle grenades and Lewis guns. The rifle grenade (No. 23) had a range of 80 yards and could be particularly effective if aimed at a loophole. Each specialist rifleman carried twelve grenades. It was as well that these attacks proved so successful, for over half the tanks which might have dealt with these stubborn little forts slid off the track into shell holes or mud from which they could not be extricated.

The 2nd Anzac Corps forced its way into German-held territory past Messines near Gapaard, captured Hollebeke and advanced east of Battle Wood. The New Zealanders captured La Basse Ville after a very intense and bloody battle.

Haig recorded in his diary: '*Tuesday July 31.* Glass steady. Morning dull and coldish. The bright weather reported as coming is slower in its progress than expected by our weather prophet.' One imagines that much the same thoughts were expressed by the Australians and other attacking infantry, but with different words and emphasis. Haig continued:

Zero for all of Fifth Army except 14th Corps was at 3.50 a.m. [i.e. 2.50 Greenwich time]. For the latter Corps and the French it was 20 minutes later.

The heavy firing near here at 4.15 woke me up. The whole ground was shaking with the terrific bombardment. During the night the Fifth Army was to discharge 80,000 gas shells. The French also kept up a heavy fire.

In the afternoon I visited General Gough with C.G.S. He had been to H Qrs of 19th and 2nd Corps.

According to the official history, II Corps 'had, it was generally recognized, the hardest task of the day'. Their brief was to capture the entire Gheluvelt plateau, considered the most strongly defended area along the whole front. Among the German forces defending it were the formidable 16th, 17th and 20th Bavarian Regiments. Whatever could be done to make this area an impregnable system of defence in depth had been done, and in addition there was a massive concentration of artillery behind it in support. Even to reach it, the attacker had to get through the wreck of three woods: Shrewsbury Forest, Sanctuary Wood and Château Wood. The mixture of fallen tree trunks and shell holes would be sufficient to stop any tanks which tried to break through here. Four months earlier Haig had suggested to the Tank Corps that, as the ground would be firmer in this sector, a massed breakthrough by tanks should be possible. Firmly, the Tank Corps pointed out the error of this assumption.

As it was impassable for tanks it was obviously going to be a hard task for infantry, and it is astonishing that at this stage of the war British infantry should be fighting as well as it did here. Even though most of the soldiers were conscripts, they showed enterprise and tenacity which veterans would have been hard put to match. But they were carrying far too much – rifles, ammunition, grenades and equipment – to move fast, and in consequence the creeping barrage went on well ahead of them, leaving the machine gunners in their path free to pick targets at will. Instead of receiving support from their own artillery, the attackers found steady and concentrated German shellfire falling among them when they reached Sanctuary Wood and Château Wood. Unbelievable though it may seem, when the divisional commander had told Corps that a creeping barrage of twenty-five yards a minute was too fast and that it should be no more than twenty, he was told it was too late to alter it.

It was, of course, almost impossible to maintain a line of advance. Sometimes heavy shelling compelled the leading troops to swing one way or the other, at other times the presence of undamaged German machine gun posts made an advance along the original line nothing less than mass suicide. But once a unit diverged it was likely to become mixed up with another body of men, such as when elements of eight battalions all became huddled close in what had appropriately been nicknamed Clapham Junction. When confusion had occurred, it was impossible for those behind to know exactly where anyone was, and which objectives had been gained. Almost all the telephone lines from the forward signallers and forward gunnery observation posts were cut by shellfire, wireless would not work under those conditions, and signalling by lamp or flag became impossible because of smoke. Pigeons were used extensively, but their casualty rate was high, and it was the courage and determination of the 'runner' – as the human messenger was invariably called – which established any communications at all. Many were killed, and even when they did reach their destination much of the information carried was already out of date.

In spite of the enormous masses of metal which were pounding everything and everywhere to rubble, it was the human factor which enabled many of the most important successes to be won. A second lieutenant with the acting rank of captain, T.R. Colyer-Ferguson, led six men of his 2nd Northamptonshire Regiment up on to the Bellewaarde Ridge. His unexpected arrival caused the Germans to fall back, thinking they were about to be over-run, but as soon as they realized how small the party was they counter-attacked. Colyer-Ferguson picked up an abandoned German machine gun and used it to kill thirty-five of them; the remainder fled. He was awarded a Victoria Cross but was killed soon afterwards.[5]

The road from Hooge to Clapham Junction was covered by a huge German pillbox and no amount of shelling was able to put it out of action. Sixteen tanks tried to force a way past it, but all were knocked out by anti-tank guns. Fortunately for II Corps the other nineteen tanks had many successes before all being stopped by shellfire, mechanical trouble or soft ground.

All along the Front it seemed that nothing could stop the determination of the infantry. At St Julien the 13th Battalion of the Royal Sussex captured seventeen German officers and 205 German soldiers from the dugouts and pillboxes. Another VC was won here, this time by an officer in the Hampshires, Second Lieutenant D.G.W. Hewitt, but he did not live to wear it for he was killed by a German sniper soon afterwards. The Scots in the 51st Highland Division were luckier. Private G. McIntosh, of the Gordon Highlanders, felt that the battalion was not advancing fast enough when they came to the Steenbeek, which was continuously swept by machine gun fire. He crossed the river without waiting for orders and, armed only with a revolver and a grenade, worked around to the back of a German machine gun post, killed two occupants, wounded a third, and returned to his battalion with the machine gun. He too received a VC. Sergeant A. Edwards of the Seaforth Highlanders earned his VC by capturing a machine gun post and, in spite of being wounded, continuing to lead his men. The Welsh showed that they were not to be outdone. Corporal Davies of the Royal Welsh Fusiliers won his VC by capturing a machine gun post single-handed and, despite his wounds, leading an assault on a heavily fortified house. Here he was wounded again and died. Sergeant Rees of the South Wales Borderers captured a machine gun post and killed the occupants with rifle and bayonet. This not being enough, he moved on to a concrete emplacement where, after killing five Germans, he captured thirty, including two officers, and also acquired a machine gun. Other VCs were won by Sergeant R. Bye of the Welsh Guards, who captured a blockhouse, and Private T. Whitham, who captured a German machine gun post by dodging from shellhole to shellhole until he reached it and killed its three occupants, one of whom was an officer. And there were others, such as Corporal T.F. Mayson of the King's Own and Lieutenant-Colonel B. Best-Dunkley of the Lancaster Fusiliers. Other individual actions, no less brave, did not end in success,[6] and of course the price of all the successes in the advance was summed up in what was officially referred to as 'heavy casualties'.

By midday the situation had become what in military under-statement is described as 'confused'. Regiments were trying to consolidate areas which they had won, at a cost of nearly half their original numbers. Artillery support stopped, mainly because the gunners had no clear idea of what their targets should be. The Royal Flying Corps, which had been unable to gain a clear picture of the battlefield earlier because of low cloud and poor visibility, had now been allocated to bombing and strafing troops behind the German lines. They found plenty of targets, but were not able to work out from the troop movements they observed what plans the Germans had. So, far from being able to deduce what was going on 'on the other side of the hill', the British units did not even know what was happening on their own side and where everyone was. The Germans were, of course, forming up for a counter-attack. The rain, which had slackened off, began again steadily.

That counter-attack came without warning, and fresh lines of German infantry hurled themselves on to the Allied regiments who were clinging on grimly to their newly won positions. As their countrymen appeared, German prisoners, who shortly before had put down their rifles and raised their hands, now grabbed their rifles again and opened fire. This could have been very dangerous, but fortunately the German artillery chose this moment to deliver a supporting barrage which came down impartially on both sides. However as more German infantry appeared, some hard-won territory had to be yielded up again: what was left of St Julien once more passed into German hands. During the afternoon the rain settled into a relentless torrent; although it made the establishment of a new defensive line extremely difficult, it also rendered impossible the German attempts to regain much of their lost ground. And when they reached the point beyond which they could advance no further, they met such a barrage of Allied artillery and machine gun fire that they turned and once more retreated. The German regimental histories of the time record that many of their rifles and some of their machine guns were now so clogged with mud as to be unusable.

Back in GHQ, when the events of the day were pieced together it was decided that it had been a very satisfactory opening to the battle. Compared with the first day of the Battle of the Somme it was, for the casualties had been fewer and the territorial gains considerably greater. The Germans had undoubtedly had a bad day: their casualties had been high, 6000 of their soldiers had been taken prisoner, and many guns had been lost. Subsequently it was found that the German divisions in the front line had been so badly affected that they were withdrawn and replaced by others from elsewhere on the Front. So, unbeknown to GHQ, some part of the original intention of this offensive – to draw off pressure from the French – had been successful. The Gheluvelt plateau and much of the area between Bellewaarde and Pilckem, from which the Germans had operated with impunity for so long, were now in British hands. This, the Germans had felt, was their most important possession in the whole area – and now they had lost it. Overall the average Allied gain along the Front had been about 1000 yards – good, but slightly disappointing. Haig instructed 5th Army to consolidate ground won, make more and better use of artillery, and continue the infantry attack as soon as the artillery had achieved sufficient ascendancy.

The cost so far: in 5th Army some 4000 had been killed and three times that number wounded. But figures were only part of the story. Most of the units involved had lost up to 60 per cent of their fighting ability in terms of men, equipment and, not least, exhaustion. But Haig decided that the attack would be renewed at dawn on 2 August. What was left of 1 August would be spent preparing for it.

All over the battlefield dying and wounded men were lying, hoping that someone would find them and take them back to safety. For most that hope was never realized. But many were rescued by Captain N.G. Chavasse of the Royal Army Medical Corps, who was attached to the King's Regiment. Chavasse had already won a Military Cross and a Victoria Cross earlier in the war and on 31 July he won another Victoria Cross – signified by a bar to his existing one – for attending the wounded and rescuing them under heavy fire. In doing so, he himself was wounded so badly that he died soon afterwards. He was the only man in the entire war to win two Victoria Crosses.

Notes

1 Two of these pillboxes may be seen today in the Tyne Cot Cemetery, surrounded by gravestones, and the viewer can judge

how formidable a defence they made, even when exposed on a forward slope.

2 One exploded in 1955, was thought to have been set off by lightning, but the other is now lost because the papers describing its exact position were inadvertently destroyed.

3 It was the Allies' intention to remove them later, but this never took place and as far as is known they are still in position. However, they probably offer a lesser hazard than many of the unexploded shells and grenades which have been dug up and heaped in piles for the interest of visitors to the battlefields. There is an impressive collection of these at Croonaert, Wytschaete, in what is termed the Museum of Peace (see Chapter 14). Next to the museum is a well-preserved section of German trenches. Hitler served here in 1914, as a corporal in the German Army, and is said to have revisited it in 1940. Visitors are warned not to stray from the marked paths, and not to handle any of the lethal relics they might stumble over if they do.

The largest of the craters (now a pool) is at Spanbroekmolen, midway between Wytschaete (known to the soldiers as White Sheet) and Messines, near Lone Tree Cemetery. The crater, called the Pool of Peace, is now owned by Toc H, having been bought and presented to them by Lord Wakefield. It is 250 yards wide and forty feet deep.

4 Norton Griffiths was made a baronet after the war, and lived till 1937. His Rolls Royce also survived till the 1930s in spite of having been hit by a piece of shell while in France.

5 Nowadays Britain maintains a small regular Army with certain Territorial units in support, and fewer and fewer people are familiar with Army practices and etiquette. Until the late 1930s promotion for officer ranks occurred only when there was a vacancy. It was possible to remain a lieutenant or captain for fifteen years or more. Nowadays, however, there is a system of promotion – up to and including the rank of major – based on duration of service in a particular rank. In peacetime a man normally holds the rank of second lieutenant for 18 months before he is promoted to lieutenant. After a further five years he becomes a captain, and after a further five years he may expect to become a major. Any rank above that of major will be determined by selection. However, even in peacetime he may some-

times hold a temporary, or acting, rank above his own. Holding a rank above his substantive one does not usually mean he gets paid for his extra duties and responsibilities.

In wartime promotion is quicker, and a second lieutenant could find himself an acting major if there were heavy casualties among those senior to him. However, at the first opportunity he will be brought down to a rank appropriate to the time he has served in his substantive rank. This procedure suits the Treasury very well, even though it may be quite unfair to give a man certain responsibilities, not pay him for them, and then reduce his status at the first possible opportunity. At the end of both World Wars large numbers of officers suddenly found themselves reduced by several ranks to fit in with a peacetime establishment. But the military practice of emphasizing that a rank is only an acting and temporary one, as opposed to a substantive rank acquired by time, seems a particularly tasteless custom when used in citations or even on gravestones.

6 In order for its perpetrator to receive a recommendation for a VC an act of bravery needed three independent witnesses, and the risk of death had to be 90–100 per cent.

5

Everywhere Successful

The steady downpour which had begun on the evening of 31 July lasted for the next three days and nights. Those who have attempted to defend Haig's tactics affirm that this was exceptional even by Flanders standards. All weather is, of course, exceptional in temperate zones: only in the tropics does there seem to be any consistency, but it is seldom the better for that. There are, however, two points to be made about the rain in Flanders that summer. Rain was expected, and even a moderate rainfall would have turned the battlefield into a swamp once the drainage pattern had been destroyed. The fact that the rainfall was pitiless and unrelenting certainly made a bad situation worse, but it was command errors, rather than the unexpectedly heavy rainfall, which made this the worst battlefield in history.

The immediate effect of the rain was to separate the newly established front line from the rear areas by a swamp over two miles wide. All the streams which ran across the battlefield had overflowed. The only possible way to cross this swamp was by the very few roads, all of which were both under observation by the enemy and full of shell holes, usually several feet deep. Movement was therefore virtually impossible. In consequence, the attack planned to take place on 2 August was postponed until the weather changed. The weather did change, in so far as the rain stopped on 4 August, but the battlefield remained totally sodden. Resumption of the offensive was required at the earliest possible moment: every time a postponement was asked for on account of the weather, the need to do something to take German attention away from the French was given as a reason why attacks must resume soon. The two main tasks were to silence the ring of guns which menaced the Gheluvelt plateau and to prepare the route for the next big push in the central sector. Unfortunately for the Allies, the effect of artillery fire on the Germans was hardly noticeable and the enemy batteries remained as persistently dangerous as ever. Their ability to shell the Menin Road day and night was totally unimpaired.

At the end of the first day of battle the Gheluvelt plateau was divided as if by a line down the middle, with equal portions being held by both sides. The line ran through Clapham Junction and left Inverness Copse and Glencorse Wood in German hands. As a first step II Corps was to advance 800 yards and capture a series of German strongpoints, including the two woods, which as a preliminary were shelled with 3000 rounds on the 8th. The 9th turned out to be the first clear day of the month. When the attack went in, Glencorse Wood was found to be a mess of broken tree trunks lying on black, slimy mud pitted with shell holes. Nevertheless the advance went fairly well. The Germans countered by putting down a barrage behind the advancing troops, thus cutting them off from reinforcements, food, water and ammunition. That evening a German force assembled in Polygon Wood and, following a heavy barrage on Glencorse Wood, was able to push the British out of all but the north-west corner of that wood. At the end of the day the new Front, which had been won at great cost, was consolidated; the attack which had been planned for the next day was postponed. This really amounted to failure, for the whole of the Gheluvelt plateau needed to be in British hands before the main attack could go in. Anything less would mean that the main attack, scheduled for the 14th, would be constantly harassed by artillery operating from the Gheluvelt area.

On the 14th there was another heavy thunderstorm. As the battlefield, which had shown signs of draining off, was now saturated again, the attack was postponed till the 16th. At 4.45 a.m. that day the forward troops were all in position on their start line, the barrage began, and the morning looked like being sunny. However, the ground was too wet for tanks, the Germans were well dug in on carefully sited posts and the assaulting troops were already exhausted by the effect of reaching their start line. Most of the regiments had suffered heavy losses in the earlier fighting. Eighth Division had had 3000 casualties on 31 July and was now back in the line after a mere fourteen days to restore it to an effective fighting force. It was up against first-class German troops, who managed to infiltrate and work round to the rear of some of the leading British battalions. The Germans also succeeded in recapturing some of their machine gun posts, from which they delivered devastating fire on the flank of other advancing British troops. Then followed a further assault by fresh German troops. One British brigade used up all its ammunition before being forced to withdraw. It was not a very happy start. Some battalions were down to half their original numbers, and the survivors had spent the last two weeks in a swamp under constant shellfire.

Nevertheless they pushed on. The worst part of it was that when they took ground from the Germans they had no one to spare to mop up the points over-run. In consequence, Germans were able to come out of pillboxes in which they had taken refuge and fire into the backs of the leading British troops. Elsewhere the attack was held up by wire, by machine gunners, by German barrages which included gas shells, and, as ever, by the nature of the ground. Some of the assault troops moved forward through slime which came up to their knees. But, almost unbelievably, ground was won, and a number of Germans surrendered quite happily. More VCs were earned in these attacks – by Private F.E. Roon of the Royal Irish Fusiliers, whose courage as a stretcher-bearer saved the lives of many wounded; by Sergeant Cooper of the 60th Rifles, who single-handed captured a German pillbox containing 45 men and seven machine guns; and by Private E. Edwards of the King's Own Yorkshire Light Infantry, who captured a German blockhouse containing 36 Germans and thereby removed a considerable obstacle to the advance. Another 36 Germans were captured when Sergeant W.H. Grimbaldston of King's Own Scottish Borderers, although wounded, reached the entrance of a blockhouse and threatened to throw in a hand grenade unless the occupants surrendered. He was awarded a VC, as was his Company Sergeant Major for leading a force of six men to clear two blockhouses and capturing a total of 60 Germans.

On the 17th the Corps Commanders in 5th Army were told that, as this attack had now been halted, a fresh offensive would be launched on the 25th. In the interim local actions would be fought to establish a suitable start line for that date.

But the unexpected arrival of fine weather on the 17th and 18th meant that fighting was almost continuous. On the 20th seven tanks, shielded by an intensive barrage, captured four valuable German strongpoints: Hillock Farm, Maison de Hibou, Triangle Farm and the Cockcroft. Two more strongpoints were added on the 22nd. Unfortunately plenty more remained untaken and, as these were carefully camouflaged with mud, they remained a hazard which would be all too apparent later.

An attempt to occupy Inverness Copse was made by 43 Brigade. The Somerset and the Cornwall Light Infantry made good progress but were eventually halted by strong resistance in heavy rain, which made the use of tanks impossible. The Cornwall also experienced strong German counter-attacks in which flame-throwers were used. They hung on grimly for three days and nights, but eventually their attack resulted in nothing but casualties to about half the brigade.

At this point Haig realized that further limited assaults in the area were not going to pave the way for a 5th Army breakthrough as had been hoped, and he therefore decided to involve 2nd Army as well. General Plumer was told that the Gheluvelt plateau must be captured at all costs, and that 2nd Army, rather than 5th Army, should now accomplish this task. Plumer pointed out that preparing for this massive task would take three weeks, which was agreed. It did not, however, mean that 5th Army would now be able to spend three weeks resting and recuperating; although it would transfer II Corps to 2nd Army for the new offensive, this would only take place after the members of that hard-worked corps had occupied all the places for which they had been battling for so long: Inverness Copse, Glencorse Wood and Nonnen Boschen. The remainder of 5th Army was given the task of advancing towards Poelcapelle, which lay nearly three miles east of St Julien. A distance of a mile – or fifty yards – was of course a totally different concept on the battlefield from what it appeared to be on a map in GHQ at Montreuil. Fifty yards might mean an impassable swamp; a mile might include some firmer ground, but one could be certain that, the more approachable it might look to the attackers, the more heavily defended it was by the Germans.

The offensive planned for 25 August was cancelled; instead, everything was now to be concentrated on a major thrust on 20 September. But the intervening three weeks was not to be left unoccupied. First, II Corps was detailed to capture Inverness

Copse and Glencorse Wood on 27 August. When that day the leading brigade set off at 4.45 a.m., it was after a night of heavy rain which showed no signs of stopping. Even before the downpour changed to a mixture of heavy rain and gale force winds, the four links which had been allotted to assist the attack had all failed to get past Clapham Junction. The infantrymen who struggled on to the objective were thus either killed or driven back. The other three Corps in 5th Army had an even more dispiriting time. The plan was that they should not launch their attack until 1.55 p.m., but the battalions allotted to the attack had all been marched up the night before during the heavy rain. After they had reached their positions they had to stand for ten hours up to their knees in mud and slime, all the while being shelled. The rain stopped for a short time during the morning, then began again in torrents just before the assault was due to begin. When zero hour came and the troops set off, their progress was so slow that the creeping barrage which was meant to shield them soon moved far ahead and ceased to be any practical use. The 15th and 61st Divisions led the assault from the XIX Corps sector but made little progress. After half the officers and one-third of the men in these units had become casualties, the remainder were withdrawn to their original start line. XVIII Corps, using 11th and 48th Divisions, did slightly better, gaining Springfield and Vancouver Farms. At the start this attack had promised well, for the Germans showed themselves more inclined to surrender than to fight to the death. (They, of course, found this battle as gruelling as the British did and would have been happy to be taken prisoner and escape from the nightmare.) However, when they saw the desperate plight of the British as they tried to advance over ground on which they could scarcely stand upright the Germans decided to put up a more spirited resistance. XIV Corps, using two brigades, were also left behind by the creeping barrage, and as they were exposed to fire both from their front and their flanks withdrew to their original start line.

As an attempt to prepare positions for the next major offensive these attacks had been a dismal failure. Men had been asked to do the impossible and had almost succeeded. They were trapped in a situation in which, whether they advanced or stayed in their original position, they would experience a steady and high number of casualties. By this time many were almost hoping for a bullet to put an end to their misery. Meanwhile, back in GHQ the operations staff moved their pins on their maps and felt a natural disappointment that the preliminary moves for the next large offensive had met so little success. It was, however, recognized that unless certain objectives were gained before the next big push the chances of success were limited.

The weather on 28 and 29 August was, if anything, worse than it had been on the 17th. An attack which had been planned to take place on the Gheluvelt plateau on the 31st was cancelled, but at the same time it was emphasized that the woods in that area must be captured before the main offensive, whatever the weather. On 28 August an order to 5th Army from GHQ, signed by Lieutenant-General Kiggell, Haig's Chief of the General Staff, stated that preparations for the main attack must be completed within three weeks, but that 'the Commander-in-Chief considers it inadvisable that you should attempt any operations on a great scale before the Second Army is ready to co-operate'. It continued:

> He therefore desires that in the present circumstances your operations may be limited to gaining a line including Inverness Copse and Glencorse and Nonnen Boschen Woods and to securing possession by methodical and well-combined attacks of such farms and other tactical features in front of your line further north as will facilitate the delivery of a general attack later in combination with the Second Army. Proceeding on this principle he trusts that you will be able to arrange for reliefs, and for the rest and training of your divisions, as to ensure having a fresh and thoroughly efficient force available for the severe and sustained fighting to be expected later. He considers these questions of relief, rest and training to be of great importance.

Kiggell, as mentioned earlier, was the officer who, seeing the battlefield some time after Passchendaele had finally been reached, broke down and wept, saying: 'Good God, did we really send men to fight in this?'

He had had a remarkable army career. Born in Limerick in 1862, he was educated in Ireland and went on to Sandhurst. He was then commissioned into the Royal Warwickshire Regiment and in his entire military career never served in anything except staff or administrative appointments. From being Director of Home Defence at the War Office in 1914 he had become Chief of the General Staff of the British Army in France between 1915 and 1918. He received a number of exotic foreign decorations such as the Italian Order of St Michael and St Lazarus (Grand Order), the Order of Danilo from Montenegro, and the Japanese Order of the Sacred Treasure (Grand Order); there seems, however, to be no record of his ever having held any post in the armies of those countries or even visited them. His literary output was a revised edition of Sir Edward Hamley's *Operations of War*. (Hamley wrote extensively about the Crimean War which, after a few indecisive battles, settled down to an extremely uncomfortable form of trench warfare.) Major-General J.F.C. Fuller, the distinguished proponent of mobile warfare, wrote in his introduction to Leonard Woolf's *In Flanders Fields*:

> General Kiggell, a tall, gloomy and erudite soldier, was Commandant of the Staff College when I was a student there in 1914 and the only thing I distinctly remember him saying was: 'In the next war we must be prepared for very heavy casualties.' His theory of war was to mass every available man, horse and gun on a single battlefield and by the process of slow attrition wear down the enemy until his last reserves were exhausted and then annihilate him.

According to Fuller, Kiggell never went near a battle but 'concocted Napoleonic battles on paper which, on the ground, turned out to be slaughter-house dramas'. Kiggell survived not merely the First World War but even the Second.

Of course, Kiggell cannot take all the blame for the ineptitude of the Ypres campaign. Haig was the architect.[1] Fuller said of Haig: 'He lived and worked like a clock, every day he did the same thing at the same moment, his routine never varied. In character he was stubborn and intolerant, in speech inarticulate, in argument dumb.' Unfortunately, like Kiggell, Haig had studied the tactics of past wars and could not see how hopelessly unsuited they were to contemporary battles. Fuller considered that Haig's staff were all yes-men and that the only person who had any influence with the Commander-in-Chief was General Charteris, 'a hale and hearty back-slapping fellow, as optimistic as Candide, who conjured resounding victories from each bloody hundred yard advance like rabbits from a hat: he fed Haig on false news – anyhow false to the men at the front – and completely misled the Press and the British public'.

On 1 September 2nd Army was given its instructions for the main offensive. Its task was to capture Passchendaele Ridge

> from Broodseinde southwards to Hollebeke, including Polderhoek and Tower Hamlets Ridge at an early date in order to facilitate the further advance and at the same time protect the right flank of the Fifth Army.
>
> The Fifth Army will advance simultaneously with the above operations. . . .
>
> The operations will be carried out by the following troops:
>
> | | |
> |---|---|
> | I Anzac | 1st, 2nd, 4th and 5th Australian Divisions. |
> | X Corps | 21st, 23rd, 33rd, 39th and 41st Divisions. |
> | IX Corps | One division north of Ypres–Comines Canal (19th Division). |
> | II Anzac (In Reserve) | New Zealand, 3rd Australian, 7th and 49th Divisions. |

The objectives were then listed: they included the notorious Polygon Wood.

Before the next offensive could begin there was, of course, much to be done. The casualties during the first four weeks had amounted to just under 70,000, and ammunition had been used up so fast that replenishment would take time. These factors were bad enough, but another, less tangible, one also had to be considered. That was morale. During the previous month thousands of men had been launched forward to fight against well-prepared positions from a battlefield on which there was no shelter and on which it was an effort to remain upright. The casualty figures for dead and wounded were high in relation to the small tactical and territorial gains; the figures for normal sickness remained low because normal ills were not counted as sickness at all. The criterion of what constituted sickness was shown when reinforcements were taken from venereal disease hospitals. Some apprehension was indeed voiced that this might lead to the spread of infection but, in view of the fact that the men were otherwise able-bodied, the risk seemed justifiable – to those not in contact with them.

In the First World War the art of public relations had not been taken up by the Army. In the Second, Montgomery showed himself frequently in the forward areas because, he used to say, in the First he had never seen anyone above the rank of lieutenant-colonel anywhere near the Front. In 1917 GHQ assumed that, because the Germans had not launched any further heavy attacks on the French, the battle of attrition in Flanders was achieving its purpose by drawing divisions away from the French-held sectors. As it happened, this was true, for the Germans had also withdrawn from the Flanders sector thirty divisions too exhausted for further use in the near future, and taken ten from the French sector as replacements. These facts might have given comfort to Allied troops floundering around in the slime and corpses of the battlefield if they had been available to them; on the other hand, they might have been received with complete indifference. One of the ironies of the situation was that Haig might be destroying the last remnants of the British Army in order to assist the French, for whom he made no secret of his dislike.

GHQ was not entirely happy with the general situation at the beginning of September 1917. Pétain was said to have the French Army back under control after the events of six months earlier but, according to report, could not vouch for their behaviour if the Germans launched another Verdun-type attack. He had, however, staged a limited offensive in that area in late August with some success. More disquieting was the news that the Russian Front was

61

now giving the Germans minimal trouble and that they were withdrawing divisions from the East in order to launch an offensive in the West. Meanwhile, the Americans were not likely to be in France in adequate numbers before 1918 and even then would need to be equipped from British resources. A gleam of light shone in Italy, however, where the Austrians, under great pressure, were appealing to the Germans for help: this Front might divert some of those divisions now being released from the Russian Front.

Haig had other problems: politicians and journalists. Foremost among them was Lloyd George who, although a civilian, had the temerity to criticize the way the war was being fought, the allocation of resources and much more. Lloyd George thought that a holding operation was the best tactic in France now, allowing the British and Imperial troops to recuperate, the French to get back into full fighting trim, and the Americans to become available in large numbers. He thought that in this quiescent period at least a hundred guns should be sent to assist the Italians. As there was already an acute shortage of certain types of gun and ammunition in Flanders, this suggestion nearly gave Haig apoplexy. However, when it was agreed that the Passchendaele offensive should be allowed to continue, Haig reluctantly arranged with Pétain that some French guns should be spared for the Italian Front. Although the conditions of the battlefield did not appear to have penetrated to Kiggell's ivory tower, Haig had been told more times than he liked that, if the weather in Belgium had been bad so far, in the remaining months of the year it could hardly be better and might be even worse. Manpower was also a problem. The call-up was now reaching deeply into reserves who might well have expected to avoid active service altogether, and yet there were still shortages running into thousands. Plenty of people now felt, of course, that the more Haig complained about shortage of manpower, the better for the survival of the nation. France had apparently already reached the end of her manpower resources, which was why Pétain was saying that, in spite of the success of his recent limited offensive, morale was worse than ever and if the Germans made an attack he would be unable to hold it. There was a distinct possibility that if France were put under further pressure she would try to make a separate peace. In hindsight it is now known that if peace negotiations had been begun in 1917, when there seemed to be a general stalemate, they might very well have ended successfully and some of the more unfortunate aspects of the later Versailles settlement been avoided.

On 9 August Haig had written to Robertson, Chief of the Imperial General Staff:

> Unfortunately Lloyd George has got the French with him as well as the Italians. Foch is hopeless. . . . He seems to have made up his mind that it is hopeless looking for good results on the West Front. That will make my task much harder.
>
> The French keep rubbing it in that it is necessary to have a central staff at Paris. I can see Lloyd George in the future wanting to agree to some such organisation so as to put the matter into French hands. However, we will see all about this. His game will be to put up the (useless) Foch against me as he did Nivelle against you in the spring. He is a real bad 'un. The other members of the Cabinet seem afraid of him. Milner is a tired dyspeptic old man, Curzon a gas-bag, Bonar Law equals Bonar Law. Smuts has a good instinct but lacks knowledge. On the whole he is best, but they help one very little.
>
> This rain is cruel luck but it will get fine in time.

But it was not fine on 1 September and he recorded in his diary: 'Heavy showers of rain fell throughout the day. Owing to bad weather there has been little military activity.' On the 7th he wrote:

> Foch seemed on arrival at Amiens to have all his 'hackles' up but my few friendly words quickly calmed him, and we were all on the best of terms. His experiences in London should have done him good. He had gone there behind the back of Pétain and myself to get the British War Cabinet to sanction 100 French guns being withdrawn from *my* command. The War Cabinet then handed the questions for me to arrange with Pétain. This we have done satisfactorily for all. I found Pétain straightforward and most businesslike.

Haig was in fact something of an expert on people going behind other people's backs. He had criticized Kitchener when he thought the Secretary of State was opposing him, but became very friendly when it seemed that Sir John French was likely to lose the post of Commander-in-Chief. Haig's attitude to French had been totally correct until it seemed that there might be a chance for him to replace his superior officer. If Haig had been as devious in his military strategy as he was in devising his own personal advancement, the Battle of Passchendaele would have cost many fewer lives.

On 14 September he wrote:

> Sir F.E. Smith came to lunch. He is now Attorney General. After several glasses of wine, port and old brandy, he was most communicative and very friendly. He stated *privately* to me after lunch that he, Lloyd George and Winston Churchill dine regularly together once a week and that although he [Smith] is not in the War Cabinet, he is in a position to influence the Prime Minister very considerably. He assured me that he [Smith] is all out to help us soldiers on the Western Front because he has seen the splendid work which has been and is being done by the Army under my orders.

F.E. Smith, the future Earl of Birkenhead, had a mind of remarkable brilliance. Unfortunately, just as his career reached its peak so did his drinking. His lapses of concentration were notorious, but it seems unlikely that, despite his reference to 'us soldiers on the Western Front', he visualized Haig as a foot-slogger in the swamps of Passchendaele.

Haig found Winston Churchill, the Minister of Munitions, amenable but more difficult to manipulate than Smith. 'I have no doubt that Winston means to do his best to provide the Army with all it requires, but at the same time he can hardly help meddling in the larger questions of strategy and tactics; for the solution of the latter he has had no real training, and his agile mind only makes him a danger because he can persuade Lloyd George to adopt and carry out the most idiotic policy.' This astonishing statement is a measure of Haig's self-deception. Churchill had been through

Sandhurst, served in Cuba, in the Tirah expedition, in the Sudan and in the Boer War, and had commanded the 6th Battalion of the Royal Scots Fusiliers in France in 1916 in the Ploegsteert sector – in Flanders itself.

Of Asquith, Haig wrote: 'He said he had been immensely struck with all he had seen and particularly with the grand spirit of confidence existing from top to bottom in the army. I felt the old gentleman was head and shoulders above any other politician who had visited my Hd Qrs in brains and all-round knowledge. It was quite a pleasure to have the old man in the house. So amusing and kindly in his ways.' He was talking about the man who had been Prime Minister up till the end of the previous year. Asquith no longer had any real power, but he might, as Haig knew, still have influence.

On 20 September, just after the start of the new offensive, Haig wrote: 'About midnight General Gough proposed that operations be postponed on account of rain, but General Plumer, between 1 and 2 p.m., after consulting his Corps and Divisional Commanders, decided to adhere to plan. Zero hour was 5.40 a.m. The attack was launched on a front of about 8 miles from Langemarck on the North to Hollebeke on the Ypres–Comines Canal on the South. Our attacks were everywhere successful.'

Note

1 It should, however, be remembered that most of the criticisms of Haig came after the war.

6

Did We Really Send Men to Fight in This?

The plan for the assault on 20 September had been carefully designed by Plumer, who had been a general when Haig was still a captain. Plumer had been in charge of the final Staff College exercise when Haig was a student there, and his comments on Haig's performance were far from flattering. But now Haig was the senior man, and whatever Plumer did must earn the Commander-in-Chief's approval. This, however, did not deter Plumer, who decided that capturing the Gheluvelt plateau would require four separate attacks at intervals of six days. These gaps would be needed to ensure that all the necessary supplies and ammunition were brought up for the next attack. Each step would take the assault divisions 1500 yards further forward, and each division would be attacking along a 1000-yard frontage. Knowing that the Germans would counter-attack briskly as soon as the 2nd Army paused, Plumer arranged for strong counter-barrages and fresh infantry to be put in to meet it. Haig's envisaged attack frontage of 6800 yards was shortened by Plumer to nearly 3000 yards. This was concentration of force indeed, and it was supported by 1295 guns and howitzers – although 44 guns and howitzers fewer than Plumer had asked for, nevertheless considered to be enough to break up all the German fortifications in the way of the infantry, as well as to give them support while they were advancing. For the preliminary bombardment and the first day of the attack, three and a half million shells were allocated. As these were mostly aimed to fall on a plateau, rather than in a swamp, it was felt that they would be adequate to destroy most of the dense German defences in the area. To ensure that every shell fell on or near its appointed target, a careful plan for air and ground observation of the German positions was arranged.

Plumer had made a thorough analysis of the Messines operation which had run into trouble in the later stages. He decided that more flexible arrangements should be made for the infantry at Gheluvelt, so that assault, outflanking movements and mopping up were all catered for. The opportunities for outflanking would appear to have been somewhat limited on such a concentrated battlefield. Mopping up did not merely mean clearing out pillboxes which had been over-run and bypassed – it also meant holding certain points against the inevitable counter-attack. All these arrangements made heavy demands on junior commanders, whether officers or NCOs. Every unit was given specific briefing and training for its rôle in the forthcoming battle. Meanwhile more small-scale attacks were made on the objectives considered desirable for the establishment of an effective start line. However, as the first series of these proved unsuccessful, merely leading to casualties without gain, the later ones were cancelled. Instead, everything was focused on preparations for the offensive.

Preparations were certainly needed, and not merely in training and supplies. The scale of the offensive and the enormous quantity of guns and shells involved required railways, roads and dumps in rear areas, linked to an adequate system for transferring them to the Front as needed. The latter need proved an almost impossible task. Some of the original tracks, including the notorious Menin Road, had been shelled out of existence. Repairing them properly with road-mending materials was a long and arduous task; a better method was to use planks, which were easier to lay and handle. The planks were of elm or beech, two and a half inches thick, nine feet long and one foot wide. First the shell holes underneath had to be filled in, then a platform of planks laid lengthwise formed a foundation on which a track of cross planks could be laid. The road was held firm by pine logs which were laid along the edges. Fortunately, much of September was fine, and roadmaking became slightly easier as the swamp dried off.

It may not sound too difficult a task. But it was carried out at night, and the Germans knew exactly where the tracks lay and what was likely to be happening to them: constant shellfire destroyed both roads and roadmakers. The roadmakers also had to compete for space with men, supplies, guns and ammunition already using the tracks in order to hold on to their existing gains.

Much of the roadmaking was done by engineers and pioneers and men of the Labour Corps; the last two categories are normally thought of by the public as having a safe, easy job: in this area they had one of the most dangerous and exacting tasks on the whole Front.

Captain O.H. Woodward of the 1st Australian Tunnelling Company had been involved in mining operations, and when these ceased he was employed on roadmaking in the forward areas. 'These timber roads,' he wrote:

> were like a ribbon stretching across a sea of shell holes and so were easily discerned by the enemy Observation Balloons. It is an axiom of War that interference with the enemy's lines of communication is highly profitable, and so the enemy artillery paid particular attention to our work. We must have presented a fine target. Our roads ran practically at right angles to the Trenches so that an enemy gun placed in line with our road had a simple task. So long as the aim was right length did not matter. If the range were too long for the working party the probability was that a portion of the newly made road would suddenly leap skyward. Thus it was a case of building and repairing over and over again until our patience was almost ended. . . . the slow but steady increase in our casualty list was disheartening. To reduce casualties we did most of our work in the early morning usually arriving at the Road Head before daybreak. We made our best progress on dull foggy mornings, as under these conditions the visibility was, as regards the enemy, bad.

The trials of those fighting on the Ypres Salient were not limited to the enemy, or even the weather. In an ideal campaign – if that can be imagined outside a staff officer's daydreams – members of a unit all know each other and have a clear idea of what they are expected to do and how they will do it. Passchendaele was not an ideal campaign and the Artillery, which had such an important rôle to play in the battle, was only too well aware of it. Mark Severn,[1] who was serving in a siege artillery battery in the salient, recalled that up till November 1917 each group of batteries in siege artillery was commanded by a colonel

who in times such as these, had barely got to know his Battery Commander by name when the whole group was reorganised, and he found himself as the nominal head of an entirely fresh set. What chance had the most efficient C.O. of commanding, in any real sense of the term, a number of scattered units, whose position, personnel, armament and numbers were changed about once a week. The siege battery therefore tended to become a self-contained command and the Battery Commander, like the Rajah of an independent state, was inclined to look on all colonels as emissaries of a superior foreign power who must be placated and hoodwinked or totally disregarded, according to the length of their stay and the force of their personality.

On arrival in the Ypres area 2XX siege battery became part of the nth Heavy Artillery Group and, as soon as the battery was in action, the battery commander went in person to Group HQ to report to the Colonel. He seemed a pleasant and kindly old gentleman with an intimate knowledge of the salient. He gave Shadbolt a lot of excellent advice, and some even better beer, and, congratulating himself that at last he had got a C.O. whom he could respect and like, Shadbolt returned to the battery. The next day an entirely different C.O. appeared in the position and announced that the battery had been transferred to his group. He was a much younger man than the C.O. of the day before, and far less human. Though the day was very hot, he declined the proffered refreshment, and at once launched into a long lecture on calibration and its effect on shooting. Tall and cadaverous, his nut-cracker face ornamented with a long drooping moustache, he theorised on the science of gunnery for nearly two hours. After the first half hour Shadbolt found it hard to pay attention. As in a dream, he heard the far-away monotonous voice saying 'ballistic coefficient – muzzle velocity – angle of projection –

69

temperature of propellant – elimination of error' and he awoke with a start to find the zealous theorist was taking his departure. Needless to say he did not inspect the position, nor take any interest in the practical working of the battery in action. Within a week his place was taken by another Colonel who appeared in the battery daily in the rôle of a kindly district visitor. He said a few comforting words to everyone, spoke hopefully of the prospect of leave, inquired after the men's health, and related any local gossip he had collected on his rounds. He never talked 'shop' except with an apologetic air, as if he were some good-hearted bailiff sent by a remorseless landlord to demand the last instalment of the rent.

The 'district visitor' did not stay long either. He was followed by a colonel 'of the grandmotherly kind who issued a little booklet to all the batteries of his group packed with detailed instructions which covered any possible and impossible contingency'. He was most particular about the safety of ammunition and the prevention of fire. To this end, one of his orders read that a tub of water should be kept in each gun pit, and another that instantaneous fuses should be kept separate from the ordinary delay action fuses. . . .

And so it went on. But Severn soon noted that the Ypres Salient had established that it was not the machine gun but the heavy howitzer which had become mistress of the battlefield. It was certainly the dominant factor. First of all, heavy shellfire had completely ruined the terrain for normal infantry tactics; secondly, the concentration of shellfire had caused the Germans to build blockhouses so strong that they could only be destroyed by a direct hit from a heavy howitzer; and thirdly, the guns had demonstrated that they could inflict a steady stream of casualties which eventually exceeded those of the most desperate infantry attacks. In fact, on the Western Front in 1917 there was a steady toll of 7000 casualties a day, irrespective of any larger numbers resulting from set battles.

Artillery duels increased in intensity as the war continued. There had always been problems over the supply of shells, at first because manufacture was badly organized, and later because of the vast numbers used. Mark Severn wrote:

On his way to the O.P. about 7.30 a.m. one morning Shadbolt passed close to the Cavalry barracks at Ypres and watched a six-gun battery of 9.2 m. firing salvoes. It was a fine sight to see those six monsters in line all firing as one. About an hour later the enemy replied with eight batteries and for four hours rained down on them an incessant torrent of shells. When he returned about midday four of the howitzers were standing on mounds of earth completely surrounded by shell holes. The ground round the other two was not too cut up to prevent them being moved, but the gun barrels had so swollen with the intense heat of the enemy shells that they could not be run out of their cradles. All the ammunition had been blown up or destroyed and the whole area was a welter of havoc and destruction.

At Trois Tours the six 6 inch howitzers concealed among the trees were rapidly reduced to five and then to four and then to three. Night and day the shells burst in the little wood with a terrifying crump and the casualties mounted and mounted. After dark, the ammunition fatigues, the long programme of night firing, and the incessant gas shelling from the enemy, flayed ragged nerves and put an end to sleep.

During the First World War the Artillery was divided into two principal groups: the Field Artillery, which was a combination of the Royal Horse Artillery and the Royal Field Artillery, and the Royal Garrison Artillery, which had a variety of weapons including heavy, siege, coast defence and mountain artillery. Although both groups employed guns and howitzers, the particular function allotted to a unit determined which type of artillery they would be most likely to use.

'Guns' included all those weapons with a long barrel which sent off their projectiles at great velocity on a low trajectory. Howitzers fired at a much steeper angle – the high trajectory of their shells made them particularly suitable for use against blockhouses and trenches. When the war began the Germans had more howitzers and the British and French had more guns. The most famous guns were the 18-pounders (four miles range), manned by the Royal

Field Artillery, which in this rôle became known as the Divisional Artillery; the 60-pounders, of which there were never enough, which had a range of six miles; the 4.7, with a range of five miles; and the 2.75, which could fire a 15 pound shell three and a half miles and could also be disassembled and carried on mules.[2]

Among the longer-range guns, which became available in the later stages of the war, was the 6-inch Mark XIX which had a range of ten miles but, as it weighed over ten tons, was a problem to transport. The 9.2s (not to be confused with the 9.2 howitzer), the 12-inch and the 14-inch all had ranges varying between 15 and 20 miles, but were so cumbersome that they were all fired from railway mountings.

Howitzers included the 6-inch 26 cwt, with a range of six miles, and the 9.2, which travelled in three sections but when fired had a range of up to seven miles. The weapon itself weighed 15 tons and the shell it fired weighed 290 pounds. Needless to say, transporting any of these weapons through the Passchendaele area was a task which ranged from the difficult to the impossible.

German weapons were roughly equivalent to those of the Allies, though some, particularly in the early stages of the war, were superior. A few days in the battle area were usually sufficient for a man to learn to distinguish what type of weapon the Germans were using against him. Some, like the 5.9, were especially disliked. Nearly as unpopular was the Minenwerfer howitzer, which fired twenty rounds an hour of high-explosive shells, each weighing over 200 pounds. Its range was from 220 to 600 yards and it seemed uncannily accurate in finding its target.

By 1917 most artillery units consisted of officers and men whose entire experience of the Army had been in wartime. On occasions they were inspected by senior officers who appeared to belong to a different world. As regular soldiers they had learnt their soldiering in pre-war times, often in stations like India, to which new equipment and ideas were slow to penetrate. Some of them were now revelling in the fact that all the equipment used in this war was new by their standards, and they became extremely enthusiastic and knowledgeable about it. Having been starved of technical information themselves for so long, they wished to share their new-found knowledge with as many audiences as they could and seemed unaware that their listeners might not be so enthusiastic.

The others knew that all their knowledge, such as it was, was long out of date and therefore took care not to inspect equipment which might invite questions they were unable to answer. Instead they had pet subjects, such as clean corks in water bottles, gun platforms or sanitary arrangements.

At each end of the ranking ladder there were extremes. Some men contrived to find a joke whatever the circumstances; others concentrated on making a bad situation seem worse. There was one young man who, according to Mark Severn,

> treated every contingency of war as a pleasantry devised by fate for his special entertainment and amusement. With his large mouth and cheerful grin this youthful mathematician used to juggle successfully with figures while the skies rained shells. Next to him was Gunner Thomas, a Welshman whose superior education had turned sour inside him. He suspected all those who were superior to him in military rank, if not in mental ability, of bearing him a personal grudge. All officers and sergeants came automatically under this category . . . in the morning he would allow no smile of greeting to relax his melancholy features, but invariably produced some dismal prophecy about the weather or some well-founded complaint anent the discomforts of life in war-time.

Not that it was easy to be cheerful:

> It was still raining, and guns and howitzers had to be manhandled over the sodden spongy ground. Ever and again they would sink to their axles, and lines of tired, blaspheming men would heave and heave under the remorseless downpour. The blinding flash of a shellburst would light up their glistening helmets and bowed forms, and etched against the surrounding blackness you saw a sudden picture of the slowly moving howitzer, the sandbags of the shattered trenches, the dismembered stumps of blasted trees, and caught the green shimmer of water in innumerable shellholes. Straining at the ropes like

beasts of burden condemned to unremitting toil, they would lose all fear of death in the hopeless misery of living and, when daylight broke, would sink to sleep in the mud, unmoved by shellfire or rain.

The difficulties of ammunition supply became more pronounced as the rain turned the churned up countryside into a morass where wheels sank deep and animals laboured up to their hocks in clinging mud. The task of the Army Service Corps was no sinecure for the only road from Poperinghe to Ypres was shelled every night by the enemy. The officer in charge sits in a lorry full of explosives which, in the pitch dark, endlessly jolts forward, stops and jolts on again like a London bus in a traffic jam. He has an eerie feeling that he is being shelled with silent missiles from a noiseless gun, for the rattle and roar of the engines drown all but the nearest shell bursts. The long column arrives without mishap at the road junction where the leading lorry skids heavily into the ditch. Cursing heartily, he orders the cargo of heavy shells to be unloaded, and with ears straining to hear the ominous whine of approaching shells, watches the frantic efforts of the men to get the lorry on the road again. This is done at last, the load is replaced, and he heaves a premature sigh of relief. Then the next in the line skids in the same place. A column of mules and limbers going up with 18-pounder ammunition tries to pass, and is met by a battalion of utterly weary infantry marching down. With uncanny prescience the Boche chooses this inauspicious moment to put down his half-hourly concentration. Wild confusion ensues, a pandemonium of bursting shells, kicking mules, and yelling men, the whole lit up in the glare of blazing cartridges as a lucky shot sets fire to a lorry load. Finally, a harrassed but ever cheerful A.S.C.[3] subaltern arrives in the battery dug-out, swallows a much-needed drink, exchanges the news of the day, pockets his receipted tally and is off again on his dark and dangerous journey home. His parting thought is 'Thank God, I'm not like these poor devils, condemned to live in this accursed spot.' Their thoughts about him are 'What a life. Thank God, we are safe and snug in our dug-out and are not compelled to go up and down these dangerous roads at night.'

In August, life for artillery in forward positions had become so unbearable that relief of officers and men took place every twenty-four hours.

The night before a battle was spent working out barrage tables in the evil-smelling little pill-box. At intervals the guttering candle would be blown out by the concussion from a nearby explosion or the threatening plop of gas shells would interrupt mathematics whilst respirators were put on and men warned on the guns. Just before dawn, a copy of the completed tables was given to the No. 1 of each gun. This showed the angles and elevations and times for each successive lift. When the barrage began all hope of issuing orders by word of mouth vanished and the blast of the whistle or a wave of the arm was all that the officer on duty could achieve. On these occasions the only casualties sustained were due to rare prematures from the 18 pounder gun muzzles immediately in rear. Six evil-looking mouths would spit and crack in deafening unceasing clamour, and the shells pour over their bigger sisters like flocks of birds in whirring flight. To the right and left, in front and rear, a thousand others would join in to mingle their strident barking with the deep bellow and boom of the howitzers. First the bass and then the treble would lead the chorus until the whole swelled into a rending, rolling thunder of sound shattering the ether and annihilating thought.

But they knew well enough what happened when shells landed, because it often happened to themselves; 2XX had 100 per cent casualties in three months, but somehow the spirit of the battery survived even though most of its original members had gone:

Merredew and Cooper were binding up the wounded in the Battery Command Post when a direct hit landed on the roof. There were ten men inside and instantly eight of them were blown to shreds. The other two, the two officers, staggered out from under a heap of human flesh, shattered sandbags and twisted iron, miraculously untouched. A few moments later another shell landed on a detachment dug-out killing all the occupants and overturning the gun alongside. . . .

A common grave seemed the only solution to the grisly problem of burial and in silence the earth was heaped over the pitiful remains. The B.C. post was moved into a pillbox some distance to the flank, the guns replaced on their platforms and by midday the battery was firing again.

The Colonel came up a few days later and sent for the Battery Commander in a towering rage: 'Why have I had no ammunition returns from you for a week? Why are they always wrong and always late? And why do you bury your casualties in the battery position. Can't you see how demoralising it is for the troops?'

The Colonel was very senior indeed but unfortunately he had been passed over for promotion so often that his natural humanity had withered. His sole passion was returns. It was no good trying to explain to him that all the papers, war diaries and records had been blown up three times. He blamed it all on these young battery commanders who showed absolutely no grasp of essentials and in peacetime would be no more than second lieutenants.

During the week before the assault (from 13 September onwards) an intensive bombardment of the German lines took place: two-thirds of the allotted ammunition was fired by night and the remainder by day. This method was used in order to exhaust the enemy, giving him no time for rest. The barrage was also directed to cut off the German garrison from its own supplies and reliefs. The results were noted by spotter aircraft of the Royal Flying Corps, by the Balloon Companies and by ground observation. In addition to conducting air and photographic reconnaissance, the Royal Flying Corps carried out bombing raids on villages behind the enemy front, where it was known that German reserves would be waiting prior to moving up to the Front. During the bombardment the Germans withdrew some of their artillery to a safer area, but this still left them with plenty of guns with which to harass the British front line positions. German aircraft were very active at night, often bombing camps around and behind Ypres: on several occasions their raids caused heavy casualties. And just as Allied shelling at night was exhausting the Germans by depriving them of sleep, so did the German bombing have the same effect on British troops temporarily in reserve.

As the 20th drew nearer, all the forward brigades moved forward to areas from which they could quickly approach the front line. In the early evening of the 19th, the troops set off to their allotted destinations. Most of them marched across country, guided by white tapes and direction markers. As far as possible roads were avoided, for these were already congested with essential supplies. Everything to be used on the battlefield had to travel up along roads which were constantly under shellfire. Every drop of liquid used on the battlefield had to be carried there: although constantly soaked by rain and stumbling through pools of water, a man would be ill-advised to take water out of pools or shell holes for washing off the mud: it was all contaminated, partly by corpses underneath, partly by the gas shells which were used by both sides. In many ways the Ypres Salient gave an indication of what a battlefield would become in a nuclear war: widespread devastation, and everywhere and everything contaminated.

Although the 19th had been a sunny day, a drizzling rain began as the soldiers set off; drizzle turned to steady rain later. At midnight the sky cleared, leaving the battlefield rather lighter than was desirable as the leading troops moved into their pre-assault positions. They were bunched up closely, so that all might reach the enemy line by the time the Germans realized what was happening and put down a heavy barrage on the British Front. As it happened, the Germans did put down two brief barrages at 4.30 and 5, but fortunately they caused few casualties: these barrages were the result of German nervousness, rather than suspicion of an imminent attack. During September, when there had been no large-scale fighting, the weather had been much drier, much of the water had drained off the battlefield and, in consequence, the Germans had been expecting further British attacks. They had been surprised when none came, but did not relax their general attitude of expectancy. In the event they did have warning of this one, for at 3 a.m. an Australian officer, carrying operation orders for the 2nd Australian Division, had strayed ahead of his assembly position in the dark and been captured by a German patrol. The German 121st Division, which was opposite the Australians, promptly ordered a bombardment of the Australian Division and at the same time sent a general warning to other German divisions in the area. However, this useful information seems to have taken rather long to circulate and by the time action was being taken the British assault barrage, using a mixture of high-explosive and gas shells, came down with devastating force. And as dawn broke, the first British and Australian troops suddenly appeared in the German lines. It was a misty morning and they approached unseen. What was to become known as the battle of the Menin Road Ridge had begun.

There were four Allied divisions in the 2nd Army assault, the 41st and 23rd being British, and the 1st and 2nd being Australian. They were attacking on a 4000-yard frontage and their objective was the Gheluvelt plateau, on which so many of their comrades had died before them. On this occasion their chances were better than those of their predecessors, for Plumer had insisted on an artillery barrage massively greater than any which had preceded it. It is interesting to compare the horror and shock which was felt by all when the Germans had first used gas at Ypres in 1915, with the general acceptance two years later that any barrage by either side would contain a good proportion of gas shells, mainly mustard. However, acceptance of gas did not make its effects any less appalling.

So devastating was the barrage and so unexpected the arrival of the leading assault troops, who, for the first time in weeks, were able to move on fairly firm ground, that many of the Germans surrendered as quickly as possible; those who did not were soon persuaded to do so by a mixture of hand grenades and phosphorus bombs flung around or into their shelters. Most of the Germans in this area had been in the line for three weeks and were looking forward to being relieved within a few days; that fact might have made them slightly less alert than usual. Even so, as on other occasions the Germans were quick to recover and, in those areas which had been missed by the British barrage, put up a stubborn defence. There was one particularly dogged strongpoint in Dumbarton Wood, which caused a lot of casualties before it was captured; Inverness Copse, by now a wilderness of junk and wire entanglements, provided other pockets of resistance. Officer casualties were particularly high: four company commanders in the 11th Northumberland Fusiliers were killed in Dumbarton Wood, and the 9th Green Howards lost two company commanders and six other company officers in Inverness Copse. The Australians found Glencorse Wood less difficult than expected until its southern edge was reached, but there several machine gun posts put up strong resistance. Two of these were captured by Second Lieutenant F. Birks, who was subsequently awarded a VC for the outstanding bravery and skill he showed at this point. A similar feat was accomplished by Private R.R. Inwood, who captured one strongpoint one day and another the next; he too was awarded a VC.

By this stage in the war Nonnen Boschen, the Nuns' Wood, was no longer a wood but a mass of shell craters each full to the brim with slime and stinking water. The problem here was to cover the ground without falling into one of these death traps. Polygon Wood, being on a slope, was slightly better, though all but a few straggly trees had disappeared into shell craters. So devastating had the bombardment been on this area that several machine gun posts were captured with their machine guns intact and unfired, their crews too shocked and dazed – though otherwise unhurt – to operate them. To the west of Polygon Wood the land falls away into what was then known as the Sans Souci valley, which contains the Hanebeek; through this valley runs the Westhoek–Zonnebeke road. (Any word ending in 'beke' or 'beck' signifies the presence of a stream, and words ending in 'steert' indicate a drainage canal.) Here again the Australians were more successful than they had dared hope: they stormed up the eastern slope of the valley on to what became known as the Anzac House spur, captured several machine gun posts, which offered little resistance, and took numerous Germans prisoner. The Anzac House blockhouse was a particular prize, for it was the chief German artillery observation post for the Steenbeek valley. Among other points captured were many which had seen capture and loss, success and failure, in previous bloody battles, such as Tower Hamlets (a mass of concrete, dugouts and pillboxes), Inverness Copse and Broodseinde.

After the capture of Anzac House blockhouse, a two-hour halt was called to enable the leading troops to prepare for the inevitable counter-attack. Before it could be mounted, the supporting barrage once more drenched the German lines with shells, reaching well back into the support area. The effect was again overwhelming, and the expected attacks did not come. However, the forward troops had enough to contend with in the shape of sniping and machine gun fire from outside the occupied area. Rifles and machine guns could be devastating up to 1000 yards, and many a man has been killed by a rifle bullet fired a mile away from him. As the Australian casualties mounted, action was taken to capture the most menacing strongpoints, which included Black Watch Corner and Garter Point. But resistance was stiffening again, and before the Australians reached their final objectives at approximately 10 a.m. they suffered a number of casualties. It had been a magnificent morning's work by the Australians, though it was feared that some of their casualties had been the result of their following up the barrage too closely.

Elsewhere along the Front, fortunes were mixed. In 39th Division, the 16th Rifle Brigade and 17th King's Royal Rifle Corps were suffering heavily from machine gun fire as they forced their way to their objectives: the former lost all its officers and 95 other ranks, and the latter were so cut up that two of its companies were eventually being commanded by corporals. Three VCs were awarded in the attacks: one to Sergeant W.F. Burman of the Rifle Brigade who, among other feats, killed a German machine gunner and then used his gun to cover the advance; a second to Corporal E.A. Egerton of the Sherwood Foresters, who cleared some German dugouts which were holding up the battalion; and a third to Second Lieutenant H. Colvin of the Cheshires, who cleared a number of German dugouts single-handed and then took 50 prisoners on his own.

Fifth Army had a wider frontage to cover and therefore thinner artillery support than 2nd Army. Ninth Scottish Division had to advance through the Hanebeek valley, which at that point was a mixture of swamp and shell holes filled with water. Nevertheless, Hanebeek Wood was captured by the 6th King's Own Scottish Borderers, who took 50 prisoners and various machine guns; Berry Farm and Potsdown House by the South Africans; and a variety of pillboxes by the Royal Scots. Captain Reynolds of the Royal Scots added a VC to his MC by capturing a pillbox single-handed: he forced a phosphorus grenade through one of its apertures and set it on fire, before leading his company to its final objective.

As every fighting soldier knows, Victoria Crosses are usually deserved at least twice over by those who live long enough to wear them. Usually the winner of a VC has been wounded, often more than once, in that particular action. But every soldier who is involved in fighting which is intensive enough to produce a VC knows that many a man has been killed performing deeds which, if he had not been killed before they were completed, would equally have merited a VC. There is also the problem of witnesses. An action may be supremely brave, but unless there are witnesses of sufficient standing and reliability to register it, it is not acceptable; even so, when soldiers say: 'That man deserved a VC', they are not usually exaggerating.[4]

One of the most unfortunate units in the fighting that day was the 55th (1st West Lancashire) Division which had begun the battle under-strength. It was caught by a heavy German barrage just as the attack began and sustained further severe casualties when its leading troops, moving forward through the morning mist, passed German pillboxes and strongpoints without seeing them; they became all too well aware of them later when the occupants emerged and attacked them from the rear. All this contributed to the division not being able to reach its first objective. In consequence, as the South African Brigade advanced its left flank was unprotected – 'in the air', as the Army likes to describe this dangerous situation. It was dangerous indeed for the South Africans, who were vulnerable on two fronts, but, in spite of sustaining casualties amounting to half the brigade strength (1250 out of 2500) they captured Bremen Redoubt and Waterend House in the valley of the Zonnebeke, and subsequently established a strong defensive position. Lance-Corporal W.H. Hewitt won a VC by crawling up to a German pillbox, in the course of which he was wounded twice, and putting a grenade through a loophole, thus clearing an obstacle in his regiment's advance.

Meanwhile 55th Division was doggedly pressing on to its objectives in spite of a variety of disasters, such as a breakdown in communications and encountering particularly strong German defensive positions. At the end of the day the right flank had succeeded in linking up with the remains of the South African Brigade, although the centre and left were still some way short of their final objective.

Further north, XVIII Corps were allotted a daunting piece of territory between the Poelcappelle and Gravenstafel spurs (the latter was subsequently nicknamed London Ridge). Their assembly area was liquid mud. Commanding the right-hand brigade was Brigadier-General B.C. Freyberg, VC, a New Zealander whose service had been with the Foot Guards and who would earn great distinction in the Second World War as well as in the First.

Thirty tanks had been allotted to XVIII Corps for this attack, but the ground was so hopelessly unsuitable for them that only one attained its objectives. Inevitably, tanks were not having much success in this terrain. At this stage in the war they were Mark IVs, described by one of the section commanders as

> unwieldy monsters, each weighing thirty tons, and having a maximum speed of only three or four miles an hour. When closed a tank was pitch black inside, but could be lit by small electric lights where the sides and the top met. The sides were filled with racks containing shells and ammunition, and forward on the left side, next to the officer's seat, was a built in tank for drinking water, while opposite on the right side was a locker for maps and sundries. As in a battleship there was a place for everything and everything was so fitted that nothing was dislodged when the tank was in motion. This economy of space was essential for each tank required a crew of an officer and seven men.

The writer of those words, Captain D.E. Hickey, had been born of British parents in the Argentine and had lived in that country until he was ten. Somewhat unusually for a boy, he had a horror of all things military, which gave him nightmares about being called up for compulsory military service in the Argentine. He was sent to school in England and in 1914 promptly applied to join the Army. Eventually he found his way into the Tank Corps, then still in its infancy. His description of contemporary tanks went on:

The officer and driver occupied two raised seats in the nose of the tank, and the rest of the crew was confined to two narrow gangways. The gangways were one foot wide and eight feet long and ran the whole length of the tank on either side of the engine and machinery. It was impossible to stand upright, for the height of the roof and the gangways was only about five feet. The 100 h.p. petrol engine reached almost to the roof, but there was a small platform behind it, covering the machinery. Over this platform was the starting handle, which it required four men to turn. Two of the crew were known as gearsmen. It required the officer, driver, and the two gearsmen to swing the tank when its course was to be altered. One of the gearsmen was understudy to the driver. Each track had its own set of two secondary gears, in addition to neutral, and by manipulating these the tank was steered.

It is only too clear that manoeuvring the tank even on firm ground must have been an extraordinarily difficult and uncertain procedure. Its chances of taking evasive action would appear to be non-existent. It seems a miracle that such cumbersome monsters were able to operate at all on the Ypres terrain, let alone do any damage to the enemy. However:

Between the officer and gearsman on one side, and between the driver and the other gearsman on the other side were the gunners, two in each gangway.

There were two types of tank – Male and Female.

A male tank had slightly more room on account of the projections on either side, where each of the two 6-pounder guns was mounted. The gun-layer and gun-loader of each 6 pounder partly occupied these projections. The projections were called 'sponsons'.

The female tank had only machine-guns and each of the four gunners worked one of them.

In both types of tank, the officer had a machine-gun in front.

Although there were reflectors and sight-holes in the armour plating through which to peep when the portholes were closed, and a small hole for a periscope, the crew of a tank could see very little of what was going on outside unless they used the portholes and revolver loopholes. This, of course, made it possible for an enemy to approach close to a tank unseen and then to drop in a grenade. However, it required considerable courage to approach one of these monsters as it lumbered towards you at walking speed. There was always a fear that it might suddenly slew in its tracks and pin you beneath it like some vast primeval beast seizing its prey.

> It was no easy matter to get in and out of these steel boxes. The doorway was only two feet by four feet. In the male tank one entered in a more or less upright position, for the door was vertical. But the door in the female tank was placed horizontally, so that the only way to get in was to lever oneself in on one's stomach. It was like getting in to the witch's oven in Grimm's fairy tale. As I had four tanks under my command, I had plenty of practice, and became skilled in the art of negotiating these holes without too much damage either to myself or my clothes.

The day of the tank was to come, but it had not done so by 20 September 1917. The official history contains a laconic note on the subject: 'An additional task, to assist in the capture of Schuler Farm, on the right boundary of the division [58th (2/1st London)] with the help of two tanks failed. The tanks stuck in the mud before their arrival on the scene, and the platoon of infantry was held up by machine-gun fire from the farm.'

The Londoners certainly distinguished themselves on that day. Although Territorial units, they had trained themselves to be the equals – if not superiors – of their regular contemporaries. Their success owed much to co-ordination and precision of movement: they outflanked the main strongpoints on their path, and then turned back and captured them from the rear. The official record states: 'Once outflanked a strongpoint was as good as captured.' Among their trophies here were six German officers, 285 prisoners and 50 machine guns. The spearhead of this notable attack were the 2/8 Post Office Rifles, the 2/5 London Rifle Brigade and the 2/6 P.O. Rifles.[5]

A somewhat unusual postal worker was Sergeant A.S. Knight of the 2/8 Post Office Rifles. He was awarded a VC, according to the official citation, 'for his extraordinary good work, exceptional bravery and initiative during this advance. Single-handed, he rushed twelve of the enemy in a shell hole, bayoneted two and shot a third: the remainder scattered, leaving behind a machine-gun. Shortly afterwards he alone rushed an enemy machine-gun in action, bayoneted the gunner and captured the gun.' Rushing a machine gun and capturing it meant approaching a weapon with an effective range of 600 yards, which at the time was probably traversing and spraying the ground with a lethal arc of bullets coming out at a rate of approximately ten per second.

By midday on the 20th the assault seemed to have been unusually successful. Second Army had established a foothold on the Gheluvelt plateau and 5th Army had reached virtually all its objectives on the left. However, no one was complacent. It was known that German tactics were to hold the forward areas fairly lightly with a complex system of pillboxes and other strongpoints and, if these were over-run, to counter-attack with massed infantry kept in reserve for just that purpose. As soon as an objective was gained by a British or Australian unit, therefore, the first need was to establish an adequate system of defence. It had to include an adequate signalling system. Wireless was installed at all key points, but the noise and effects of artillery made reception very poor, and wireless was much less effective than lamps, runners, messenger dogs and pigeons.

Somewhat optimistically, two tanks filled with wireless equipment had been lent to 2nd Army for what the official history describes as 'subsidiary inter-communication with the forward area'. One, attached to X Corps, was sent up to Clonmel Copse and the other, with the I Anzac Corps, to the south-west corner of Glencorse Wood, where it received a direct hit with a shell almost at once. D.E. Hickey wrote: 'It had been instilled into us that a tank commander's duty was to stick to his tank to the end, his whole object being to protect it. If need be, he must, like the captain of a ship, perish with it.'

Hugh Quigley was serving with the 12th Royal Scots (9th Division) at this time. Subsequently he wrote:

> Our friends at home expanded chests at the thought of the heroism of Passchendaele but was it heroism that should ever have been demanded of the Army? Now that the business is over, the soldier cannot look back on shell-holes and acres of dead Germans as monuments to the heroism of the British Army; he has a dim sense of shame as at some unnatural, disgraceful thing he was forced to do, which neither instinct, sentiment, nor reason could invest with pride. With that comes the ironic feeling of sacrifice to the political intrigue of worthless statesmen: we could not explain the Passchendaele offensive from a military point of view, consequently we could only see it as political, a calm cold-blooded sacrifice of life for miserable diplomatic advancement. The only image of it that came to the mind was that of a man patting [someone] familiarly on the back but in reality seeking the right place to put the knife.

Quigley's contempt for the politicians and commanders who had put them in that bloodbath was not tempered by the heroism he often witnessed there. He freely confesses how terrified he was as he went up the line:

> It seemed the best solace for excited nerves to keep going, no matter whether or not out of danger. Yet luck stood by us: in spite of over-zealous artillery not a shell dropped near us until we reached our trenches, and then we had it stiff. A sergeant and two privates were blown to pieces twenty yards from me: all that night and early morning we lay in the shallow trench, trying vainly to keep knees from shaking and teeth from chattering with a deadly sick feeling in the stomach as bits of shrapnel hit the side of the trench with a thud and earth was shaken over our faces. All we could do was to lie motionless on our backs and pray that the enemy had not seen us. I tried to sleep but nervous excitement kept me awake all

day until night, when we dug out a new trench. While plying the spade I encountered what looked like a branch sticking out of the sand. I hacked and hacked at it until it fell severed and I was picking it up prior to throwing it over the parapet when a sickness, or rather nausea, came over me. It was a human arm.

That did not complete my experiences that night: about eleven o'clock we set out on patrol but had to take refuge in a deserted pill-box in No Man's Land because the enemy had sighted us. This pill-box had been used at one time as a charnel house; it smelt strongly of one, and the floor was deep with human bones. From there we watched the Véry lights flickering outside and, casting a weird light through the doorway, the red flash of bursting shells. Occasionally a direct hit shook us to the very soul. While sitting there the odour overcame me and I fainted. Waking up an hour afterwards, I found myself alone without the faintest idea of my whereabouts, uncertain of where the enemy's lines were or my own. Some authors practise the description of fear but nothing they could do could even faintly realise my state. It went beyond fear, beyond consciousness, a grovelling of the soul itself. For half an hour I stood inside, wondering whether to venture out or stay in at imminent risk of daylight coming to disclose me to the enemy. At last bravery returned and I went out only to stumble over a derelict wire a hundred yards further on, and find my hands clutching a dead man's face. But on the other side of it lay our trenches and I was able to calm down in readiness for the morning barrage.

Our road to Company HQ from Ypres is shown in places by dead men in various postures, here three men lying together, there a dead 'Jock' lying across a trench, the only possible bridge and we had to step on him to get across. The old German front line, now behind our reserve, must be the most dreadful thing in existence, whether in reality or imagination, a stretch of slimy wicker-work, bordering a noisome canal of brown water, where dead men float and fragments of bodies and limbs

project hideously as in a pickle. The remembrance of one
attitude will always haunt me, a German doubled up
with knees under his chin and hand clutching hair above
a face of the ghastliest terror.

But, like his contemporaries, Quigley became inured to such
experiences for the time being, even if they did return in nightmares
later. Fear was never absent, but a sort of jaunty fatalism often
sustained men and prevented them from going mad. After the
battle of 20–22 September, Quigley wrote:

I shall never forget that afternoon in Ypres, when every
officer and man we met asked how our division did in the
attack. I was proud of it too, in some kind of perverse
delight, not keen on fighting yet glad to be in it. Even
then, among all that sordid mass of ruins we call Ypres,
memory and recollection have given a romantic aspect,
as of some monument worthy of valour and enshrined in
our deeds, where our bravest fought to the last and never
yielded. It may be a cemetery, a horrible cemetery at
that, but an air of nobility blows round it yet. The
horrible remains a characteristic, instance that story of
'Hellfire Corner' where two battalions of an English
regiment lie buried, shelled to death.
    Holding the line is fairly safe, except in a hot corner,
but our artillery have the enemy so much on the qui vive
that hot corners become more their privilege than ours.
How he manages to exist at all when a discriminating
barrage licks up every yard of ground in his vicinity and
over him must be one of the great mysteries of warfare. . . .
    However, there is good stuff in him yet – but I think he
is on the down grade, like a street singer dressed in a
frayed frock coat and tattered linen. The old glory
smacks of him, but it's worn and threadbare. The idea of
conquest and victory may bemuse him and place a
narcotic in his soul, thus concealing from him the fact
that the hell he once thought to plan for us has been
planned most effectually for him. The variety of weapons

he uses is bewildering. I have walked along a railroad after a barrage and found the weirdest conglomeration of dud shells – 'flying pigs', 'boches', '5.9s', 'pineapples', 'whizzbangs', 'oilcans' etc. Gas shells lay about just burst at the nose caps, with the gas oozing out very gradually. I remember one of the type which fell between two branches and lodged in the fork of a tree down the Somme. Everyone passing that orchard where the tree stood remarked on the sweet smell of this dud, and very few apples. Beside the shells there were 'flying darts', gaudy red things with a long flanged tail to balance (the slightest wound from them is deadly, owing to their being poisoned), clumsy pomegranate-shaped bombs with huge four-leaved appendices of no earthly use (to my idea), the usual 'stick bombs' in hundreds (I used to alarm the nervy people by unscrewing the tin-can and then pulling the string to set the fuse going), boxes on boxes of machine-gun ammunition and powerful machine-guns with the main parts lacking. Belgium is sown with nothing else but those souvenirs of German occupation and with them helmets, body plates, and thigh protectors of enormous weight held together with leather straps. I should imagine a German dressed in the armour with that strange helmet would be the image of a Lanzknecht of Wallenstein's time. The armour does not really protect them. I found in a mine crater two men bayoneted together, a 'Cameron' who had been caught in the stomach and a German in the throat, both locked irrevocably, dead at the same time. Such statues appear frequently; one man told me of two he saw at Beaumont-Hamel, not lying down but standing up as if wrought in iron.

Of course, if one dwelt on such horrors any length of time, nervous cowardice would ensue, and the result would be disaster. The main idea is to be an Epicurean, get the sum of enjoyment from the smallest detail and trust to the general disposition of fate.

Quigley, who a short time before had experienced unbearable

terror, had hardened quickly – or perhaps, one should say, acquired a working philosophy.[6]

P.J. Campbell, a Gunner subaltern in the same area, came from a more privileged background[7] than Quigley but, at the age of nineteen, quickly adapted to the appalling conditions. He wrote:

> I did not want a way out. I wanted to stay where I was. For as long as the war lasted this was where I belonged. At first I had been an individual, now I was part of the battery, the battery was part of the brigade, and the brigade was part of the B.E.F. All my friends were in France, and all the men in France were my friends.
>
> All the men in France. I had no enemies, or only the Staff, and they lived so far away that we did not think of them as a part of us. Life was very simple at the front, you just served.

Many men preserved their sanity by retreating into a dream world, their minds resolutely detached from the horrors around them. The Editor of *The Boy's Own Paper* offered to send spare copies to soldiers serving in France and was astonished at the number of requests and grateful letters he received. Certain regiments maintain standards whatever the conditions, and it has been said appropriately of the Guards, 'They die with their boots clean.' But even Campbell, educated at Winchester, was rather surprised when he was temporarily attached to the Grenadier Guards.

> Was I a regular soldier, was the Colonel's first question.
> 'No, Sir,' I said.
> Had I been at Eton, his second.
> 'No, Sir,' I said again.
> He appeared to take no further interest in me but I was impressed by him and what I saw that night. I admired the Guards, but did not feel at home in their company.

The fact that one could be asked whether one was a regular,

when one's military career might be ended at any moment by a German shell and when the battlefields of Passchendaele bore little resemblance to the playing fields of Eton, where Waterloo was alleged to have been won, might strike the modern reader as bizarre, but the test of this sort of philosophy is whether it works. It certainly works for the Guards: their fighting efficiency and reliability are unsurpassed by any regiment in the world.

And fighting efficiency was at a premium when the German infantry were moving up for a counter-attack, as they were at 3 p.m. on 20 September 1917. Fortunately the weather was now sunny and clear and the air observers of the Royal Flying Corps were able to spot targets and radio the news to the artillery: a total of 394 radio messages was sent by air observers that day. It was a change for the Germans to have their every move under observation; for a long time they had had that advantage over the Allies. The British barrage came down with such ferocity that the Allied infantry, waiting for the Germans to arrive, felt robbed as well as relieved when the enemy failed to appear. Remarkably, this was the same all along the line. No one was more relieved than 55th Division, which was now able to see the enemy take a taste of his own medicine.

In the following days the Germans made many attempts to recover patches of lost ground but on every occasion were driven back with heavy losses. One of their most vigorous attempts was against 55th Division on the 21st. Their objective was Hill 37. The attack began at 6 p.m. following a barrage and, by accepting heavy losses, the forward troops made a few inroads into the Allied line. However, 55th Division fought back with such force that by 9.15 p.m. the Germans had all been killed or pushed back and the line was back in its former position. German war diaries describing the position at this stage made it clear that the British barrage was so concentrated and complete that their infantry was quite unable to penetrate it. British artillery was now demonstrating its ability as a war-winning factor, and certainly this was the way to use it. The mistake which had been made earlier was to use artillery in the preliminary bombardment of the battlefield, destroying the irrigation system and reducing the area to a flooded swamp.

In order to reach the remaining final objectives, two more assaults were launched, one on 21 September and another on the

23rd. The first attack, which was made by 41st Division, had the Tower Hamlets spur as its objective; but in spite of heavy shelling and repeated infantry attacks this feature was not captured. On the 21st, 20th Division had set out to capture Eagle Trench, which lay beyond Langemarck, but its tanks were unable to get past Langemarck village and the operation was cancelled. A second attempt was made on the morning of the 23rd, and, after a massive bombardment by Stokes mortars and rifle grenades, the objective was captured by the 12th Greenjackets and 10th Rifle Brigade.

The 21st brought the death of Brigadier-General F.A. Maxwell, VC, who was commanding 27th Brigade. Frank Maxwell had won his VC in the Boer War. Subsequently he was ADC to General Kitchener, and his cheerful disposition and shrewd judgement enabled him to make his somewhat austere charge rather more sociable; in those days he was nicknamed 'the brat'. On the battlefield he was not merely brave but apparently so indifferent to danger that he had a remarkable effect on the troops under his command. According to the official history, he was sitting on the front of the parapet of a trench watching wiring parties when he was killed by a sniper, as were many of the bravest men; according to his orderly, writing an interesting letter to General Maxwell's widow, he was shot when inspecting an outpost in No Man's Land:

> 27th Brigade,
> 5th October, 1917.
>
> Dear Madam,
>
> I was very glad to hear from you. I will try and tell you about the fateful 21st, when I lost my beloved General. There was Major Ross and myself along with him. We went up to the front line to see if everything was all right and carried on down the line of our brigade front. We went out into 'no-man's-land', as the General wanted to have a good look round. We were from 80 to 100 yards in front of our front line. A captain of the Scottish Rifles came along with us to his 'out-post'. The General was showing him the land. I think the General wanted to have a machine-gun posted at this particular part. I was about five yards in front watching for any movement in shell-holes. I was lying flat with my rifle ready to shoot.

The first bullet that was fired by the Huns went right into the ground below my left elbow. I shouted to the General to get down, as he was standing at the time, and he did so. He sat for about two minutes, then he got up again to show what he was saying to this Captain, and he was just opening his mouth to speak when he got shot. I caught him as he was falling, and jumped into a shell-hole with him. I held his head against my breast till all was over. Madam, I cried till my heart was like to burst. If I could only see you I could tell you something about the General. He was a King among men and loved by everyone; in fact, Madam, next to yourself, I miss him more than anyone, for I would have done anything for him.

Perhaps I can speak better than anyone of his personal bravery, for I was his personal orderly in all the fighting the brigade did.

I can say no more just now, but if God spares me, I will come and see you some day.

> I am,
> Your faithful servant,
> (Signed) A. LAIRD
> L/Corporal

With the exception of the Tower Hamlets spur, all objectives had been gained by 25 September, and the operation had clearly been a brilliant success. The Germans had at last been pushed off the important parts of the Gheluvelt plateau, 3243 prisoners had been captured and casualties had been inflicted on the enemy on a massive scale. It was a triumph of good battlefield organization; the correct tactics had been used; the assault divisions had completed the task and been relieved within three days of setting out.

Unfortunately this success gave the impression that the campaign was now going on the right lines, and that Haig's original grandiose idea to break out from the Passchendaele Ridge, race through the countryside in a series of cavalry-like charges and capture Bruges, Ostend and Ghent was about to be realized. The fact that it was late September, after which there was really no hope of good weather, was conveniently overlooked. So too was the casualty list for the period 20–25 September – 12,000 in 2nd Army and 8000 in 5th Army. In these figures an average of 15 per cent had been killed, the remainder wounded, in many cases too severely ever to return to the Front. All statistics are potentially misleading, and nowhere does this apply more than on the battlefield. The heaviest casualties invariably occur among the most essential fighting troops, the specialists such as machine gunners and, of course, junior officers and senior NCOs. This sort of loss had never been easy to absorb at any time in the war, but, now that both sides were calling up many who had previously been exempt on grounds of health or other disabilities, the outlook was not encouraging. Haig believed absolutely sincerely that if he had another 500,000 men he could bring the war to a successful conclusion. Lloyd George believed that if Haig was able to get his hands on that extra half a million he would feed them into the slaughterhouse for little real gain, and the end of the war would be no nearer.

Notes

1 'Mark Severn' – the pen-name of Franklin Lushington, a regular soldier (Eton and the RMA Woolwich), became a successful author in the 1930s. In 1939 he commanded the Kent Yeomanry in France, was subsequently evacuated at Dunkirk and fought in the Western Desert. Later he became a colonel commanding troops in Cyprus, and stayed on there all through the EOKA troubles. He was killed in a car crash in England in 1964.
2 A visit to the Imperial War Museum in London is recommended, where many of the guns and other weapons used by each side may be seen.
3 Army Service Corps.
4 There were, of course, many other gallantry awards of which the citations were printed in *The Times* during the war.
5 The first figure gives the number of the Regiment, i.e. the 2nd London Regiment, and the second the number of the battalion. A regiment which in peacetime might have had only one battalion

was expanded by additional battalions in wartime: thus the Royal Northumberland Fusiliers reached the astonishing total of 52 battalions.

6 He survived. After the war he took first-class honours in modern languages at Glasgow University and subsequently had a distinguished career in the electricity industry, eventually becoming Chief Statistical Officer in the Central Electricity Board. A prolific author with a very wide range of interests, he described himself as an 'economist and farmer'.

7 P.J. (Patrick) Campbell went up to Oxford after the war, vowing that he would never become a schoolmaster. However, that is what he did, and eventually became Headmaster of the Westminster Under School. In the later stages he had to fight hard to save the school from extinction by the London County Council, as well as to obtain backing from the Westminster Governors. In the Second World War he served in the Home Guard. Married, with three sons, he died in 1986. He is remembered by generations of boys for his insight and wisdom, and his ability to make work – even elementary mathematics – enjoyable.

7

See You Again in Hell

Haig was so pleased with the results of the assault on 20 September that the following day he gave orders for the next phase of the attack. It was to take place on the 26th and would pave the way for the final capture of the ridge, which would be completed in October.

The plan for the battle on 26 September, to be known as the Battle of Polygon Wood, was essentially simple. The main thrust would be made by I Anzac Corps, which would advance 1200 yards. On their right would be X Corps, which would be attacking on either side of and along the Menin Road; and the left was allotted to 5th Army which was to reach, and capture, Hill 40 at Zonnebeke. This assault might cause the German line to crack and disintegrate, for which possibility five cavalry divisions would be assembled, ready to charge through the gaps and turn defeat into rout. The operation would be greatly assisted if a force could be landed at Ostend and contribute to the subsequent clearing of the coast.

Following a successful battle on the 26th, 2nd Army with the addition of II Anzac Corps would take over the area previously held by V Corps in 5th Army, thus bringing the ridge up to Passchendaele village within its area of attack. That would be Stage 3. Stage 4 would put 2nd Army in occupation of the ridge from Passchendaele to Broodseinde. However, that would follow only if, in Stage 3, the Broodseinde sector and Gravenstafel spur had already been captured by the two Anzac Corps, and the remainder of the Gheluvelt plateau had already been captured and consolidated by X Corps. Should the German Front not have crumbled at this stage, Haig planned a thrust from 5th Army towards Roulers and Staden.

Having issued his instructions, Haig was able to make up his diary. The only entry for 21 September was: 'Professor Haldane (brother of Lord Haldane) arrived to-day. He stays the night. He is an expert on gas and gas masks. A curious quiet shy fellow but full of knowledge. Quite unlike his brother Lord Haldane.'

One imagines that Sir Douglas Haig and John Scott Haldane would find little to talk about. J.S. Haldane was an expert on the physiology of breathing and the physiology of the blood; most of his studies had been made in connection with safety in coal mines. He was also an expert on decompression for making deep-sea diving possible. *The Encyclopedia Britannica* described him as 'a notable thinker who throughout his life tried to clarify the philosophical basis of biology, its relation to physics and chemistry, and the problems of mechanism and personality'. Plenty for after dinner discussion in that, one might think, but not perhaps with Haig. His son was J.B.S. Haldane, the brilliant scientist who became a Marxist, edited the *Daily Worker* and then, disenchanted with Soviet science, emigrated to India where he took Indian citizenship. In the 1930s his alarming forecasts of what gas might do to cities in a future war (one small bomb destroying 50,000 people) gave much encouragement and help to pacifists and others wishing to stop British rearmament, although the Nazi threat was already obvious.

Haig did rather better on the 24th, when the soldiers in the Ypres Salient were moving to their start lines for the assault. He wrote:

> I found Mr Gardiner (Editor of *Daily News*) waiting for lunch. It is over two years since I saw him at Hinges – just before Loos. I gather that Lloyd George has often tried to win over the *Daily News* to his side, but has failed. L.G. was for many years solicitor for the paper.
>
> Gardiner says L.G. never reads anything or thinks seriously. How unfortunate the country seems to be to have such an unreliable man at the head of affairs in this crisis. I thought Gardiner much above the usual newspaper man who visits France.

Among the preparations for the battle planned for the 26th was a rapid, widespread extension of the plank roads which, though not ideal, met immediate requirements. The need was not merely to enable the guns to approach nearer to the German line but also to ensure that their voracious appetite for ammunition could be satisfied. This period of roadmaking reflected enormous credit on the Engineers and Labour battalions, who worked day and night, often at considerable personal risk, to complete the task.

On the 25th the Germans counter-attacked between the Menin Road and Polygon Wood. At 5.15 a.m. they opened up with an artillery barrage, using a mixture of shells which included gas, and fifteen minutes later the German infantry came in. But this counter-attack was beset by troubles. In order to delay the next British move long enough for heavy German reinforcements to be massed in the line of advance, the response had been mounted as quickly as possible, even though the experience of the last one had not been encouraging. The opening barrage had been the heaviest yet produced by the Germans, but an attempt to synchronize it with the infantry advance went badly wrong and many of the shells fell among the leading troops. Few experiences are more calculated to discourage infantry waiting to attack than a brisk shelling from their own guns firing short.

It was to be expected that a counter-attack of this weight falling on freshly prepared positions would have some effect, but it was less than the British had feared. The centre of the line held, the southern flank was pushed back a short way and the northern flank fell back several hundred yards before stabilizing again. Losses among the attacking German infantry were very high, and scarcely less so among the reinforcements which tried to force a way through a box barrage to replace the casualties. However, this situation was common to both sides. Heavy German shelling of the British supply lines interfered badly with the delivery of ammunition, in spite of heroic efforts by individuals who ran the gauntlet. One man with unlimited courage and a charmed life was Lance-Corporal J.B. Hamilton of the Highland Light Infantry, who not only carried supplies of ammunition through the German barrages but also distributed it in full view of enemy snipers and machine gunners. He was awarded a VC.

The assault went in as planned at 5.50 a.m. on the 26th. The drive to clear the remainder of the Gheluvelt plateau was led by 4th and 5th Divisions of the Anzac Corps, who had the unusual experience of advancing through clouds of dust raised by the shelling. The plain below was, of course, still a sodden swamp, but up on the slopes the recent sunny weather had dried the light soil which easily turned to powdery dust. This was by no means ideal terrain for infantry work, but it was a thousand times preferable to the conditions they had recently left behind and were all too soon to experience again. The Australians capitalized on the fact that they were advancing unseen by coming forward so quickly that many German machine gun posts were outflanked before they realized what was happening to them. Great courage and enterprise were shown as the Australians forced their way into what remained of Polygon Wood. An outstanding VC was won by Private P. Bugden, who led parties of his comrades through heavy German fire and captured enemy pillboxes with grenade and bayonet. Subsequently he rescued five wounded men, but was killed by machine gun fire while attempting the sixth. In addition to much of Polygon Wood, the Australians captured the Butte where the Germans had an important observation post. The only drawback to a successful day was that 98th Brigade in the 33rd Division was completely pinned down at the start by an intense German barrage; as a result, when this shelling lifted they had lost the protection of the initial British barrage. When 98th Brigade was able to start it was once more deprived of the benefit of a covering barrage, for some men were known to have penetrated well forward and would be in the target area, even though surrounded by Germans.

A second VC was won by the Australians on this day. Sergeant J.J. Dwyer of the Australian Machine Gun Corps rushed a German machine gun at Zonnebeke, killed its crew, captured the gun and used it against German counter-attacks that day and the next.

But the spur at Tower Hamlets, at the southern end of which was a block of defence known as the Quadrilateral, proved as intractable as ever. Before the assault it had been pounded by a relentless bombardment, which led to the top of the spur being captured in the first hour. However, the Quadrilateral continued to hold out. In contrast to other places in this area, the approach here was through a deep swamp which quickly accounted for the two tanks detailed to assist in the operation. After many delays the Quadrilateral was reached and penetrated by battalions from the Black Watch and Cambridgeshire, but they were unable to hold their gains in the face of intensive machine gun fire and determined counter-attacks. Recognizing the importance of the Quadrilateral, the Germans were determined to hold it at any cost.

The Germans also clung on to the important observation point known as Hill 40, which lay north of Zonnebeke. Here the terrain was the deciding factor, for the *beke* which gave its name to Zonnebeke lay in the direct line of the British advance and had long since transformed that area into a swamp. As the infantry struggled through it in the morning mist, there were long delays and considerable bunching at the points where the stream was not actually impassable. The creeping barrage went on ahead, the German machine gunners were able to raise their heads again, and the infantry was halted some 600 yards short of the objective.

The 59th Division (a North Midland unit) was more fortunate and reached its objective between Waterend and Schuler Farm with comparatively light casualties. Following this success, 5th Army decided that the attack should press forward along the Gravenstafel Ridge to the point known as Aviatik Farm, but the advance was halted some 400 yards short of the objective. The opportunities for confusion in the mist, as soldiers struggled over difficult ground and tried to bypass strongpoints, may be imagined – in nightmares.

As experience had shown that initial gains in thinly held areas could easily be lost again in determined German counter-attacks, it was decided to consolidate captured ground as quickly as possible. Most of the points which had been won that day were of great tactical importance and it was unlikely that the Germans would not make a wholehearted attempt to recover them, regardless of casualties. By midday the weather had become warm and sunny and the air observers were able to send messages about the strength and direction of the German counter-attack: it was formidable. However, all the possible approach roads and assembly points were already known to the Allies, and as the German infantry reached them they were hammered with bombing and artillery barrages; these did not stop the Germans, but they caused considerable disruption. The full weight of the German counter-attack came in the mid-afternoon, and the British artillery was soon beset with requests for covering fire. The line of the attacks seemed to be from Becelaere and Reutel in the general direction of Hooge and Polygon

Wood, about half of which was in Australian hands. The German infantry which survived the artillery barrage was in each case met by intensive machine gun fire, and ultimately bayonets. Although this reception blunted the German attack, it had clearly not removed the danger and, as expected, further attacks began to develop during the early evening. The final effort was on the Front extending from Tower Hamlets to Polygon Wood. Here and at Zonnebeke the Australians clung on with stubborn tenacity, which surprised those who had always considered them excellent in attack but less effective in defence. By 8.30 the Germans decided that nothing further would be achieved by trying to continue the attack into the night, and, except for the normal exchange of artillery fire, the Front settled down. Nevertheless both sides realized that this was only a lull and that further attacks by either could begin without warning.

Subsequently the German historians had much to say about the intensity of the British barrages, which had inflicted German casualties and made the counter-attack a matter of advancing through a wall of flying steel. The effect on the British artillery of firing virtually non-stop all day long was predictable. Not only were guns worn out, but casualties among the gunners, who were often in exposed positions, were twice as high as would have been expected under normal conditions. The 'butcher's bill' for the second half of September gave German losses (official figures) as 38,500, but this was in fact only marginally more than the British and Australian, which amounted to 36,000. Nevertheless the Allied losses had been incurred in gaining ground, and those of the Germans in losing it and failing to recapture it. Unfortunately the successes of this attack were less valuable than GHQ assumed. There was no longer enough time to make any strategically significant gains before the winter; the Allies would, of course, be left in possession of the ridge if they succeeded in clearing the last Germans off it, but that would be the limit of an achievement of incalculable long-term cost.

However, Haig and his close companions were jubilant at the result of the latest phase of these murderous battles. The possibility that the resources wasted in small tactical gains might have been used more profitably elsewhere did not seem to have entered into anyone's calculations. Confident predictions were made that the size of the German losses would make them unable to maintain their existing front line: those forecasts were proved wrong when it became clear that the Germans had not merely replaced their exhausted forward troops but had also added an extra division to the line. In fact this efficiency had certain disadvantages which soon became obvious. By abandoning their policy of defence in depth and, instead, defending the front more strongly, the Germans put their best troops well within reach of Allied artillery, which took full advantage of that fact.

On 2 October Haig wrote in his diary:

> I held a Conference at my house at Cassel at 11 a.m. Kiggell, Davidson and Charteris accompanied me. Generals Plumer and Gough were also present with their senior Staff Officers and General Nash (Director General of Training). I pointed out how favourable the situation was, and how necessary it was to have all necessary means for exploiting any success gained on the 10th, should the situation admit, e.g. if the enemy counter-attacks and is defeated then reserve brigades must follow after the enemy and take the Passchendaele Ridge at once. Both Gough and Plumer quite acquiesced in my views, and arranged wholeheartedly to give effect to them when the time came. At first they adhered to the idea of continuing our attacks for limited objectives.
>
> Charteris emphasised the deterioration of the German Divisions in numbers, morale, and all-round efficiency.

Charteris was Brigadier-General John Charteris, whom Haig had selected for his Chief of Intelligence when he himself became Commander-in-Chief. Before that Charteris had been a lieutenant-colonel. He has been heavily criticized for his habit of making wildly optimistic forecasts and telling Haig what he thought the Commander-in-Chief wished to hear rather than what he should have told him. Intelligence officers, at any level, do not have an entirely happy time in the Army, but Charteris seems to have been so widely criticized for facile optimism that he must share with Kiggell and Haig the blame for the waste of life at Passchendaele. In Charteris's defence, it may be said that intelligence officers are scorned if their pessimistic forecasts are found wrong, but rarely commended if they prove to be right. The main criticism of Charteris was that he encouraged Haig to continue when he should have advised caution. Advocating caution to an ambitious and stubborn cavalry officer is never an easy or productive task. It should perhaps be borne in mind that, although the strategy and tactics advocated by Haig and his staff now appear wasteful, futile and appallingly stupid, those of their opponents were no better. Crown Prince Rupprecht of Bavaria, Commander of the Northern Group of German Armies, could see no better way of advancing than by massed infantry charges against positions protected by intensive ground and artillery fire.

On 3 October Haig wrote:

> I got back to Blendecques about 2 p.m. Lord Herschel came to lunch. He is in France on secret service duty for the Admiralty. Most talkative and looks like a Jew.
>
> A great bombshell arrived in the shape of a letter from the C.I.G.S. [Robertson] stating that the British Government had 'approved in principle' of the British Army in France taking over more line from the French and the details are to be arranged by General Pétain and myself. This was settled at a Conference at Boulogne on September 25th at which I wasn't present. Nor did either Lloyd George or Robertson tell me of this at our interview [when they had visited Haig immediately after the conference on 25 September].
>
> All the P.M. said was that 'Painlevé [the French Minister of War] was anxious that the British should take over more line.' And Robertson rode the high horse and said that it was high time for the British now to call the tune and not play second fiddle to the French, etc. etc. and all this when shortly before he must have quietly acquiesced at the Conference in Painlevé's demands. Robertson comes badly out of this, in my opinion, especially as *it was definitely stated (with the War Cabinet's approval) that no discussion re operations on the Western Front would be held with the French without my being present.*

It was unlikely that Robertson cared greatly whether he should have explained the situation more fully to Haig, even if he actually remembered the original statement being made. Robertson had had a career in the Army which even now seems scarcely credible. He had enlisted as a trooper in the 16th Lancers in 1877 at the age of seventeen; he was, in fact, three months too young to be accepted, but he was tall and his age was entered as eighteen. Life in the ranks of the Army at that time was harsh and brutal, but he was intelligent and determined, his ability was recognized and he was promoted. He mastered several languages, but never altered his own version of English which was blunt and usually devoid of aitches. He was afraid of no one. Although he lacked money, influence, a privileged background and social accomplishments his complete mastery of his profession took him to the rank of field-marshal. In 1917 he was Chief of the General Staff. Doubtless he and Lloyd George saw eye to eye on most things, even though one was an orthodox soldier and the other a subtle politician.

On the assumption that the Germans were near breaking point, that the Russian Front had now stabilized to the extent that the Germans would be unable to transfer divisions from that area to Flanders, and that the weather would stay fine long enough for the Allies to sweep over the Passchendaele Ridge and drive forward to Bruges and Ghent, the next attack was planned to begin on 4 October. Even if these optimistic forecasts were not entirely fulfilled – if the Germans still put up a strong resistance, if the Russians did make a separate peace and if the weather did not remain fine – there were still good grounds for optimism. The Allies had shown that they could outfight the Germans under even worse conditions; even if divisions were transferred from the Russian Front it would still take over three months to get them to Flanders; and if the weather proved unsatisfactory, conditions could not be worse than those experienced – and overcome – previously.

On 4 October Haig wrote in his diary:

> Glass fell ½ inch from mid-day yesterday to mid-day to-day. High wind all night with slight rain, increased to a gale during the day. Storm in Channel so boats did not cross. Wet afternoon, fine night.
>
> Attack was launched at 6 a.m. this morning by eight

divisions of Second Army and four divisions of Fifth Army (Gough). On the right of the attack was 37th Division (9th Corps) south of the Menin Road. Next on the north was 10th Corps with the 5th, 21st and 7th Divisions. Some hard fighting took place here. To-day was a very important success and we had great good fortune in that the enemy had concentrated such a large number of Divisions just at the moment of our attack with the very intense Artillery barrages.

Over 3,000 prisoners and six guns are already reported captured.

In order not to miss any chance of following up our success if the enemy were really demoralised, I met General Plumer and Gough with their Staff officers at my house in Cassel at 3 p.m. Plumer stated that in his opinion we had only up-to-date fought the leading troops of the enemy's Divisions on his front. Charteris, who was present, thought that from the number of German regiments represented amongst the prisoners, all Divisions had been seriously engaged and that there were few more available reserves.

After full discussions I decided that the next attack should be made two days earlier than already arranged provided Anthoine could also accelerate his preparations.

At 4 p.m. I saw the latter. He was most anxious to do everything possible to hasten matters. Finally it was found only possible to advance the attack by *one* day.

Euphoria, orchestrated by the irrepressible Charteris, was clearly the order of the day at GHQ. Up in the line, in the rain, attitudes differed somewhat.

The battle, which began on 4 October, passed into the record books as the Battle of Broodseinde. It was seen as a preliminary to the battle for Passchendaele itself, which was expected to begin on 10 October. Plumer and Gough, as was seen from the reference in Haig's diary, tended to take a more cautious view. They had listened patiently while Haig explained that, as soon as the remainder of the Gheluvelt plateau had been captured and Broodseinde secured, there should be little problem in pushing on to the top of the ridge at Passchendaele, and then without delay following up the retreating Germans with infantry, artillery, tanks and cavalry. Especially cavalry. Gough, although a cavalryman himself and an enthusiastic believer in the possibilities of that arm, had however been in command of an Army which had been fighting an enemy whom he was not inclined to under-rate.

Both generals were then asked to state their requirements for the forthcoming offensive. Each sent a letter expressing doubts about Haig's extended plans. Plumer emphasized that the capture of the high ground might involve more difficulty and thus time than was evisaged, and Gough felt that the necessarily slow final stages of the struggle for the summits – low hills though they were – would enable the Germans to withdraw their artillery and many other troops; these would then be positioned to make it nearly as difficult for the Allies to get off the eastern side of the ridge as it had been to capture it from the west.

Haig's optimism was in no way dimmed by these prudent remarks from field commanders who had every reason to know what they were talking about, and who were undoubtedly under-stating their case. Disregarding entirely the fact that the weather might suddenly close down the entire operation, Haig merely commented that if there were delays these would not alter the forecast, but merely delay its timing. He elaborated this point at a conference he held on 2 October, emphasizing that this golden opportunity must not be lost as – in his opinion – other opportunities in the war had been lost by both sides through failing to exploit the moment of victory through the fear that the Army was too exhausted to press ahead rapidly. So important did he feel this present opportunity was that he had arranged to strengthen the Ypres Front with ten divisions from other sectors. All other potential areas for a breakthrough were to be disregarded. Six of the transferred divisions would be allotted to 5th Army and the other four, which formed the Canadian Corps, would be added to 2nd Army when the breakthrough was imminent. The Canadians were rated very highly indeed by the British commanders, possibly because they were equal to the Australians in fighting ability but considerably more disciplined. A plan for alternating leading troops with reserve troops was drafted, so that the latter could make rapid thrusts forward when the first objectives had been reached. Experience at varying stages in the war had shown that switching reserves into the line while the former front-line troops retired and the enemy artillery continued to shell briskly could create a confusion to which imperfect roads and intermittent rainfall would add their not insignificant contribution. However, such gloomy thoughts were not allowed to enter the planning schedules of GHQ. One cavalry division each was allotted to 2nd Army and 5th Army to make any necessary moves after the expected successes of the reserve divisions, and two were to be brought up and held in reserve close to the Yser Canal, from which they could be brought forward rapidly to exploit the capture of Passchendaele and its immediate surroundings.

Five tank battalions were brought up to join the reserves. Haig, like many a cavalryman of his time, had initially taken a distinctly sceptical view of tanks and refused to accept them as in any way a substitute for real cavalry. In consequence, tanks had been expected to perform miracles in impossible situations, but had never been employed with any degree of imagination. Now, however, they were in favour. Realism was not a characteristic of planning for the exploitation of the capture of the Passchendaele Ridge, but the belief that the 'better going' on the eastern side of Passchendaele would enable the tanks to swarm forward in intimidating numbers – at least three miles an hour if they did not break down, get stuck in trenches or meet a reception from German artillery – seems one of the less conservative prophecies. Perhaps it was as well for everyone's peace of mind that Charteris did not disclose information which had been brought to his notice – but which he preferred to discount – that the Germans had prepared a strong defensive line from Staden to Roulers. Both Plumer and Gough felt that the time allotted for the preparation of such a massive all-out thrust was insufficient, and that the attack should not take place till 6 October. Haig, however, felt that the dry weather with which the month had begun might not last much longer and therefore urged them to be ready by the 4th.

The Germans, well aware that the Allies would now be making a final desperate push to gain possession of the entire ridge, decided to impede the Allied preparations by a series of varied but intense artillery barrages, interspersed with unheralded infantry attacks.

That the latter failed to make headway was due to the lively responses of the regiments in their path: the Sherwood Foresters, Green Howards, Royal Welsh Fusiliers and Leicestershire Regiment earned special distinction for their resilience. The commanding officer of the Leicesters (9th Battalion), Lieutenant-Colonel P.E. Bent, won a VC by leading a counter-attack and regaining vital ground with the remnants of his regiment, but he was killed at the moment of victory. The stage was set for the Battle of Broodseinde but, as Haig noted in his diary, there was now every sign that the weather would break.

In the Second World War generals such as Wavell, Slim, Patton, Auchinleck, Horrocks and some others were often to be seen in the forefront of the battle, but on the whole the First World War generals felt that they were best positioned several miles behind the front line. Some, such as General Birdwood, were often in the forward area, and had an excellent effect on morale, as described by the Australian Captain O.H. Woodward:

> On the following day the Company was reviewed by General Birdwood and we received our issue of 'Birdwood Soft Soap', so famous in the A.I.F. We had always realised that we were a very efficient unit but after the General had addressed us we felt that there were only two units opposing the Hun on the Western Front – ourselves and the embryo Yanks. After rum issue that night we were fully prepared to dispense with the assistance of the latter.

To be fair, the majority of generals kept away from the Front not through any lack of personal courage but because they had been trained to believe that if they became too closely involved in the battle they would lose their sense of proportion and perspective. Even in the Second World War it was impossible for a general to stay in the line for more than a short visit if he was to do his job properly, and he therefore lived in a different world from the fighting soldier.

Between 1914 and 1918, then, very few fighting soldiers ever saw a general, though they saw plenty of everything else. In the course of the war soldiers who survived became different beings from the men they had been at the outset. Some, of course, had been schoolboys; they acquired maturity very quickly. After the war, the lucky survivors found that their new personalities were not easily adapted to peacetime. They also had memories, and the effects of wounds and exposure to contend with. Some found the chilly ingratitude of peacetime Britain more than they could bear and either committed suicide or retired into closed-up personalities. A few lucky ones were able to come out of the trenches and adapt once more, apparently unchanged. They had been through hell and come out at the other side.

One of these was Desmond Allhusen, who by 4 October 1917 had reached the rank of major. Before the end of the year he was wounded and permanently disabled. He had kept a diary for most of the war and he was able to supplement it later when enforced leisure gave him all too much time to ponder on his memories. After his death his papers were presented to the Imperial War Museum. He wrote:

> At the beginning of August 1914 I was in camp near Aldershot with the Eton College Officers' Training Corps. I was a Lance Corporal and incredibly inefficient. The average Etonian took little interest in the war scare till it dawned on him that a European conflagration might entail the breaking up of the Public School Camp. When on August 1st we were given the order to pack up, there were scenes of wild enthusiasm. We were taken back to Eton and dismissed. A form of parting much used was 'Good-bye. See you again in hell.'

As he had been in the Officer Training Corps and was probably rather more efficient than he acknowledged, he was quickly commissioned into the 3rd Devonshire Regiment, part of the Special Reserve. At this time the belief was widespread that, once the Germans realized they were now up against the British Empire, France and Russia, they would soon acknowledge their mistake, peace would be made and everyone would be home by Christmas. Nevertheless the public took the declaration of war very seriously. For many years spy stories had been popular: the principal villains had been Germans, with the Russians as close runners-up. There were, of course, quite a number of ingenious German spies in Britain, but not nearly as many as were imagined, and German waiters or even shopkeepers who could speak no German but had German-sounding names were immediately suspect. The 3rd Devons were at Plymouth, and Allhusen wrote:

> At this time Plymouth was a great spy-hunting centre. People were being arrested or shot at by sentries all day. The victims were usually old women. Two officers were shot dead in a motor car in Plymouth. I never discovered whether there were any genuine spies or not. Once some sailing ships came into the harbour and ignored signals, as their masters had not yet heard about the war. A gun was fired across their bows. One shell demolished a summer house on the opposite shore.

The regiment was next sent to Exeter for 'further training'. Here he learnt that his company commander's previous military experience had been limited to summer training with the militia in England during the Boer War. Fortunately there were six regular NCOs to help with the 280 new recruits who were all bursting with enthusiasm to learn. 'We taught them musketry with borrowed rifles. Everybody taught the men anything they could remember or invent. After a month or two a number of old red uniforms were unearthed and in these the men were clothed. By degrees boots appeared and then a few rifles. There was no discipline but immense good will.'

A few weeks later they were all given embarkation leave and told they would be going overseas soon after they reported back. Nothing happened. The following weekend they all went home, as they had been accustomed to do before the embarkation leave. On Monday morning when they turned up again they were genuinely surprised to find themselves under arrest.

When the regiment eventually went overseas Allhusen was in bed with influenza and so missed the draft. As nobody knew quite what to do with him, he was sent to Sandhurst. Although commissioned, he was only eighteen and a half. He records the experience as follows:

Above left: Left to right: Thomas, Haig, Joffre and Lloyd George.
Above right: Crown Prince Rupprecht of Bavaria.

Below: Left to right: Hindenburg, the Kaiser and Ludendorff.

Above: German blockhouse in the remains of Remus Wood.

Above right: This was once Kemmel Château.

Below: Gun crew at Pilckem Ridge.

Above: Norton Griffiths, the mining expert, with the 2½ ton Rolls-Royce in which he toured the battlefield.

Below: Allied sappers using a geophone to detect counter-mining.

Germans counter-mining

View from inside the Spanbroekmolen crater, the result of mining, before it filled with water.

Above: A Mark IV tank with its track blown off by gunfire, 12 October 1917.

Below: Soldiers at Zonnebeke, October 1917.

Above: Duckboards over the mud at Pilckem.

Below: Stretcher-bearers at Pilckem Ridge.

A trench in the Ypres Salient, October 1917.

The New Submarine Danger

" They'll be torpedoin' us if we stick 'ere much longer, Bill "

A typical Bairnsfather cartoon.

Above: Ypres in 1914.

Below: Ypres after the bombardment, a German photograph taken from Hill 60, two and a half miles away.

Right: The choir of Ypres Cathedral in 1914.

Below: The choir in 1917, reduced to rubble.

Above: The medieval Cloth Hall of Ypres in 1914.

Below: The Cloth Hall in ruins, seen from the cathedral.

Above: All that remained of Hooge in 1917.

Below: Passchendaele village, November 1917. The gentle hillock in the centre background once held the church.

Above: Passchendaele today – the low hill in the background is the vantage-point for which so many thousands on both sides died.

Below: Seventy years after the battle, this gentle-looking pastureland near Sanctuary Wood is still too dangerous to enter.

I can't recollect having learnt anything but the time passed very pleasantly.

At Sandhurst my Company Commander confined his attention to the Under Officer [the title given to the cadet who led the company when it was on parade and at other times performed many of the routine tasks which fall to a sergeant in ordinary regiments] and four Cadet Sergeants, and completely neglected the remaining forty odd cadets who used to amuse themselves in the background by throwing fir cones at each other. As the Company Commander was a particular enemy of mine, I was rather surprised when he sent for me and said he was now going to make me a corporal 'if I would promise to be clean on parade in future'.

This was really an old, not very funny joke. Allhusen had arrived wearing the uniform of the Devons and refused to wear the Sandhurst issue, which in any case was for cadets and not for commissioned officers. In every other respect he had set his commission on one side, and he was sure that his promotion was due not to a sudden change of heart by the company commander, but to the fact that he had been strongly recommended by the officer who was second in command. The uniform from the Devons was certainly very old and battered; it had had other owners before Allhusen. Nevertheless he refused to change it and said: 'This must, I imagine, be the only known instance of promotion for dirtiness.' It must also have been the only occasion when a second lieutenant was promoted to corporal. Allhusen formed a poor opinion of his contemporaries: 'The Under Officer was a complete nonentity, and most of the others were quite unfit to become officers. One was too frightened to ride a bicycle.'

After Sandhurst he was posted to the 60th Rifles,[1] with whom he travelled to France where, in spite of having learnt French for several years at Eton, he found he could not make himself understood at all. He arrived just too late to be sent to the Battle of Loos in September 1915. Had he got there in time for that battle, in which there were some 60,000 casualties, most occurring within the first twenty-four hours, it is unlikely that he would have survived to record his later experiences in the Ypres Salient.

Although they had been drafted to France, the 60th learnt that they were not to be sent to the trenches there. Instead they were sent to Amiens and given Serbian phrasebooks. Allhusen recalls that the phrase learnt most quickly was: 'Give me more wine.' With the phrasebook came pack transport and some instruction in mountain warfare: their destination was Salonika. As they arrived, he observed: 'On the pier were German spies with notebooks. The roads leading away from the port had been blocked by Greeks. An old lady asked me in a thick German accent "Vot regiment I vos" and someone threw a dead rat at a sergeant.'

The 60th saw no action at Salonika but the battalion was badly affected by sickness and Allhusen was so ill that he was sent home. After some months in hospital he claimed to be fit enough to return, but the doctors refused to let him go. They were completely baffled by his illness, which they were unable to cure. 'Only when a Rhodesian doctor with experience of tropical ills arrived did I improve. I had to see him in the mornings because after lunch he was drunk for the rest of the day.' Gradually Allhusen's health improved, and on release from hospital he was posted to the 7th Battalion of the 60th Rifles in the 14th Division, who were serving in France. He crossed the Channel and entrained for the long, laborious journey to the Front. At Hazebrouck he and another officer were having a wash in a water tank on the platform. Suddenly, 'the engine, which had shown no sign of life for several hours, gave a savage scream and started. We collected our sponges, clothes, etc, and set off in pursuit, with the railway staff cheering us on. Before long we overtook it. One man told me he had lost his train in these parts and had caught it two stations further on.'

Thence they went to Bailleul, 'the social centre of the Ypres Salient'. Some London shops had established branches there, even though once a week the Germans shelled it from long range. 'On ordinary peaceful days the club was full of clergymen so thick around the bar that the ordinary weary soldier from the line could not hope to compete with them. But on shelling days you could search the town from end to end without seeing a sign of the Church Militant.'

Allhusen joined the battalion at Neuve Chapelle and was sent up to the Messines Ridge:

Shells were falling fairly thick and when I was shown a flight of steps going down among the rubbish I went down pretty quick. At the bottom was a door and beyond it was a biggish room full of orderlies and telegraph operators. I went through this, and then came to a large room with wood-panelled walls and good furniture. This was the officers mess when the regiment was in the support position; the front line was much further on but the Ridge itself was still fairly active.

From here he was taken to D Company, whose headquarters in the line was an undersized pillbox. Next day he was given his platoon and told by the sergeant that 'it was an unlucky one for officers'.

From the top of the ridge there was a good view east and west over the valley of the Lys, the trenches, the great concrete tower of Warneton erected by the Germans as an observation post, the evil valley of Ploegsteert and Wolverghen where the front line had been for two years, all mud and wreckage. On the ridge pill boxes had been built inside the houses, giving the impression they were still standing. Messines was full of corpses, some still sitting at tables. A mine underneath was still expected to go up.

There were still several places where corpses were to be found sitting at tables. At Messines they had been killed by the shock waves from the huge explosion of 7 June. Elsewhere they were the victims of drifting or seeping gas which had not been noticed in time.

Working parties carrying stores were a normal nightly occupation when in support – one of the worst horrors of the war – endless toiling in the dark through mud, shell holes and old wire, carrying a heavy load of duckboards, rations or ammunition, always losing the man in front or being lost by the man behind, everyone hurrying, trying to pass some special danger point before the inevitable shell came. When a flare went up, everyone stood motionless cursing everybody who moved and cursing others for making too much noise, handing over stores at some company HQ, probably a well-known shell-trap, sorting out and counting things in the dark, signing receipts, everybody hanging about and lost – all in pitch darkness with every sound a crime and always with the chilling knowledge that the Germans were alert and close by in the darkness. There was a touch of mustard gas and some sniping. Some men of C Company were killed on the way back.

In the line 200 yards ahead of Company HQ we had no dugouts. One of the subalterns and I shared a small hole cut in the side of the trench. It was like a torture cage, too small either to sit up or lie down.

Night was the very busy time, an officer was on duty of one sort of another all the time.

Shelling was continuous but comparatively little of it was intended for the front line. The Germans always began the day with a bombardment in which a few gas shells were always included. Every morning we sat in gas masks watching our breakfast getting cold. Unfortunately it was considered necessary by the generals who lived out of range of the guns to draw the attention of the Germans to our part of the front so as to help the battle further north.

In deep dugouts you could just hear the barrage above, sounds like the rolling of a drum, hence the words 'drum fire'.

One night he went on patrol in No Man's Land to investigate a German sap – a trench reaching forward from the normal trench line. He was accompanied by a corporal. Taking merely gasmasks, revolvers and bombs, they began crawling forward. 'No Man's Land was always the best part of the front. There were no shells there, only, perhaps, a Boche as frightened as one's self.'

One night the Royal Engineers brought up a line of dummy men made of wood and canvas and fixed on a frame which could be pulled upright by a cord from the trench. Allhusen and his company then moved to a different trench, lit flares and pulled the figures upright. They drew attention to the dummies and partly obscured them. While the Germans shelled the trench full of dummies, which looked as if they were going to attack, the regiment made a raid further along, killed many Germans and took prisoners.

After a period in the line they were relieved by the Durham Light Infantry: 'The joy of coming out. Food, drink, water to wash in and beds.' They visited Bailleul, which was still comparatively unchanged but which later would become a rubbish heap of ruins.

In August the battalion had been on the Menin Road, the worst sector of the battle front at Ypres, and a nightmare through the whole army. I could see that people's nerves were all wrong still: they shivered when the Menin Road was mentioned and talked of it with a horror I could not understand. I wondered vaguely what it was like.

In the first few days of October the weather began to break. On the 6th as we started off to the Menin Road, the rain began in earnest. There was deep gloom beyond all description.

We marched by Shrapnel Corner and Zillebeke lake. At Zillebeke we picked up our Lewis guns. We were now among the heavy howitzers. On the right a stack of cordite charges was burning merrily. After Dead Mule Corner the road, now made of timber, began to rise. Here we came into the first of the barrages. The road was slippery. We slithered and stumbled and fell over things. We were all heavily loaded and the pace was awful. At last we came to the end of the road and turned to the right along a track. There were broken trees on the ground and I was told this was Sanctuary Wood. We were still going upwards. Here a man in my platoon was hit: I have never seen anyone so pleased. Then we turned on to a causeway hardly recognizable and looking like a long irregular ridge. This was the Menin Road.

It leaves a confused memory of bursting shells, treading on dead men, frantic calls for stretcher bearers long after the stretcher bearers had gone, losing the way, getting mixed up with stray parties of other battalions, then awful delays while the guide admitted he was lost and made futile remarks such as 'There ought to be a broken tank here.' Men were being hit right and left. Then we came to a black mass and the guide guessed it might be battalion headquarters. Strangely enough, he was right. 200 yards on was Company HQ. It was a machine-gun post and full of men. The Bedfords, whom we were relieving, looked like ghosts, pale and wild-eyed, with long beards and coated with mud from head to foot.

I took my platoon down a shallow trench with a foot and a half of water in it and put them in the sodden ditch where they were to live. Men of different regiments were wandering about and swearing.

He went back to the pillbox which was promptly hit by a shell, though not demolished. He was hit on the head by a piece of shrapnel but his helmet kept it out.

By next morning I had six casualties in my platoon. Our surroundings were unpleasant enough. Even the mud was different from what we were used to. It had lost all form and consistency and all resemblance to the honest stuff one finds in peaceful lands. It was just the shapeless mess that remains when everything else has gone. It rose in squashy heaps out of pools and lakes of slimy liquid, which were sometimes black, sometimes yellow from lyddite, sometimes bright green, but never the colour that water ought to be. Mixed with everything were stores, arms, equipment and dead men. Sometimes these were in groups, sometimes single, and sometimes only bits of them.

The landscape was always the same, and it made people feel ill; and then there was the smell. But the strongest memory of all is the indefinable horror, the hunted, haunted feeling that made men restless and sullen, wandering aimlessly about, and ultimately drove them mad. There was nothing to do, but people always seemed to be in a hurry. There was no rest or conversation or escape of any kind. It always seemed that the other place was a little bit safer.

We buried the nearest corpses, English and German. We set the men to work improving the trench, a hopeless task as every shovelful of mud thrown out slithered slowly back again. We stood behind our own pill box and stamped our feet. We were already cold and wet and weary and it was only the first morning.

Between our pill box and my platoon there was a waterlogged trench and a short-cut over the open. The latter, we were told, was commanded by a German sniper who never missed, and several corpses on the path testified to his efficiency. On the first morning some platoons of C Company arrived with a guide from the Bedfords. I warned them to keep to the trench and the guide laughed and said that he knew that sniper of old. About ten minutes later I saw the guide start back from C Company headquarters by himself across the short-cut. He was killed.

We stayed there three days in the support line and then received orders to take over the front line. Our casualties had been comparatively light so far. Two men had gone down with shell shock, one in the pill-box. He shook all over like a jelly and couldn't speak. The other, in a post near the pill-box, became paralysed and was not expected to live. Three out of the four quartermaster sergeants of the battalion had been killed bringing up the rations, and the R.S.M. was not expected to live. The company was still fairly strong but we were all feeling worn out. Our feet had been numb and cold since the first day.

Being second in command I went up to the front line with an N.C.O. to make arrangements for the relief. There was a communication trench of a sort, full of liquid mud which made every step an effort. The etiquette was to go across the open till the sniper had at least one shot: he was less deadly here and so far had had only one man. We started off at a brisk pace. I would have enjoyed the walk a good deal more if I had not known that someone was aiming at me. The bullet came close enough and I dropped down. After that we took to the trench. The mud and water reached to our waists and it took us about half an hour to do a hundred yards.

At last we reached the front line and I saw the Company Commander. He was standing up to his knees in water with his teeth chattering. Soon after he went out of his mind.

It had clouded over and the rain began again in earnest. The water in the trench rose quickly. We were far from happy.

Another company had a man drowned. We often had to pull men out. We had no pill-box. Our ears and eyes were full of mud, our legs numb and without feeling. We shivered violently day and night and couldn't stop.

All day the Germans used to shell their own front line with all manner of guns. There was nothing quite so satisfactory as watching the shells meant for us burst among the Boches. All day the rocket known as 'Golden rain' went up – the German signal that their shells were falling short. We used to amuse ourselves by firing rifle grenades at the men who fired the rocket and the latter would reply with vane bombs, a missile between a rifle grenade and a trench mortar. I don't suppose much damage was done but it helped to pass the time.

There was a little mild excitement when we discovered that an entirely new form of gas was being used against us. I remember sitting in the mud, sneezing hard, and thinking nothing of it until I noticed that everyone else was sneezing.

They never found out what the new gas[2] was and there were no further effects from it. He continued: 'Those days were the longest I remember. By the end we had been six days without sleep for however weary you may be sleep is out of the question when your limbs are numb with cold and your teeth are chattering. We were all near the limit and a good many had passed it and collapsed. What made things worse was the knowledge that to reach salvation we must drag ourselves somehow or other along six miles of tracks and the Menin Road.'

Haig's diary reveals a somewhat different viewpoint:

Monday October 8th:
    I called on General Plumer and had tea. It was raining and looked like a wet night. He stated that 2nd Anzac Corps (which is chiefly concerned in to-morrow's attack) had specifically asked that there should be *no postpone-ment*. Plumer was anxious lest the French should want to postpone. . . . The bombardment had not been satisfactory but Anthoine would cover the left flank of the 14th Corps. He would not, he thought, be able to carry out his *full task*. I said all he was asked to do was to *cover the flank of the Guards* who are attacking on his (Anthoine's) right. Gemeau said Anthoine did not want a postponement on any account. Later Kiggell brought me Anthoine's letter – a very mean document. He is evidently keen to save himself and to place the risk of failure on me. I am ready to take the responsibility and have ordered him to carry on and do his best. The French seem to have lost their chivalrous spirit if it ever existed out of the story books. Gough telephoned to Kiggell as to postponement: he said Cavan was against it, but Maxse wanted to postpone. I ordered them to carry on.

The trials of the 60th Rifles, as described by Allhusen, did not enter into the consciousness of either Haig or the compilers of the official history, *Military Operations in France and Belgium 1917*, so ably edited by Brigadier-General Sir James E. Edmonds, CB, CMG, RE. Edmonds, who had been a contemporary of Haig at the staff college, was one of his greatest admirers. There were, of course, many other regiments in the same desperate, squalid conditions as the 60th, and it would have been impossible to have mentioned them all. The official history, whose version of events has some-times attracted critical comment, records that: 'At dusk on the 3rd the assaulting brigades began the march up the line: most of the Australians, of whom three divisions were going into battle side by side for the first time, passed out of Ypres by the Menin Gate. . . . The chief concern was a possible break in the weather', it con-tinued. 'Possible' seems unduly cautious: there was already a gale, and the forecast had predicted more rain. 'The approach march during the midnight hours was made across ground rendered greasy by the rain and for the most part the duckboard tracks had to be used to enable units to reach their destinations up to time.' 'Ground rendered greasy by the rain' was undoubtedly not the phrase used by the Anzacs who made their way over it, and it is of interest to note that an infantry brigadier said: 'The tanks were elated.'

If the tanks were elated, they managed to control their emotion very well. Captain T. Price, DSO, MC, recorded:

> Ypres was the triumph of King Mud; all conquering mud, clinging viscous slime against which neither man nor machine could wring more than an hour's progress by a day's agony of toil.
>
> The tons of mud collected by the tanks were not of such an adhesive kind as the mud slung at them by disgruntled commanders of other units seeking a scapegoat for the untoward happenings of plans gone awry.
>
> The men who floundered through the successive bogs or trod warily the greasy duck boards on their daily lawful occasions gradually became acclimatized; but they were only carrying their own weight plus equipment. A Mark IV tank was obviously out of drawing in that picture. It was like an elephant in a quicksand. There was nothing solid for the tracks to grip . . . no one proposed that 15 in. howitzers should be dragged through the swamps up to Broodseinde, but the powers seemingly did expect a like miracle to be worked by the Tank Corps staff. Passchendaele: in that epic the infantry had, without doubt, the worst of it in every way, but at least their martyrdom was crowned at last. The tanks, however, for the most part, gathered the bitter conviction that their failures were not even regarded as splendid failures – they were just futile. Besides the common lot of losing their best men, they were losing as well their, as yet, insecure footing as a fighting Corps.
>
> They were Nobody's Darling, and so were left unloved

and untended in No Man's Land to be billets for wandering detachments. The Fifth Army hated the very sound, as well as the smell of a tank. The drawing room and smoking room experts of Mayfair and Pall Mall were chanting, for once united, the solemn requiem 'Scrap them, scrap them and let us get down to clean Victorian soldiering'. It was a near thing for the tanks.

'Elated' on 4 October 1917 the tanks certainly were not, even though they avoided being ditched in the early stages. Nor was anyone else, as men lay crowded together on the wet ground waiting for zero hour, which had been fixed for 6 a.m. They had all reached their start lines by 4 a.m., having come forward early in order to meet any German defensive barrage that might be expected to fall on the approach lines. When one came at 5.20 a.m., even more heavily than had been expected, it fell on the front of I Anzac Corps and lasted for forty minutes. In the leading brigades of the Anzacs one man in every seven was either killed or wounded. Subsequently the Allies learnt that the barrage had been put down not to deter the Anzac attack but to serve as a preliminary for a heavy German counter-attack which had as its aim the recapture of the territory lost in the battle of 26 September and was timed to begin at 6.10 a.m.

But at 6 a.m. the British barrage crashed down on the three German battalions who were waiting to attack. And as the Anzacs crossed No Man's Land they came across Germans waiting everywhere for the order to advance. Both sides had bayonets fixed and the encounters which took place were described as 'sharp and merciless'. The Anzacs had by far the better of them and were soon swarming around the pillboxes and strongpoints behind. A few pillboxes were so surprised at the sudden change from attack to defence that they surrendered quickly; others proved more resistant and caused many casualties before they fell. As the Anzacs came closer to the Broodseinde Ridge they found a number of command and observation posts linked by trenches. Using the latter for cover, the Anzacs were able to work in behind two battalion headquarters and capture their staff. Broodseinde itself was no longer a village but a heap of rubble: Zonnebeke was no better, but each was surrounded by machine gun posts and even anti-tank guns; these were captured or bypassed. However, the Anzacs were still 200 yards short of Passchendaele itself and on the way lay Celtic Wood, Daisy Wood and Dairy Wood, which the Germans had prudently filled with machine gun posts.

II Anzac Corps had a task as formidable as that being undertaken by I Anzac. Although Zonnebeke village was not in their zone, the Zonnebeke spur was and so, indeed, was the notorious Gravenstafel spur. The approaches, particularly by the Zonnebeke itself, had been covered with duckboards wherever these did not float away or sink out of sight. Hill 40, which had been for so long an unattainable objective, was first pounded with a heavy artillery barrage and then taken by a fierce infantry assault. Here again bayonets were the principal weapons. The ferocity of the Anzac assault caused many Germans to run back panic-stricken to rear areas, where they tried to take refuge in a barrage described as 'like a wall of flame'. But other Germans still stuck to the pillboxes and took a heavy toll before they were over-run. Two VCs were won in the assault. One was by Lance-Corporal W. Peeler, a member of a Pioneer battalion who led a wave of attacks and himself killed 30 Germans. Pioneers are not normally used as combat troops – their job is to dig trenches and act as a labour force. Peeler was having none of that: what the infantry shock troops could do he could do too – and better. The other VC went to Sergeant L. McGee, who, leading an attack armed only with a revolver, captured an entire German machine gun post on his own. On the Gravenstafel spur the New Zealand Division had the formidable task of taking the prominent point nicknamed Abraham Heights. They swept over this, then continued into the upper Stroembeek valley. At the end of the day they had killed an unknown but large number of Germans, taken 1159 prisoners and captured 59 machine guns.

Fifth Army's objective was to gain Poelcapelle and to press on, if possible, to what was now called the Flanders line, a line which ran due north from Gravenstafel and which, if gained, would give 5th Army a commanding position on the ridge. The Flanders line was some 3000 yards behind Poelcapelle.

The attack was led by Midland regiments and they gained their objectives quickly. To everyone's surprise, not least the Tank Corps, tanks played a successful part here. The slope up to Poelcapelle contained numerous machine gun posts and strongpoints, with which tanks dealt very effectively. They continued into Poelcapelle itself and demolished several more strongpoints with shells from their 6-pounder guns. During the battle a VC was won by Private A. Hutt of the Royal Warwickshires, who took command of his platoon (30 men) when all the officers and NCOs had become casualties. As they advanced they came to a strongpoint; telling the platoon to wait, he ran forward himself, shot an officer and three men inside the pillbox and took the surrender of the other 40 occupants. After handing over his prisoners, he occupied himself by rescuing the wounded under heavy fire, for there were no stretcher-bearers still available for the task. Two other VCs were won. Sergeant H. Coverdale of the Manchester Regiment led a party which wiped out two machine gun posts, showing complete indifference to danger. Corporal F. Greaves of the Sherwood Foresters was a member of a platoon which was checked by a strongpoint, at which his platoon officer and the sergeant were killed. He ran round to the back of the strongpoint and threw in grenades, which resulted in the capture of the position and its four machine guns.

It should perhaps be emphasized that assaults could only be carried out by fresh troops who had been brought up from the reserves and still had the energy for such activities. As was seen in the account of Allhusen's company on the Menin Road, the worst strain was felt when the line became static. When troops were left standing in water, regularly shelled and gassed and worn down by lack of sleep, such efforts were completely impossible. Nevertheless by holding the line they were preserving the position for another thrust forward.

On the northern flank XIV Corps found the going very hard indeed. In spite of tremendous efforts only one battalion, the Dublin Fusiliers, gained its objective. (Sergeant J. Ockenden won a VC for capturing a vital strongpoint.) The 10th and 11th Brigade took very heavy casualties on a forward slope, but were unable to make the desired headway. X Corps on the right flank was more fortunate. Their task of capturing the eastern edge of the Gheluvelt plateau was made easier by a devastating preliminary barrage which killed many of the Germans defending the position and demoralized the rest. Six hundred prisoners were taken easily. X Corps established its southern flank between Polygon Wood and the Menin Road. In peacetime the area was drained by the Polygonbeek and the Reutelbeek, shallow streams a few feet wide; however, the continuous bombardment had turned this area into a valley of mud over half a mile wide and of unknown depth.

In 21st Division the Queen's, and the King's Own Yorkshire Light Infantry, managed to cross the Polygonbeek under heavy fire, although losing many men, and to work around to the back of the main German strongpoints. Four tanks were allotted to this operation, which was described as follows by Captain T. Price and Captain D.E. Hickey:

> At 3 a.m. on October 4th Captain Clement Robertson had brought them all to the starting point. His zero hour was 6 a.m. and he led the van, after continuous lack of rest since 30th September. The infantry were moving steadily forward, alternately swimming and jumping over the rain-sodden quagmire from edge to edge of the shell-holes. What had once been a road was now, of course, a mass of broken cobbles, muck and debris, human and mechanical.
>
> Over this Via Dolorosa Captain Robertson moved forward, and on foot. If a tank missed the way it missed the battle too, for there was no recovery once the so called track was left.
>
> Strait was the way and narrow, and Robertson walked alone in front of his tanks, otherwise no one would have escaped submersion.
>
> He was no light-hearted boy doing a stunt. He knew what it meant, but it was up to him to bring his tanks into action at any and every cost. The swampy nature of the ground made it necessary to test every step of the way to prevent the tanks being ditched.
>
> Captain Robertson walked in front of his leading tank, prodding the ground with his stick, in spite of machine-gun bullets and heavy shell-fire against the tanks. He must have known that under these conditions his devotion to duty meant, sooner or later, certain death for him. He knew, however, that the success of the attack depended upon his making sure of the ground over which

his tanks were to go. They had crossed the stream, and were approaching their objective when he was killed by a bullet through the head while still leading.

He was awarded a posthumous VC.

Another VC won in this attack was that of Lieutenant-Colonel L.P. Evans, commanding the 1st Lincolnshire Regiment. When he saw heavy casualties being caused by the fire from a pillbox, he ran up to it and fired his revolver through the aperture. This surprise attack made the occupants surrender. In spite of being wounded and losing much blood he continued to lead his battalion to their objective.

The 5th Division, which was on the right of X Corps, advanced 800 yards; the Cornwall Light Infantry, assisted by a tank before it became stuck, managed to occupy Cameron Covert. Polderhoek Château, which had now been made into a concrete fortress, proved a formidable obstacle. I King's Own Scottish Borderers reached it and got inside, but at the end of the day had to fall back with the other members of their (13th) Brigade. The same misfortune occurred to the Somerset Light Infantry and Lincolns, who managed to force an entry into the defences on the Tower Hamlets spur but were driven back by intensive German machine gun fire from three sides. Gheluvelt Wood and Gheluvelt itself still resisted capture, although much of the plateau was now in Allied hands. All the gains were at the expense of heavy casualties: 62 Brigade lost 74 out of 86 officers; as early as midday on 4 October, the Northumberland Fusiliers had lost their commanding officer and all four company commanders. Among the many men who gave their lives that day none showed greater self-sacrifice than Private T.H. Sage of the Somerset Light Infantry. One of his fellow soldiers was shot just when he was about to throw a grenade; Private Sage promptly threw himself on to it, thus saving the lives of his fellows at the cost of his own.

GHQ was well satisfied with the results of the attacks. Although there had been setbacks, many important objectives had been gained. German casualties had been exceptionally high; their histories subsequently described this as 'the black day of 4 October' and 'the worst day of the war'. German morale had been badly affected by the relentless barrage and attacks, and thousands had been taken prisoner without offering much resistance. Charteris's optimisim became greater than ever and he persuaded Haig to let him press Plumer for more vigorous exploitation of this success than the original plan allowed. Plumer was, of course, much nearer to the fighting than GHQ and had had considerable experience of the German ability to bring up reserves quickly and turn a disastrous reverse into a brisk counter-attack. He suspected that only a part of the German Army in Flanders had been engaged in the fighting in this sector and that there were substantial forces in reserve backed by massive artillery support. Previous experience had also taught him that the Germans defended their forward areas with pillboxes and strongpoints, but had a more thorough and formidable defensive system behind. However, he gave the new idea consideration and ascertained the views of his Corps and Divisional Commanders. There was little support among them for the idea of rapid exploitation; most thought the best policy was to continue with the methodical approach of the original plan. Charteris's ideas were therefore dismissed.

However, at 5th Army HQ Gough and his advisers felt that there were still gains to be made – though not, perhaps, substantial ones. Gough ordered his Corps commanders to continue the attack in the late afternoon of the 4th, but cancelled the order quickly when there was some confusion between units withdrawing and units advancing. By now the Germans were replacing the losses in their front line units by a stream of reinforcements, although these were making their way forward with some difficulty in the face of determined Allied artillery and machine gun fire. They reoccupied Reutel and Cameron Covert and reinforced Poelderhoek Château. Passchendaele itself was already in ruins, but there was still considerable cover on the ridge from hedges and trees; this was now being systematically torn away by British shellfire. The Germans responded by thoroughly pounding the lost territory on the Broodseinde Ridge and Gheluvelt plateau; this made the existence of its new occupants exceptionally difficult and unpleasant. Rain, of course, fell intermittently.

Having held their line and been bypassed, the 60th were now relieved and started back on 'what used to be known as "the Menin Road handicap". We went along well enough until Inverness Copse,' wrote Allhusen.

See You Again in Hell

Then some men in the middle were blown off the path by
a shell. By the time they had picked themselves up the
front part of the platoon had gone. Here there was heavy
shelling and wounded men were lying around everywhere. It was an awful pandemonium, something like
the medieval idea of hell, pitch-dark apart from the evil
flashes of bursting shells, screams, groans and sobs, men
writhing in the mud, men trying to walk and falling
down again and everywhere figures scurrying like lost
souls, backwards and forwards, blaspheming and im-
ploring someone to tell them the way. It seems that when
a man turns his back to the front he is on the road to
panic and when his mind and body have reached
breaking-point the road is not so long. Parties would
leave the trenches marching in order like soldiers but
with every step towards the safety of which they had
almost despaired, discipline and tradition and self-
respect would ebb away, left behind in the front line – the
men who fell were unable to pick themselves up again
and there were heartbreaking delays in which we pulled
them out of holes in which they would have been
drowned. When we reached the pick-up point there were
no lorries. They were six hundred yards further back,
halted by the shelling. The thought of hot cocoa kept
men going. When they reached the canteen they were
told the cocoa was finished.

When they finally reached their destination men simply sat and
wept. Allhusen slept, but some men kept themselves awake through
fear of the nightmares which came once they closed their eyes.

After a short period of rest, the 60th were sent back into the line.
Before they began the march back 'we were lectured about British
pluck and determination by a Corps Commander who then got into
a Daimler limousine which rolled away in the opposite direction'.
When they returned they found the Front was frozen. One night
the stove in a hut they were using overturned on to a box of rifle
grenades; they put the fire out just in time. Passchendaele village
was now being shelled by both sides day and night. When the 60th
reached it they were surprised to find there was nothing there: the

127

village had entirely gone, and where the church had been there was only a low mound.

Allhusen never became indifferent to the sufferings of others, as so many did under those conditions. In his company was a man called Quinn, the last of six brothers. When the other five had been killed, his mother had tried to get the last survivor a transfer to a regiment in a less dangerous situation, but her request had been turned down by the authorities. Allhusen appointed him company runner and kept him inside the pillbox most of the time, where he was safe from anything but a direct hit.

But eventually Allhusen himself was hit, receiving a wound which left him permanently disabled. As he was recovering he caught scarlet fever, a highly dangerous disease in those days. Somehow he survived that too, though he would never be fully fit again. By what seems a miracle he managed to preserve something of the cheerful philosophy with which he had begun the war.[3]

The attacks on 4 October had been only a preliminary in the minds of the planners: a decisive assault was to be made on the 9th, and the final effort on the 12th. This next stage of the attack would pass into the record books as the Battle of Poelcapelle.

Notes

1 The King's Royal Rifle Corps, also known as the Greenjackets and now amalgamated with the Rifle Brigade and Oxford and Bucks Light Infantry to form the Royal Greenjackets (RGJ).
2 Diphenyl chlorasine. See p.155.
3 Allhusen remained in the Army until 1922, even though he had been severely wounded at Passchendaele and later shot through the elbow when serving with the British forces at Murmansk. He stayed on in Russia for a while in a diplomatic role, as Assistant Agent to Sir Robert Hodgson. Had the war not interrupted his career, he would himself have gone up to Cambridge in 1914 and subsequently taken the Civil Service examination for the Diplomatic Service. After Russia, however, he entered the business world and produced a book entitled *The Market Problem* which was published by Peter Davies in 1938.

In the Second World War he was recalled to be Adjutant of the 2nd Battalion of the Queen's Westminsters. In 1941 he became Commandant of the Middle East Intelligence School. On demobilization he contested the West Bristol constituency in 1946 as a Liberal; he was not elected, but did not lose his deposit either. He married the same year.

In 1939 he published *Money is the Decisive Factor – Britain's Handicap in the Economic Race with Russia.* It advocated today's ideas of monetary control – then unfashionable – and was even published in Japanese.

He was deeply religious, but not a church-goer. His experiences in the First World War made him determined to try to make the world better for all. He died in 1977, alert, humorous and compassionate to the end.

8

The Difficulties
Were Greatly Underestimated

On 8 October, Haig sent a memorandum to Robertson:

> Though the French cannot be expected to admit it
> officially, we know that the state of their armies and the
> reserve manpower behind the armies is such that neither
> the French government nor the military authorities will
> venture to call on their troops for any further great and
> sustained offensive effort, at any rate before it becomes
> evident that the enemy's strength has been finally and
> definitely broken. Though they are staunch in defence
> and will carry out useful local offensives against limited
> objectives, the French armies would not respond to a call
> for more than that, and the authorities are well aware of
> it. In these circumstances, since the British armies alone
> can be made capable of a great offensive effort it is
> beyond argument that everything should be done by our
> Allies as well as ourselves to enable that effort to be made
> as strong as possible, and for this as much training, leave
> and rest as possible is absolutely essential for our men.

Having established that the forthcoming battles would be fought
by the British and Anzacs alone, Haig went on to explain that in no
circumstances should the British/Anzac Front be widened to take
over more of the French sector. He pointed out:

> They are in a foreign country, the French are at home.
> They get little leave and at long intervals: the French
> soldiers get ten days leave every four months and their
> government dare not refuse it. Our men have borne more

and accomplished more than the French this summer and though France may plead that the weight of the war has fallen on her it cannot be expected that the British soldiers in the field who have done so much and borne so much and who have come voluntarily from the ends of the earth to fight in France will be content to see preferential treatment being give to our allies.

Here he was using a political argument to bolster what he thought to be a military need. Haig was determined that the British (in which he included the Anzacs) should win the final victory and be seen to be doing so. Under no circumstances did he intend that the British effort should be thinned by acceding to a request to cover a section of the French Front, which the French were perfectly capable of looking after themselves. Prejudice apart, it seems that at this stage in the war Haig's attitude to his allies was tempered more by experience than by personal feelings; even the most ardent Francophile could hardly expect the British to extend their burdens merely because the French were unwilling to honour their commitments. After all, he thought, it was not the British fault that the French armies had mutinied: it was mainly because of the stupidity of giving Nivelle so much authority. Haig claimed that the plea for the British to take over an additional section of the French line was a political rather than a military decision. What his memorandum disguises, however, is his absolute determination not to be deflected in any way from his ambition to capture the Passchendaele Ridge and then, even at this late stage, to sweep beyond it with his cherished cavalry.

'The actual extent of front measured by miles is no test of what we should hold. The true test is the relative number of enemy divisions engaged by us, and still more the rôle to be allotted to us in next year's campaign.' 'The rôle to be allotted to us in next year's campaign.' Before the end of 1917 Haig would have so completely missed the opportunity created by the successful tank action of Cambrai that another year of war was now certain – and one which almost produced defeat for the Allies. But Haig had no time for variations on his own principal plan. The war would be won by infantry and cavalry. He continued:

For these reasons it is necessary, in my opinion, to refuse to take over more line and to adhere resolutely to that refusal, even to the point of answering threats by threats if necessary.

One more indispensable condition of decisive success on the Western Front is that the War Cabinet should have a firm faith in its possibility and resolve finally and unreservedly to concentrate our resources on seeking it, and to do so at once. To gain decisive success, especially under the conditions postulated by the Prime Minister, we have need of every man, gun and aeroplane that can be provided, and of taking their training in hand as early as possible this winter. To ensure this we must take risks elsewhere and cut down our commitments in all other theatres to the minimum necessary to protect really vital interests. This principle applies equally to our dealings with our allies.

It is clear from this last paragraph that Haig's eye was now roving hungrily over all the other areas where British troops were committed: Palestine, East and West Africa, Mesopotamia (Iraq) and Egypt were clearly of less importance to him than Ypres; the Italian campaign could be left to simmer; and there would no doubt be scrapings to be made from garrisons elsewhere. He saw no point in waiting for the Americans to come into the war. Their only resource was manpower; they had few arms and aircraft and would need to rely on the British and French for these and other equipment. He was returning to the point made on 19 June to the War Cabinet:

I strongly asserted that Germany was nearer her end than they seemed to think, that *now* was the favourable moment for pressing her and that everything possible should be done to take advantage of it by concentrating on the Western Front *all* available resources. I stated that Germany was within six months of the total exhaustion of her available manpower, *if the fighting continues at its present intensity*. To do this more men and guns are necessary.

Unfortunately four of those six months had now elapsed. In that time the British and Anzacs had already sustained over 200,000 casualties for advances of less than three miles. The Germans might be at the end of their resources but the French had already reached the end of theirs, and if the Passchendaele battles continued to use up soldiers at their present rate (some 20,000 on 4 October) there would soon be very few men of fighting age in Europe, British included. Haig, of course, did not see that the war could be won anywhere but in Belgium, with France as a secondary theatre. It seems that he did not take into his calculations the fact that if Britain withdrew troops from other theatres the Germans there would have a distinct possibility of gaining swift victories against a heavily outnumbered opposition and then withdrawing troops to bolster their defences in France.

Robertson replied to Haig's memorandum immediately:

> Your memorandum is splendid. I gather from Lord R. Cecil that you are perhaps a little disappointed with me in the way I have stood up for correct principle, but you must let me do my job in my own way. I have never yet given in on important matters and never shall. In any case, whatever happens, you and I must stand solid together. I know we are both trying to do so.
>
> He (Lloyd George) is out for my blood very much these days. Milner, Carson, Curzon, Cecil, Balfour, have each in turn expressly spoken to me separately about his intolerable conduct during the last week or two and have said they are behind us. Since then he has got my Future Policy Paper and your Memo. A Cabinet is now sitting. He will be furious and probably matters will come to a head. I rather hope so, I am sick of this d——d life.
>
> I can't help thinking he has got Painlevé and Co here in his rushing way so as to carry me off my feet. But I have big feet. The great thing is to keep on good tactical ground. This is difficult for he is a skilful tactician but I shall manage him.

Though Lloyd George had been reluctant to support the idea of the war when it was declared in 1914, as the months passed his

enthusiasm for it grew. But with his growing determination to help
the war to a successful conclusion had developed very considerable
concern about Haig's military capabilities and political ambitions.
In 1917 he had come to regard Haig as a menace, not merely to the
successful conclusion of the war but to the survival of the British
nation. When he had learnt of Nivelle's proposed offensive earlier
in 1917 he had opposed it, but he soon came round to giving it his
support on the basis that Nivelle's advancement would help to
check Haig. He had in fact tried to put Haig under Nivelle's
command, but the plan had been frustrated, mainly by Robertson.
In consequence, in the second half of 1917 Haig and Lloyd George
regarded each other more as enemies than as allies. Each thought
that the other's policies were certain to lose the war, and felt
himself bound to use every means in his power to frustrate them.
Lloyd George believed that Haig's tactics of launching division
after division into the Ypres bloodbath and then asking for more
was more likely to defeat Britain that anything the Germans could
think of; he believed fervently that there must be some other theatre
which would be more profitable: the Balkans, the Middle East or
even Russia. Haig, grimly aware of how little had been accomplished at Salonika and Gallipoli, used all his considerable
influence with George V to isolate Lloyd George. The King, who
detested Lloyd George as much as Haig did, made the latter a
field-marshal but that merely served to polarize the situation.
Lloyd George's power, such as it was, lay on the Home Front. If he
could persuade his not very strong-minded colleagues that Haig
should not be allowed to scrape more deeply into the manpower
barrel unless he changed his apparently suicidal tactics, then Haig
would be brought to heel. But Haig had no intention of being
brought to heel in this or any other way by someone whom he
openly despised. At all those informal little receptions of politicians
and others who visited Haig's headquarters, miles behind the front
line, Haig was the essence of reasoned affability – except, of course,
when he referred to the dangerous policies of Lloyd George. Not
least of Lloyd George's deficiencies in the eyes of the Commander-
in-Chief was that, while one moment he was saying he knew
nothing about strategy and tactics, in the next he was trying to tell
the Army how to fight the war.

But in October 1917 Haig realized that he needed to redefine his objectives. Now, instead of talking about the great breakthrough which would follow the final over-running of the Passchendaele Ridge, he was talking about the value of the battle for its own sake. That value was *bleeding the German Army to death*. Unfortunately subsequent figures, very hard to elicit and to authenticate, suggest that it was not the German Army which was suffering the most at Passchendaele but the British and Anzac forces. The German generals have never been frank about their losses, but their historians have worked them out as somewhere near 250,000; the British ones were said to be slightly higher. In any event the Germans still had ample resources, as their successful offensive of the following spring so grimly proved.

On 9 October Haig wrote in his diary: 'A general attack was launched at 5.30 a.m. to-day from a point south-east of Brood-seinde on the right to St Janshoek on the left (1 mile north-east of Bixschoote). The results were very successful.' Haig's comment that the attacks were 'very successful' seems the product of wishful thinking rather than statistical evidence. The plan was for a single two-stage attack by I and II Anzac Corps in the central sector and a 1200-yard thrust by 5th Army at the northern end of the ridge. The Anzac attacks would be made with four divisions which, after gaining their objectives, would be replaced by four other divisions previously held in reserve. Two cavalry divisions would be within one day's march of the battlefield; two others would be in reserve but immediately ready to move. Two tank battalions would be held in readiness two miles south of Ypres pending their employment by 2nd Army, and four more tank battalions would be made available for 5th Army when needed. Preliminary reports on the state of the ground in the proposed assault area indicated that it was highly unsuitable for tanks: later information confirmed this, and in consequence tanks were not used at all in this battle. Nevertheless the objectives for the coming offensive were extremely optimistic. Second Army was to sweep through and past Passchendaele, driving the Germans off the north-east and eastern slopes, while 5th Army's thrust would take it to the so-called Flanders Line and therefore well on the way to Westroosbeke. At the final stage the cavalry could be launched forward to turn the German defeat into a rout. Westroosbeke was expected to fall on the 12th at the latest. Intelligence reports issued from GHQ confirmed that the Germans had been so exhausted by the battle on the 4th that they had now been obliged to put all their available resources into the line. Their morale was said to be extremely low, and GHQ was confident that if they could be stunned by a further attack in the very near future they would collapse entirely. GHQ reasoned that the sooner the next blow could be struck the greater the chance of overwhelming success. For this reason the attack scheduled for the 10th had been brought forward to the 9th.

Unfortunately the rain, of which GHQ seemed unaware, had never stopped since it began on the 4th. Occasionally it had slackened off to a drizzle, but it had usually made up for these lighter spells by relentless downpours. The entire area and the men in it were drenched. Commanders in the forward area sent back reports to headquarters of both 5th and 2nd Armies which indicated that rapid progress was out of the question – in fact any further progress looked unlikely. After pondering these reports Plumer and Gough told Haig that they did not feel anything could be achieved under present conditions, and that the Army should now settle down to consolidating its recent gains and wait for drier conditions before operations continued. Drier conditions might, of course, mean frozen ground in the winter, or improved weather in the following spring. Waiting for either would mean leaving the Army in an extremely uncomfortable position, with most, though not all, of its objectives gained, while the Germans recovered from their recent hard knocks and prepared to recover their lost ground. Haig was left in no doubt of the difficulties likely to be encountered if the present campaign continued, but he felt that, whatever the cost, the armies should now press on and capture the remaining portion of the ridge. The ridge had now become of paramount importance; it was as well that none of those fighting desperately to capture it could look into the future and see how easily their hard-won gains would all be lost again in a few weeks' time.

One more thrust. If the weary, sodden troops could drag themselves over the quagmire in front of them, kill the Germans manning the pillboxes, strongpoints and trenches, and then hold the ground they had won in the face of determined German counter-attacks, they would hold the vital ridge from Messines to Westbroeke and give the Germans the medicine they had been handing out to others during the last three years. As a task it was near impossible, but then almost every task they had accomplished during the last three months could be described in the same way. This would be no worse than the others; at least they hoped not.

Whatever doubts Haig may have had – and after talks with his Army commanders he had plenty of information on which to base misgivings – he felt he had little room for manoeuvre. He was at the point of decisive victory, even though he might even now be robbed of it and left with an Army almost as demoralized as the French, and perhaps mutinous as well. The French seemed hardly to have improved at all. Miraculously the Germans still seemed unaware of the rich dividends awaiting them if they made an all-out assault on almost any section of the French line. Pétain had been particularly anxious that pressure should be kept on the Germans; later it appeared that Pétain was thinking not so much of a massive offensive as of a series of local attacks. It was also important to send the Germans reeling backwards before they could withdraw divisions from the Russian Front and sent them to strengthen their line at Passchendaele. Everything suggested that they should continue the attack – everything but one fact: the rain.

On the effects of the rain the official history is strangely inconsistent. The final chapter of Volume II of *Military Operations in France and Belgium 1917* contains a remarkable passage entitled 'The Mud'. It runs:

> Several eminent civilian critics with the ear of the public have spread the mud legend and maintained that on account of the mud Sir Douglas Haig should never have initiated a campaign in Flanders at all, and should have certainly stopped operations in August.
>
> Mud there certainly was most of the time, but not of the degree to justify calling Third Ypres, 'The Campaign of the Mud'. Even to call it 'A Campaign in the Mud' would be little more than to call it an autumn campaign. Whenever great armies carry on operations in European autumns and winters, or in tropical rainy seasons, be it Flanders, Holland, Poland . . . Spain . . . Italy (in 1944), Burma or Virginia . . . there is mud. Yet no one has blamed Marlborough, Napoleon, Grant, or the generals of 1939–45 for carrying on over soft ground and adverse weather conditions. . . .

It continues by quoting senior officers who alleged that the mud on the Somme was worse than that at Passchendaele, and with the remarkable statement that 'Reports and photographs clearly indicate that the mud in Holland in the winter of 1944–45 was far and away worse than any experienced in 1917 in Flanders – or at any time on the Western Front. As one officer has put it, in Holland there was "hard mud, soft mud, gravel mud, mud with ice in it and also the sort you can't say if it is mud or dirty water" '.

There is much more in this vein, quoting various campaigns in past centuries when mud had proved a difficult obstacle. Of course, nothing mentioned was remotely like the seas of mud between Ypres and the Passchendaele Ridge – a revolting horror which has already been described in these pages. Brigadier-General Edmonds, the editor of the official history, had undoubtedly completed a magnificent achievement; but in 1948, when this volume was published, he was eighty-seven and had perhaps overlooked the fact that a few pages earlier the history had carried the following words:

> Three months of persistent shelling had blocked the watercourses, and the mass of shell-holes frustrated every effort to drain the water away. . . the entire area of the upper Steenbeek and its tributaries (behind II Anzac Corps) was, in the words of one divisional C.R.E.,[1] 'a porridge of mud'. On such a foundation, despite the concentrated and untiring efforts of the engineers of the two Anzac corps, no progress could be made with the forward move of the guns: the planks either sank in the mire or floated away. The field batteries of the II Anzac Corps which were to have been near the Zonnebeke–Winnipeg road to support the main attack had to remain west of the Steenbeek on hurriedly constructed and unstable gun platforms. Until these were made many of the guns were up to the axles in mud and some even to the muzzles. . . .

Supplying ammunition to the advanced field batteries was a formidable task, and could only be done by selecting battery sites within 100–150 yards of the main roadways. Shells and supplies had to be carried by pack animals from the wagon lines to the guns, and this journey, which normally took an hour, now took between six and sixteen hours. The mules and pack horses frequently slipped off the planks on to the quagmire on either side, where they sometimes sank out of sight, and the shells generally arrived coated with slime and were unusable till cleaned. The dugouts at the wagon lines and the shelterless gun platforms were soon flooded, and the men had to sleep on wet blankets or sodden straw, resulting in a rapid dwindling of artillery strength through sickness and exhaustion. . . .

> The chief cause of the great discontent during this period of the Flanders fighting was, in fact, the continuous demands on regimental officers and men to carry out tasks which appeared physically impossible to perform, and which no other army would have faced. It must be emphasized again that in all that vast wilderness of slime hardly a tree, hedge, wall or building could be seen. As at the Somme, no landmarks existed, nor any scrap of natural cover other than the mud-filled shell-holes. That the attacks ordered were so gallantly made in such conditions stands to the immortal credit of the battalions concerned.

Zero hour for 2nd Army's attack on 9 October was 5.20 a.m.: the leading units were to be 66th and 49th Divisions. The timings went wrong from the start. To reach the start line (then called the 'jumping-off tapes') by midnight they had to march two and half miles in five hours, about half the speed at which they could march on a road in daylight. But this was not daylight and the roads they were required to use were duckboard tracks. Even these were submerged, some so deeply that the unfortunate troops using them struggled through mud at best ankle deep, at worst knee high. It was dark, pouring with rain, and the Germans were intermittently shelling the approach roads. It was obvious that many units would not only fail to be in position by midnight, but would also fail to reach their start lines by zero hours, five hours later. Worse was to follow.

When the assault began, using those units which had managed to struggle up to the start line, the covering barrage was sadly inadequate. Many of the guns which should have taken part were incapable of firing, while some of those which did were on such unstable platforms that their aim could not be accurate, and of those shells which did land in the target area many buried themselves so deeply in the mud before exploding that they had minimal effect. In fact the so-called creeping barrage which was meant to cover and guide the infantry was barely discernible and almost totally useless.

For 49th (1st West Riding) Division the attack was a nightmare which grew steadily more horrific as the hours passed. Their march up to the start line was a feat which in any other place or time would have seemed a triumph over impossible odds: here it was merely the preliminary to even greater trials. Immediately ahead of them was the flooded Ravebeek, a 50 yard wide sea of mud with waist-deep water in the middle. Units struggled through and around this obstacle; the edges were little better than the centre and the opportunities for losing contact with one's fellows, as well as the general direction of the attack, were unlimited. Those who did manage to negotiate this obstacle found themselves confronted first with concentrated machine gun fire from pillboxes and then by lines of barbed wire. In addition they encountered machine guns sited in shell holes. There was no longer any chance of heroic individuals or small parties rushing up to pillboxes and strong-points and lobbing in grenades through the apertures: the pillboxes were now all protected by aprons of barbed wire. Unaware of the fact that the leading brigades had been held up, or slaughtered, among these obstacles, Divisional HQ sent up the second phase of the attack. By mid-afternoon all but one of the brigades were back at their start lines, having suffered 2500 casualties.

The 66th fared better than 49th initially, but also had its share of Ravebeek mud before being held up by flooded trenches on the eastern slopes above the stream. Here it was fully exposed to machine guns firing at up to 800 yards' range from Bellevue; these stopped 198th Brigade altogether. Moving along an easier route, 197th Brigade reached the top of the ridge. One patrol succeeded in reaching Passchendaele itself, which was deserted. When the rain stopped, German machine guns and artillery concentrated their fire on the ridge and its approaches, inflicting heavy casualties on every unit in the vicinity.

These, although part of the Anzac Corps, were British divisions. The Australian divisions fighting alongside fared no beter: they had lost so many men from a variety of causes on the way up that they had been unable to avoid leaving pockets of Germans behind as they advanced. There were also gaps in their own front line through which other Germans succeeded in infiltrating. In view of the strong possibility that some of their leading units might easily be cut off, orders were given to withdraw 800 yards. It was dispiriting enough to have to give up ground so recently gained at heavy cost, but it was made worse by the heavy casualties they took while doing so. Daisy, Dairy and Celtic Woods, mentioned earlier as likely to be difficult obstacles, now proved to be just that; the latter was penetrated by a party of 85 officers and men of whom only 14 emerged unwounded.

The danger which was now all too apparent was that the front line would fall into a zigzag pattern, giving the Germans excellent opportunities for both enfilading and counter-attacks. Fortunately this was avoided – though narrowly – just in time to check the first German counter-attack. During the evening the soldiers, now at the point of complete exhaustion, dug in and consolidated their somewhat precarious positions. Further south, another attack had been made on Polderhoek Château, this time by 5th Division, but the château was defended by heavy machine gun and artillery fire. The only bright spot in the day was the capture of Reutel village and its immediate surroundings by 2/1 HAC and 2nd Royal Warwickshire in 7th Division.

It was clear in retrospect, as well as to many of those being asked to do the impossible, that the infantry were being ordered to make attacks under conditions which in every way favoured the enemy. The British barrage, formerly so effective, was now a mere shadow of what it should have been. In consequence pillboxes, strongpoints, wire and substantial numbers of enemy troops were left untouched. The unfortunate British and Australians were asked not merely to struggle through mud and water at times up to the waist but, having done so, were thrown against carefully prepared positions without even the protection of a creeping barrage. Every twenty yards of the enemy line had a well-sited machine gun, and in addition a multiplicity of other weapons, varying from grenades to howitzers, was aiming to knock all life and spirit out of the oncoming troops. The fact that men could still press forward under these conditions is not so much miraculous as incredible. But even the most determined and undaunted human courage is, in the last resort, helpless against a solid wall of steel – a fact that the Germans had already discovered for themselves. In 5th Army the leading battalions, after a fourteen-hour march up to their start lines, were confronted with a concentration of German fire which tore them to pieces from the first moments of the assault. So much for the 1200 yards' advance scheduled by the planners living far behind the battle zone.

The extreme northern flank seemed to offer the best prospects for attaining the planned objectives. It was allotted to XIV Corps, who had the French Army on their left. Its destination was the southern edge of the Houthulst Forest, a place of sinister reputation from previous wars but which so far had been less devastated than other so-called forests. The march up had been easier, the artillery had been less affected, and even the Broembeek, though flooded, looked negotiable and proved to be so. On the right 12th Brigade, commanded by the formidable Brigadier-General Carton de Wiart, VC, who had been wounded and decorated so many times he had lost count, made some headway but could not venture further forward than XVIII Corps on their right, which had been brought to a halt. The other units in this area also made progress, in some cases amounting to a mile and a half. This, though highly creditable, merely brought them to the southern edge of the Houthulst Forest. The Germans made one not very vigorous counter-attack and seemed content to reserve their efforts for the next 5th Army thrust, which would aim at penetrating the Houthulst Forest. This was an area which the Germans had long and carefully prepared for such an eventuality: crammed with pillboxes and machine gun strongpoints, it had been organized as a major killing ground. All in all, at the end of a night and a day of superhuman effort, gains had been very slight and losses very high. Haig had clearly been deceived, or was perhaps deceiving himself, when he wrote: 'The results were very successful.'

Astonishingly, even in the conditions of 9 October there were still occasions of conspicuous heroism. Private F.G. Hancock worked his way round to the back of a German pillbox and made its 40 occupants surrender by threatening them with a 36 grenade (more usually known in those days as a Mills bomb). His reappearance, carrying a German machine gun and followed by 40 captive Germans, amazed his fellow soldiers. He was awarded a VC. Sergeant J. Lister, of the Lancashire Fusiliers, also tackled a pillbox single-handed. Having shot the machine gunners before they were aware of his presence, he was surprised to find that 100 other Germans willingly surrendered. The 101st showed signs of objecting, so Lister promptly shot him. Lister's feat earned him a VC. Sergeant J. Molyneux of the Royal Fusiliers led a party which captured a trench and a house. Fewer prisoners were taken in this private battle, but a number of Germans were killed and wounded. Molyneux was awarded a VC. Lance-Sergeant J.H. Rhodes of the Grenadier Guards won a VC for capturing a pillbox with its nine occupants, who included a German Forward Observation Officer.

Ironically the French, who were supposed to be incapable of further offensive effort, had a successful day with their 1st Army and reached their objectives on the British left. In fairness to all concerned it should be noted that the conditions under which they made their attack were much easier than in the other sectors, and the German opposition less concentrated. But at least it served to demonstrate that the entire French Army was not in the dire straits alleged.

On 10 October Haig recorded in his dairy: 'I saw General Gough at Château Loewe and had tea with him. He thinks the Second Army objectives too far distant for the next offensive. Gough's dates for reaching Westroosbeke also seem slow. So I said we cannot decide until the next attack.'

On the 11th Haig received a message from Robertson saying that he now thought that he (Robertson) should resign from his position as CIGS on the basis that Lloyd George was no longer listening to his advice but instead was calling for other opinions. Haig replied immediately, saying that under no circumstances should Robertson resign.

On the 11th Haig entertained the Editor of the *Westminster Gazette* to lunch. 'A charming fellow and I feel sure quite honest: a friend of Asquith. Because of this Lloyd George is trying to get rid of him from his paper. . . .' He also met the President of the Portuguese

Republic at Lillers station, where he saw Poincaré:

> I had a few minutes talk with Poincaré at Lillers. He looked tired. I was asked by him when I though operations would stop! He was anxious to know because of taking over more line. I said we ought to have only one thought now in our mind, namely to attack. And I hoped that the *French Army* would attack soon in co-operation with the British. He said he expected the bombardment to begin to-morrow. I thought him a humbug and anxious to get as much as possible out of us British.

The Australian history of the war, by C.E.W. Bean, records:

> The coming attack was not favoured by Gough, who was consistently averse to attacking in the west, and who had been informed by the XVIII Corps that II Anzac was not so far advanced as it supposed itself to be. Moreover, the Fifth Army, being short of fresh troops, could undertake no extensive operations. However, as Plumer had decided that an attack was practicable, Gough agreed to safeguard the Second Army's flank, pivoting on his left at Houthulst Forest. On October 10th Haig issued the order for the attack.
>
> At the moment when this order was given, little was known of the true experiences and results of the recent fight. But before the coming attack was launched there was time to ascertain what had happened and this duty rested in particular on General Godley and the staff of II Anzac. Obviously, there was every reason for caution: the advance projected for the II Anzac divisions was now not 1500 but 2000 to 2500 yards. The interval between the attacks – the time available for bombardment and other preparations of all sorts – was not six or eight days but three. Presumably the reason for this was the supposed weakening of the enemy morale. Plumer and Harington still believed that far-reaching strategic success was possible, and, at this stage, in contrast with their earlier caution, they tended to propose objectives

beyond the capacity of the troops. For example, they would have liked I Anzac at this time to carry out the extraordinarily difficult operation of seizing the Keiberg: and they hoped that at a subsequent stage, when the Canadian Corps advanced down the eastern slope to Magermeirie, I Anzac would take Moorslede. On October 8th General Birdwood had to point out that there was no hope of any of the I Anzac division being able to last through such operations. The 2nd was already exhausted; the 4th was to advance the flank on October 12th; and the 5th, after three days' carrying through the mud, would be no longer fresh. In view of the condition of the troops and of the ground Birdwood was obliged to limit the action of I Anzac to the least that would suffice for maintaining II Anzac's flank.

Plumer's high hopes seem difficult to understand. At the end of the day's fighting on the 9th he had informed GHQ that II Anzac was now in a good position for an attack on the 12th, a day on which he thought Passchendaele might finally be captured and held. II Anzac would then be relieved by the Canadian Corps who would subsequently drive the last Germans off Gheluvelt and out of Becelaere. It was doubtless these optimistic though rash forecasts which enabled Haig to make his diary entry about the results being very successful.

Plumer, surprisingly, was quite unaware of the strength and depth of the lines of barbed wire which had checked 66th and 49th Divisions. Patrols sent out on the 11th ascertained that this wire was even more daunting than had been reported. He was equally unaware of the condition of the troops holding the small gains made on the 9th. The official history reports:

> It was also disclosed that although the 49th Division had held the lower slope of the spur east of the Ravebeek, the 66th's line was about the pill boxes from which its assault had started. The conditions, too, were lamentable. The sodden battlefield was littered with wounded who had lain out in the mud among the dead for two days and nights; and the pillbox shelters were overflowing with

unattended wounded, while the dead lay piled outside. The survivors, in a state of utter exhaustion, with neither food nor ammunition, had been sniped at by the Germans on the higher ground throughout the 10th, with increasing casualties.

Prospects for a new and successful attack looked bleak indeed. The Steenbeek had been difficult enough for infantry to cross; for guns it was impossible. In the circumstances artillery could not get within proper range of its appointed targets and even if the range had been right the now familiar instability of the gun platforms would have made any chance of an effective barrage highly unlikely. Meanwhile on the afternoon of the 11th Haig was telling war correspondents, 'We are practically through the enemy defences. The enemy has only flesh and blood against us, not blockhouses.' He was now talking about 'the failure on the 9th', which he said was due to mud. Nobody, it seems, had told him of the barbed wire, although this was now extensive enough to be seen clearly from the Anzac lines.

That evening, the 11th, the leading brigade of II Anzac Corps, who had assembled behind Pilckem Ridge, moved up to their start line. For the moment the rain had stopped, but traversing the devastated ground up to the start line was a horrendous task. The only way to be sure of staying in the line was to hold on to the man in front, though if he slipped off the duckboard there was every chance that you would go with him. At midnight the rain began again, accompanied by high wind. Gough, who seemed more aware of conditions at the Front than the other generals, urgently requested Plumer to postpone the attack. Plumer gave the matter consideration, but then decided it must continue. The Germans, well aware that another attack was about to be made, bombarded the approach roads with gas shells. Now, added to the problems of negotiating mud, slippery duckboards and sheets of rain was the need to do so while wearing gasmasks. Fortunately the wind which had accompanied the midnight rain dispersed most of the gas quite quickly, and casualties from this cause were low. The wind and rain, however, both continued to increase. Firm ground had now disappeared entirely from the battlefield. It was mostly covered by a precarious platform of duckboards, though the mud swamp through which the Ravebeek crawled had now been bridged by coconut mats, a remarkable feat performed by 1st Field Company, New Zealand Engineers. But with the rain sleeting down, as it continued to do, from zero hour at 5.25 and all through the day, the chances of survival of any form of ground cover were limited.

For that Friday Haig's diary entry ran as follows:

> *October 12th* A high wind sprang up before midnight and continued till sunrise. A little rain fell about 6 a.m. Glass fell an inch between 8 p.m. and 5 this morning; it was then steady. Heavy rain fell during the day.
>
> Second and Fifth Armies continued their attack at 5.25 this morning. Troops reached points of assembly up to line in spite of the very bad state of the ground. Owing to the rain and bad state of the ground, General Plumer decided it was best not to continue the attack on the front of his Army. About 500 prisoners are reported.
>
> Sir J. Simon (late of Mr Asquith's Cabinet and at one time considered one of the 'Peace at any Price' Party) arrived and stayed the night. He is most anxious for employment in any capacity and is very humble. I found him a most charming man and very able. I propose to employ him in the Flying Corps attached to General Trenchard's staff.

Sir John Simon might well have been described as 'very able'. He was a brilliant barrister with an impressive list of achievements behind him and even more dazzling ones ahead of him – he would become Chancellor of the Exchequer, Foreign Secretary and Lord Chancellor, the later distinctions with the National Government. At the time Haig met him he was forty-four and had been a Liberal MP for eleven years. True to his word, Haig got him the job on Trenchard's staff, where he served as a major and was mentioned in despatches. Haig and Simon had a mutual hatred of Lloyd George, who once said of Simon: 'Many a man before you has crossed the floor of this House but none has left such a slimy trail of hypocrisy behind him.'

On 10 October Hugh Quigley wrote a letter to his parents from a hospital in Le Tréport:

I got that comfortable wound I mentioned in my last letter: some intuition must have told me what was going to happen. The pain is not too great, although the right leg is useless just now. . . .

I just want to tell you about that last affair. Our division had the pleasing task of making a bold bid for Passchendaele: of course our officers told us the usual tale, 'a soft job' and I reckon it might have been easy enough if we had had a decent start. But none of us knew where to go when the barrage began, whether half right or half left: a vague memory of following shell-bursts as long as the smoke was black, and halting when it changed to white. It was all the same to me. I was knocked out before I left the first objective, a ghastly breast work littered with German corpses. One sight almost sickened me before I went on: thinking the position of a helmet on a dead officer's face rather curious, sunken down rather far on the nose, my platoon sergeant lifted it off only to discover no upper half to the head. . . .

Apart from that, the whole affair appeared rather good fun. You know how excited one becomes in the midst of great danger. I forgot absolutely that shells were meant to kill and not to provide elaborate lighting effects, looked at the barrage, ours and the Germans', as something provided for our entertainment – a mood of madness, if you like. The sergeant's face struck me most, grey and drawn, blanched as if he had just undergone a deadly sickness. There was death in it, if ever death can be glimpsed in the living. A fat builder, loaded with five hundred rounds, acted the brave man, ran on ahead, signalled back to us, and in general acted as if on a quiet patrol. The last I saw of him was two arms straining madly at the ground, blood pouring from his mouth, while body and legs sank into a shell-hole filled with water. One Highlander, raving mad, shouted as us, 'Get on, you cowards, why don't you run at them?' As if running could be contemplated with a barrage going twenty-five yards a minute.

Then the enemy put up a counter barrage, something to make the hair stand on end, shells tripping over each other, gas sending out a horrible smell of mustard, shrapnel whirring just over our heads, and a strange explosive which ran along the ground in yellow flame for yards and took the feet from us. We rested in a shell-hole for a minute, just to give our nerves a rest and escape the machine-gun bullets which pattered thickly on the ground all round us. I saw one gentleman going through the pockets of a dead German, very careful to unpin the Iron Cross colours on his breast. May he have good luck for his thieving.

The lighting effect appeared in great glory, superb in a word. The enemy knew exactly when the barrage would begin for at 5.30 he sent up long streamers of green stars and a strange arabesque of yellow, red and crimson lights: Véry lights hovered all over the sky already paling in a grey, bleak dawn. Then with a continuous drumming our shells burst on him; before us the country seemed a mass of crawling flame, wave after wave of it, until the clouds were blotted out, and our men, advancing into it grew nightmarish, as if under a cliff of fire. Vaguely in the distance, several dark forms could be seen running over the ridge, the enemy retiring to be out of range. I had seen a dark blotch to the right, and was going towards it, thinking it a machine-gun post in our advanced line, when the enemy counter-barrage surrounded it and spread in long lines behind us. Thus we were shut in, and the only thing to do was to advance. Some of our shells fell short and exploded in isolated groups of men. But when the mud and smoke cleared away, there they were, dirty but untouched. The clay, rain-soaked, sucked in the shell and the shrapnel seemed to get smothered, making it useless. One from the enemy fell behind me and made me gasp as if someone had poured cold water down my back. A man beside me put his hands to his ears with a cry of horror, stone-deaf, with ear drums shattered.

We got to the first objective easily, and I was leaning

against the side of a shell-hole, resting along with some others, when an aeroplane swooped down and treated us to a shower of bullets. None of them hit. I never enjoyed anything so much in my life – flames, smoke, lights, S.O.S.s, drumming of guns and swishing of bullets appeared stage-properties to set off a great scene. From the pictorial point of view nothing could be finer or more majestic; it had a unity of colour and composition all of its own, the most delicate shades of green and grey and brown fused wonderfully in the opening light of morning. When the barrage lifted and the distant ridge gleamed dark against the horizon, tree stumps, pill-boxes, shell-holes, mine craters, trenches, shone but faintly, fragmentary in the drifting smoke. Dotted here and there, in their ghostly helmets and uniforms, the enemy were hurrying off or coming down in batches to find their own way to the cages. They knew our lines better than we. Nothing fulfils the childish idea of a ghoul more satisfactorily than those prisoners, mud-befouled, unshaven, terror-stricken, tattered and heavily booted, with their huge helmets protecting the head closely.

Then going across a machine-gun barrage I got wounded. At first I did not know where, the pain was all over, and then the gushing blood told me. The problem now lay in front, how to get through the double barrage of machine-guns and shells the enemy had put behind our advancing columns. I decided to make a run for it but knew not where to run, and followed a German prisoner to an advanced dressing station, where four men carried me on a stretcher down the Passchendaele road, over a wilderness of foul holes littered with dead men distinterred in the barrage. One sight I remember very vividly: a white-faced German prisoner tending a whiter 'Cameron' who had been struck in the stomach. In spite of the fierce shelling he did not leave him but stayed by him as long as I could see. I confess my first feeling of deadly fear arose when on the stretcher. The first excitement was wearing off and my teeth were chattering with cold. Besides, shrapnel was drumming along the line of the duckboard track. Nothing frightens one more than high shrapnel, a blow from it is almost certain death, for the bullets strike the head first and there remains no way of escaping. With a high-explosive one can side-slip or lie down beside it, letting the stuff go over. An old solider can tell to a nicety where a shell will land, and make off to suit, but high shrapnel bursts around one before the hearing or even instinct can warn. I saw two men carrying a wounded Highlander killed at the same time, while the latter got off Scot-free. I came down myself once or twice, the path being so bad, but my stretcher-bearers, R.A.M.C., were good stuff, afraid of nothing and kind-hearted, apologizing for any jolting. How they kept it up during that ghastly ten kilometre journey is a mystery. I would rather go over the top than suffer that fatigue.

Stretcher-bearers won universal admiration. It was said that it took sixteen in relays to carry a man a mile through the conditions of Flanders. In peacetime some had been bandsmen, while others had even been conscientious objectors who had been allotted this non-combatant task. They took greater risks than the infantryman, for whereas he could crouch in a trench when not required to be in action, they were always on duty and always exposed.

Doubtless there were other soldiers who shared Quigley's views, but few were as articulate. Like others whose careers up to Passchendaele and back are followed in this book, he evolved a philosophy:

The stoic doctrine remains the only pillar of faith that can support the soldier, not by the skill of his arm or his strength, but by undoubting trust in good luck and sure Fate is he able to withstand a deadly sickness of disillusionment and horror of disaster.

When an army goes into the trenches, with the resigned despair of an Oriental going to torture, 'Kismet' on the lips, then there is little hope of real enthusiastic action, or even attempt at action. The war has given birth to that weird courage which inspires a man to great

151

bravery even when he knows no reward will or can possibly accrue: the daring is reasoned, like the clarity of a man meeting death open-eyed and never wavering even an eye-lid. I can see it in the men around me – men who have been wounded and gone home, who possess no illusions about its horror, yet go willingly enough without cowardly shrinking or backward appeal. I have always that fear beside me, the fear of showing myself unworthy, cowardly, – if I had that mastered, or even shelved, I could be as resigned as the others.

Quigley, of course, is describing a feeling well known to all but a minority of soldiers, the fear of being killed or, worse, horribly wounded and maimed, but at the same time being more afraid of actually showing fear among his friends or even admitting it to himself. The dangerous moments were when the ordeal was almost over – the experience so aptly described by Allhusen as his company marched back from the Menin Road. The minority which goes into battle without any feelings of fear ranges from the fatalist who knows what may happen but does not fear it, to the person who lacks imagination and knowledge: the latter's morale is liable to collapse suddenly when he finds that war is not as simple as he expected.

But although the Passchendaele battle ended for Quigley when he was wounded on 12 October, it carried on relentlessly for others. Quigley had been with 9th (Scottish) Division. The 9th was in XVIII Corps, which in turn was in 5th Army; and its task that day was to advance the 2000 yards which would take it on to the main ridge. On its left was 18th Division of 55th Brigade, which was to move forward in parallel. In spite of the impressive firework display reported by Quigley, the official report on the barrage was that it was 'thin and erratic'. Very few of the guns due to take part had been able to reach their battle positions, and the machine guns meant to cover the advance were largely unable to fire owing to the mud which clogged the mechanisms and ammunition belts. The Germans, who were on the higher ground ahead, had none of this trouble with mud and were able to use their machine guns to full effect. According to the official report, 'very heavy losses soon resulted'. The 9th maintained contact with the New Zealanders on its right, but at the end of the day scarcely any advance had been made beyond the start lines. A few small parties, one of which had doubtless included Quigley, had reached further ahead, but these were now in too vulnerable a position and were withdrawn after nightfall.

XIV Corps had an altogether more successful time but this, as with the French successes earlier, was due to the better ground and lighter opposition. Both artillery and machine gun fire were fully effective. In consequence, XIV Corps closed up to the Houthulst Forest. Twelfth Brigade, led by the redoubtable Brigadier-General Carton de Wiart, advanced 700 yards. At one point it looked like being held up, but Private A. Halton of the King's Own single-handedly captured a machine gun post which was proving a formidable obstacle. He was awarded a VC.

Second Army was still trying to gain the objectives it had failed to reach on 9 October. The plan was for 3rd Australian Division to capture Passchendaele village itself, while the New Zealand Division took Bellevue and Goudberg. If all went well this, combined with the 5th Army programme, would represent an impressive advance all along the line.

But all did not go well. The supporting barrage proved almost completely ineffective. As the New Zealanders tried to advance towards their objective they came up to dense lines of barbed wire, none of which had been affected by the preliminary bombardment. As they tried to cut it by hand and force a way through they were caught by intense and well-aimed machine gun fire. Nearly 3000 men were cut down as the division tried, with the utmost courage, to force a way forward. At the end of the day all that was to be seen for their efforts was an almost intact wire network and piles of New Zealand dead in front of it.

The Australians (3rd Division) did no better. The 10th Brigade was soon checked by machine gun fire which swept their lines from one end to the other. This, of course, was the ground over which 66th Division had tried to advance in the first attacks and the Australians were astonished to find some of their wounded still alive in shell holes after three days in the open. One Australian patrol reached Passchendaele itself, but the rest of the division was being so badly cut up by German machine gun fire that support could not be given. The 9th Brigade did reach the top of the ridge, but there found themselves so completely exposed to German artillery and machine gun fire that it was forced to withdraw.

On 13 October Haig wrote in his diary:

> I held a conference at Cassel at noon with Generals Plumer, Gough and their staff officers. There were also present my staff officers, Kiggell, Nash, Birch, Charteris and Davidson. The Army Commanders explained the situation: all agreed that mud and the bad weather prevented troops getting on yesterday. We all agreed that our attack should only be launched when there is a fair prospect of fine weather. *When the ground is dry* no opposition which the enemy has put up has been able to stop our men. The ground is so soft in places, the Director General of Transport told us, that he has light engines on the 60 cm. railways sunk half way up to the boilers in mud. The track has completely disappeared.

In spite of these conditions Haig once again stressed the need to capture Passchendaele and Westroosbeke before the winter set in, but accepted the fact that no further attacks could be made before the weather improved sufficiently for roads to be constructed. Until that time it would not be possible to position the artillery where it could provide an adequate barrage for the next attack. At this conference he mentioned two other points. One was the need to keep the Germans busy in Belgium while the French put in their proposed attack in Champagne; the second was the possibility of a tank operation at Cambrai: for the latter 500 tanks were to be made available. He *may* have regarded these two operations as of great importance but, in view of the fact that the French now seemed able to look after themselves and that he himself was less interested in the potential of tanks than of cavalry, it seems doubtful whether he saw them as much more than excuses for continuing the battles of Passchendaele. Meanwhile he was left in no doubt as to the conditions on the salient: Gunners, Engineers and airmen all told the same story. The Ravebeek was now wider and deeper than ever: even with mats no one could now cross it. This, of course, narrowed the approaches from which new attacks could be launched, and the Germans had their machine guns positioned accordingly. Nevertheless the objectives would remain the same. Passchendaele and the surrounding area would be captured by 2nd Army, and Westroosbeke by 5th Army. The only change in the plan was that the Canadian Corps would replace II Anzac Corps in 2nd Army.

On 16 October there was a further conference and at this the general commanding the Canadian Corps, Lieutenant-General Currie, forecast that *if* the weather improved, *if* all the required artillery could be brought forward on newly made roads, and *if* most of the German wire had been cut by artillery fire, an attack could be launched on 26 October. All being well, a second attack would follow on 29 October and a third on 2 November.

Surprisingly, the weather showed signs of improvement from the 15th onwards. This enabled progress to be made with roadmaking, but it also gave the German airmen an excellent view of the preparations for the next British attack. In consequence bombing and artillery barrages were regular occurrences. Among the latter were numerous gas shells, some of which contained the sneezing gas referred to earlier by Allhusen. The gas in question was diphenyl chlorasine, and its purpose was to make the wearing of gasmasks uncomfortable. If they were removed, the recipients of the sneezing gas were vulnerable to the more lethal mustard gas which usually accompanied it.

However, in spite of difficulties created by both the terrain and German attentions, the plank roads proceeded according to schedule. An attempt to mislead the Germans over the direction of the main offensive was made by staging a heavy bombardment on the 22nd, and following it by attacks on the 5th Army and French 1st Army Fronts; but success was very slight. Whether the Germans were deceived or not made little difference in view of the modest nature of the gains. Another, more successful, attempt at deception was made by planting false information about an amphibious operation which was due to be mounted on the Belgian coastline. The Germans were, of course, well aware that plans for a coastal operation had long been discussed at GHQ and so this came as no surprise. To meet it, they put a small corps on standby. The Allies had no intention of landing a force either as raiders or as a proper invasion at this time, although on 23 April a naval expedition was launched to block the harbours of Zeebrugge and Ostend.

Though the main Canadian thrust was towards Passchendaele via Bellevue, substantial diversionary attacks were also carried out on the right and left flanks. Their aim was to make the Germans disperse their artillery fire along the entire Front, instead of concentrating it on the points where it would do most damage. The diversion on the right was allotted to X Corps, and included the capture of the notorious Gheluvelt and Polderhoek spurs and the even more formidable Tower Hamlets Quadrilateral. Only at Polderhoek Château was there any success. It was captured by the 15th Warwickshire, but at the end of a day of heroic attempts to wade through knee-deep mud and capture the other objectives the attack ended where it started, apart from the fact that over 3000 casualties had been sustained.

Two tanks had been allotted to this operation, but it was realized that unless the approach roads could be repaired the chances of their reaching their destination were slight. As a result Captain D.E. Hickey, who would normally have been commanding a tank, was detailed to take two officers and thirty men to repair a mile of the Menin Road, described as 'from Hooge Dump to Clapham Junction'. 'The equipment at my disposal,' he recorded, 'was ten shovels, ten picks and two felling axes. The party was to carry haversack rations and the job was to be finished that day.' The job, in Hickey's view, was hopeless, since the road was constantly being shelled and fresh craters appeared as fast as, or even faster than, the old ones were filled in.

> When, following instructions, I asked Gerrard (the other tank commander) to indicate the position of the worst parts of the road, he replied: 'The whole bloody road is a succession of craters and you'll have to repair it as best you can, if I am to get my tanks along it, but there are two big crumps you can't miss, – one at Hooge Dump and the other just beyond Clapham Junction. Both stretch almost across the road. How you are going to fill them I don't know.' I knew that the job was impossible, and that it was useless to attempt it. But orders were orders and I had to go forward as though believing it could be done.

Hickey managed to get two hours' sleep before the operation. He addressed the road-repairing party at 6 a.m.:

> I warned officers and men with great emphasis that under no circumstances must they tell anyone of the reason for the work, nor mention a single word about an osprey operation which might take place. (Osprey was the code word for a tank.) I also told them how important it was that the work should be completed that day. There was to be no coming back until it was done.
>
> We went to Birr Crossroads by lorry, arriving soon after 7 a.m. There was a considerable amount of movement on the road – lorries, limbers, pack mules and men. I divided the party in two. I thought it would be courting trouble to divide it equally and give each officer thirteen men. So I gave fourteen to 'A' and twelve to 'B'. I purposely sent 'A' 's party ahead as they had the farthest to go and said that as soon as I had got 'B' 's party started I would rejoin him and we would investigate the crater on the spot. I gave 'B' his instructions as, with his party, we followed about 150 yards in the rear of 'A' 's. In next to no time 'A' 's party became engulfed in the traffic and lost to view. I sent my runner to tell him to keep in touch with me. After a while Bell returned and said he had not been able to find the party. In amazement I went forward at once, expecting every moment to overtake them. But I arrived at Clapham Junction without finding any trace of them. I went on, eventually getting into Inverness Copse. The road here was deserted. There was not a living soul to be seen. I suspected that our own front line was in this neighbourhood but I could see no sign of it. The surface of the road was churned to mud. I passed a hand sticking up. Its owner had evidently been buried by a shell. I have since been told that this hand remained unburied because the troops going up to the line regarded it with superstitious reverence. They believed if they touched it no harm would come to them. At the point I reached there was a water-filled crater stretching almost across the road. I

presumed this was the crump to which Gerrard had referred. Five or six tanks could have sunk in it easily. Floating on the surface of the water were several dead bodies. As I gazed forward across a black expanse of mud where no life was visible, the desolation of the scene reminded me of a cold grey sea and deserted shore.

I retraced my steps, searching both sides of the road but without result. When I arrived back at Clapham Junction I went some little way along the plank road to Polygon Wood in case 'A' had followed it by mistake. Again I drew a blank. There were no men to be seen. There was an unnatural stillness all round. I went by the loop-way, south of Hooge, back to Birr crossroad, wondering if 'A', having lost touch with me, had returned that way. But again my luck was out. Once more I went back to Clapham Junction, but nowhere could I find the lost party. Hoping that 'A' would find his way to Clapham Junction I went back to help 'B' and his squad. I had hardly rejoined them when, without the least warning, our guns commenced a terrific bombardment. The enemy soon retaliated, and we were caught in his barrage. The Menin Road was going up in spouts of earth and smoke. If Gerrard's tanks were caught in a barrage like that they would be smashed to pieces. With one of the squad I was cut off from the remainder of the party. I waved and shouted to the men to take cover. The noise was ear-splitting. The shell-fire forced 'B' and his men one way and me and my companion another. We eventually took cover in a dug-out with some gunners. When gunners went to earth things were serious. From them I learnt it was a practice barrage our guns were putting over. With my inside knowledge, I realised it was a rehearsal for next morning's attack. The shelling was so intense that both my wrist watches stopped.

About a quarter past eleven the barrage had slightly abated and I set out on a last search for 'A' and his party, going along the Menin Road and right up to Inverness Copse again.

But he failed to find them. He went back to his party and found that the recent German barrage had completely destroyed all the work they had already done – not that anything they could have managed would have made any appreciable difference to those vast craters. Nothing more could be done, so he ordered the party back to camp, where he learnt that the whole of 'A' party had been taken prisoner.

The party had missed its way and not seeing our front line, which had been withdrawn owing to the practice barrage, had walked right on into the enemy line.

At first the enemy was surprised, and thinking it was an attacking party had put up their hands. But when they saw the 'raiders' with only shovels, picks and an axe, they had thrown hand-grenades at them.

Although the written orders had been explicit regarding road-mending equipment and haversack rations, no mention had been made concerning the wearing of revolvers. Our men were therefore unarmed.

They had picked up the grenades before they exploded and had thrown them back. In the fight one man had been wounded and had managed to escape by crawling away on his stomach.

The enemy would now know from the badges of their prisoners that tanks were in the neighbourhood, and would expect a tank attack. There was therefore no hope of its success and the plan was abandoned.

While we were on the Menin Road, Gerrard's tanks had started to move up so that they should be well forward at night for the next morning. Many months later Glanville told me how when he was moving up with the tanks that morning from Elton Point, the trees, the fields, the copses looked drab and miserable. But when they were returning home, with the attack cancelled, and going through those same fields and copses, and past the same trees, the whole world seemed bright and cheerful, and he saw things of beauty in nature which he had never noticed before.

In view of the depth of the mud in front of Polderhoek, which was the destination of the two tanks, it was as well they never reached it.

The Canadians had begun their attack at 5.40 a.m. As they assembled at their start lines during the hours before zero, the rain which had held off for a few days now started again in earnest. Prospects were not good, for although some of the wire had been cut by artillery fire, most of the German pillboxes seemed to have remained intact. As the assault went in, it was met by a strong German barrage. Even so, the 46th (South Saskatchewan) Brigade reached its objective, which was 400 yards ahead of the start line. There they were the target of both the artillery barrage from behind Passchendaele and intensive machine gun fire from the front: as a result they lost 300 of the 400 men on the objective. They were then counter-attacked by the Germans. The remnants of this courageous brigade then gave up 300 yards of their gains, but clung doggedly to the last 100. They were then reinforced and by 10 a.m. were back on the line they had gained and lost earlier.

On the left the 3rd Canadian Division was battling with an equally daunting task. In spite of the heavy rain, intense machine gun fire and German counter-attacks, they reached their objective on the Flanders line by 3.30 p.m. At the end of the day they were therefore established on higher and drier ground on the ridge.

Three VCs were won in these attacks. Captain C.P.J. O'Kelly (52nd Battalion) led two companies across 1000 yards of open ground under heavy fire and reached the crest of the hill. There he led further attacks against German pillboxes. Six were captured: this brought in over a hundred German prisoners and ten machine gunners. Lieutenant R. Shankland, a member of 43rd Battalion, was with his company on the ridge when the Germans put in heavy counter-attacks. Shankland inspired his soldiers to fight off the enemy attacks and the position on the ridge was consolidated. Private Holmes of the 4th Canadian Mounted Rifles captured three pillboxes single-handed. In the first two he killed the occupants with grenades; in the third a bomb in the entrance caused the nineteen Germans inside to surrender.

At the end of the day the Canadians were well established on ground west of Passchendaele itself. This, though a valuable gain, had its drawbacks in that supply lines were exposed and therefore completely vulnerable to enemy fire. Attempts to overcome this handicap by using mule trains at night caused very heavy losses of both mules and equipment when the unfortunate animals stepped off the plank roads in the dark and promptly disappeared into the mud. Nevertheless determined and persistent efforts ensured that there was never a shortage of supplies.

To the north of the Canadians, 5th Army was making a further effort in nightmare conditions. XVIII Corps tried desperately to advance up the Lekkerbotebeek valley, but as the mud was knee-deep could make no progress at all. Those who gained a few yards found that their weapons were so clogged with mud as to be useless and had to fall back. XIV Corps did no better.

The best news of the day had come from the Canadians; the worst was to come from London. As Haig was digesting the reports of the mixed fortunes of the day's fighting, he heard from Robertson that Lloyd George had ordered two divisions from Flanders to be sent to Italy immediately. This decision had been taken because of the Italian defeat at Caporetto on 24 October, which had caused their Army to fall back 70 miles to the Piave line. Haig was, naturally enough, furious and wrote in his diary: 'Telegram from the C.I.G.S. to-night. "H.M.'s Government have decided to despatch two divisions to Italy as quickly as possible." This decision has been come to without the War Cabinet asking me as to the effect which the withdrawal of troops from this front would have on the situation. If the Italian army is demoralised we cannot spare enough troops to fight their battles for them.'

Unfortunately for Haig, his views as Commander-in-Chief of the British forces in France and Belgium were not shared by the War Cabinet. Not only were the first two divisions sent, but soon afterwards, in early November, two more followed them and a week after that a further division joined in the exodus. Matters were by no means improved when the French despatched six of their divisions to the Italian Front also. But by the time the later moves took place the seemingly unending Passchendaele campaign had ground to a halt.

After the heavy rain during the attacks, the weather took a turn for the better. The improvement was not enough to make any significant change in the communication problem, but did enable the Canadians to make a few minor gains on the night of 27th/28th, thereby improving their line. Welcome though the cessation of the rain was to the soldiers, it also meant that the airmen could fly without hindrance, observing, artillery spotting and bombing. On the whole the British had the better of these exchanges. This could not be said for the following day, 28 October, for the fine weather was now succeeded by thick fog which did not clear. The Germans, realizing that target spotting was impossible, drenched the British lines with mustard gas. When the fog cleared on the 29th, the Germans, well aware of what was in store for them, hammered the British lines with shells and the back areas with bombs.

On 30 October Haig was able to write in his diary: 'Second and Fifth Armies attacked at 5.30 a.m. with the object of advancing our line closer to the ridge on which Passchendaele village stands. The operation was most successful and we are now round the village on the south-west and the north-west.' But they were not, of course, at the other points of the compass, nor in the village itself. However, they were now poised for the final assault.

As the Canadians closed in relentlessly on the 30th the Germans gradually yielded up points to which they had clung long and desperately. Crest Farm was one, Bellevue spur and Goudberg spur were others. But the price the Canadians paid was appalling – at some points their casualties amounted to half the troops engaged. The Germans counter-attacked five times but failed to make the Canadians give up their gains. Having got this far, the Canadians were not going to go back whatever the cost.

XVIII Corps in 5th Army suffered equally heavy casualties with less to show for them. In the earlier stages of the battles in the salient, 5th Army had – for the most part – fought over easier ground than that encountered by 2nd Army. Now, however, it was experiencing conditions as bad as, if not worse than, anywhere else on the Front. XVIII Corps, fighting their way up the Lekker-boterbeek slope, were up to their knees in mud. As their own covering barrage went far ahead of them, they found themselves receiving one from the Germans. Casualties were high throughout, but the worst occurred among the Artists Rifles, the 28th London Regiment. The Artists Rifles had been formed as long before as 1859, when England was almost at war with France and there was a possibility of invasion. All its members were volunteers and included such distinguished names as G.F. Watts, Lord Leighton,

Holman Hunt, J.E. Millais and William Morris. The concept of an artist in those days was like the Elizabethan men of action (Sidney, Raleigh, Essex and so on) who believed that the whole man was a combination of adventurer, poet, musician and sociable drinker.

In 1914 the Artists 1st Battalion had been en route for Ypres when it was stopped and taken into reserve. Fifty-two of its private soliders were taken off to be commissioned immediately as second lieutenants. For the next three years the regiment was treated as an Officer Training Unit, much to its disgust. Eventually it was given the chance to go into action in its own right and was brought in for the battle of 30 October at Passchendaele. Here it was detailed to cross the Lekkerboterbeek and its lake of liquid mud; on the first day there were 350 casualties out of 900 men. By the end of the week very few were left unscathed.[2]

On the 31st XVIII Corps was detached from 5th Army, with which it had served long and honourably, and put under command of 2nd Army. This was to ensure that the final assault should be under one command, that of General Plumer. Two days later Lieutenant-General Sir Ivor Maxse, who had been commanding XVIII Corps with notable skill, was relieved by Lieutenant-General Sir Claud Jacob.[3]

The Germans continued their counter-attacks as the Canadians clung tenaciously to their newly won territory during the following days. The British and Canadian artillery retaliated by methodical shelling on 1, 2, 3 and 4 November, and on the 5th this was increased in an all-out effort. Vigorous German attacks had little success except at one point in the Ravebeek valley; although the Germans made temporary gains elsewhere, they were ejected later. The Canadians too were mounting local attacks, principally with the aim of adjusting the line to a more favourable position for the final assault on Passchendaele. There were, of course, still important points such as Becelaere in German hands further along the ridge, but it was felt that these need only be threatened by simulated attacks at the moment: they would fall easily enough later.

At long last, on 6 November Passchendaele village passed into Allied hands. With the objective of securing not only the ruined village itself but also the land to the east and north-east, the Canadian Corps set off for the critical attack on the same day. The

Germans had guessed rightly that an attack would be coming on that day and put down one barrage in the early morning and another one minute after zero hour. Experience had told them that British attacks never began exactly on the hour or half hour but either a few minutes before or after. But this time the barrage made little difference, for the Canadian assault force had taken the somewhat venturesome step of forming up in No Man's Land, leaving their lines clear. It was a chilly morning but, for the moment, not raining; that came later. It took the Canadians an hour to reach the village and another two to gain the crest of the ridge beyond. The timing of their own barrage had been exactly right. There were still Germans in the ruins of the village when the Canadians arrived with fixed bayonets. They had no chance to surrender, even if they had wished to: the Canadians had too much to avenge from early battles in the salient. Beyond the village were numerous pillboxes, but they did not succeed in holding out for long. One was captured by Private J.P. Robertson of the 27th Battalion. He ran ahead, reached a machine gun post and killed the occupants; then, taking the gun with him and using it, he led his platoon, whose officer and NCOs had all been killed, to its allotted objective. He received one of the two VCs awarded to Canadians that day. The other went to Corporal C. Barron of the 3rd Battalion, who knocked out no fewer than four machine gun posts which were holding up the progress of his battalion.

Gratifying though it was to have achieved at long last the capture of Passchendaele and the area immediately around it, there was still the problem of retaining it. To ensure this, the area north of the village was an essential objective. It was allotted to the 1st Canadian Division, which found itself with a task as difficult as any encountered by anyone during the last four months. Much of the area in front of the position was a liquid swamp which was impossible to cross; this limited the frontage of the assault to 380 yards. The Germans, aware of the limitations put on the Canadian attack, had carefully aligned all their machine guns on the only route that the oncoming battalion could take. Both these battalions came from 1st Canadian Brigade and were 1st (Western Ontario) and 2nd (Eastern Ontario) respectively. They achieved the near impossible. Corporal Barron's action described above was typical of many courageous deeds that day. The Canadians showed a high degree of skill in the way that they outflanked enemy strongpoints even though the overall frontage was so narrow. By 7.45 they were on their first objective, having captured field guns, machine guns and over 50 prisoners on the way. The expected counter-attack came in at 9.30 a.m., but was dispersed on its way up by a heavy barrage and did not require action by the infantry.

But the Germans were not expected to give up this territory without making strenuous efforts to recover it, nor did they do so. Attack after attack came in during the remainder of the morning and all that afternoon, and when the enemy infantry were not attacking the German artillery was shelling the position. Just before nightfall the shelling was raised to such a pitch of intensity that a final all-out attack with infantry seemed inevitable. Surprisingly it did not develop; it appeared that the Germans had no more reserves or, perhaps, no heart for any more fighting in the Passchendaele area. The hardships had not been all on one side and the Germans were no doubt as exhausted as the British, Australian and Canadian troops.

On 6 November Haig wrote in his diary:

> Canadian troops attacked this morning at 6 a.m. with two divisions (2nd Division on right, 1st Division on left) north-eastwards along the Passchendaele Ridge and on the spur north and north-west of the village.
>
> The operations were completely successful. Passchendaele was taken, as were also Mosselmarkt and Goudberg. The whole position had been most methodically fortified – yet our troops succeeded in capturing all their objectives early in the day with small loss – 'under 700 men'. The left battalion of the 2nd Division had hard fighting, 21 officers and 408 other ranks were taken prisoner. To-day was a very important success.

It was not, however, the final battle. That came on 10 November. At 6.45 a.m. that day the 1st Canadian Division set off to push the Germans a little further to the north of the ridge. The Allied drive to Westroosbeke, the great thrust forward and the dramatic follow-through by the cavalry had all now been abandoned. But making Passchendaele village secure was still a paramount need.

As the Canadians set off it was, of course, raining; rain continued to fall throughout that day. However, the Canadians knew they had to advance 500 yards to achieve their objective, and advance 500 yards they did. The Germans hammered them all the way with artillery fire, but the Canadians had gained all their objectives within the hour. The Germans immediately counter-attacked and saturated the ridge with shells, but to no effect. The Canadians held on, dug in and fought back. Finally, having consolidated their positions on top of the ridge, the Canadians handed over to VIII Corps and departed back to the Avion–Mericourt Front from which they had been taken.

On the 20th, Haig decided to close down the Flanders campaign. The official history states, 'It had served its purpose', but few people could see what the purpose had been. The British forces had suffered over 250,000 casualties, and doubtless German losses were at least as bad. But the Passchendaele Ridge would never be used as a springboard for an attack on Bruges, or Ghent, nor had it exhausted the Germans so much that they would be unable to continue the war. On the contrary, they had enough reserves to blunt the next British thrust at Cambrai and more than enough for their great breakthrough the following spring. Immediately after the final battle, Plumer had departed to command the divisions sent to the Italian Front. Fifth Army was withdrawn and replaced by the 4th. The principal actors had now left the stage: all that remained, as in all tragedies, was the litter of bodies left behind waiting to be decently interred whenever possible.

Although the losses on both sides were enormous, they were never exactly, or even approximately, known. It was said that manpower was too scarce for the figures to be compiled at the time, but perhaps there were other reasons. In an official German history of the war, published three years after it ended, German losses in the Ypres Salient were not stated but the British ones were given as 400,000. This total was subsequently thought to be the probable number of German losses, although perhaps more of an estimate than an exact figure. If so, more must have been killed and wounded by artillery fire than was realized at the time. The British losses should have been larger than the German, for they were attacking and they had the worst of the terrain. It is normally estimated that the attacker's losses will outnumber those of the defender by three to one, but there is no doubt that the British artillery support must have taken an exceptional toll of the German defenders.

Although the official figure for British losses has been challenged as being an understatement, the detailed breakdown, week by week, listing killed, wounded and missing, gives a final total for 5th and 2nd Armies of 238,313.

Even before the last shots were being fired on the ridge that November, the critics were at work on the battle. Certainly there was plenty to criticize. If the campaign had followed on the heels of the Messines victory, it would have been fought in better weather. And if it had finished earlier, something more might had been made of the victory.

The official history considered the battle to be entirely justified, both strategically and tactically; but, as seen earlier, that work includes sharply contrasting views of the amount of mud on the battlefield. Even more remarkable was its justification for the manner in which tanks were used: when they failed, it was not because they should not have been there in the first place but because of the presence of shell holes. One might have thought that even GHQ would have known that shell holes were likely to occur on battlefields.

In general, the official view of the Passchendaele battles was that they represented a valuable success – not perhaps as great as it might have been, for it was not fully exploited, but successful enough to reflect credit on the Commander-in-Chief and the Army commanders. It seems unlikely that this view was shared by those required to do the actual fighting. After the battle Captain Yoxall, OBE, MC, stood on the ridge and looked back to the ground over which the campaign had been fought. Subsequently he wrote:

> One felt amazed that the Boche had ever let anyone live in our trenches. We knew we were overlooked but never thought we were overlooked to such an extent as we actually were. He must have been able to see every movement we made for thousands of yards back. Many a sore neck, gained from walking around the trenches with a bent back, I might have saved had I known that to

have escaped observation it would have been necessary
to go on hands and knees.

Notes

1 Chief Royal Engineers.
2 It saw further brisk action in the following spring and summer: at
the Armistice, members of the Artists Rifles had overall won eight
VCs, 56 DSOs, 891 MCs and 20 DFCs, among many other
awards. In 1939 there was no question of it being allowed to serve
again as a fighting battalion and it became an officer-producing
unit throughout the war. In 1947 it was happily united with the
SAS Regiment which, after distinguished wartime service, had
been disbanded but was now reborn as a Territorial unit: 21 SAS
(Artists Rifles) thus began a new phase of military history.
3 Sir Claud Jacob was the father of Lieutenant-General Sir Ian
Jacob, who had a distinguished career before and during the
Second World War, and between 1952 and 1960 was the
Director-General of the BBC.

9

The Focus of a Spider's Web

Two days before the Canadian capture of Passchendaele village, Haig attended a meeting in Paris at which Lloyd George, General Smuts, General Maurice and General Davidson were present. Lloyd George raised the question of forming an Inter-Allied War Council and Staff, and asked Haig what he thought of it. Haig informed him that the proposal had been discussed on several occasions but dismissed on the grounds that it would not work: he explained why. Lloyd George then announced that Britain and France had decided to form the Council. Haig subsequently wrote in his diary: 'I gave Lloyd George a good talking to on several of the questions he raised and I felt I got the better of the arguments. He seemed quite "rattled" on the subject of Italy. At about 12 o'clock he asked me to go for a walk. Quite a pleasant little man when one had him alone, but I should think most unreliable.'

He seems to have underestimated the Prime Minister. By this time Lloyd George had come to regard Haig as a dangerous fanatic who, if not restrained, would use up all Britain's available manpower in grandiose but futile campaigns. He knew that to remove Haig from his post as Commander-in-Chief was a bigger task than he dare undertake but he knew he could help to restrain the Field-Marshal by removing his chief supports, Kiggell and Charteris. This he was determined to do. It was, however, too late to save the victims of Kiggell's ignorance of the battlefield and Charteris's absurd optimism. Kiggell, as observed earlier, visited the battlefield when Passchendaele had already fallen and was visibly moved when he saw the horrible conditions into which men had been sent. Charteris never lost his optimism. Subsequently he wrote a biography of Haig, whom he knew well. He also wrote another book entitled *At GHQ*.

If one reads Charteris's book and another entitled *GHQ*, the author of which only gave the pseudonym of 'G.S.O.' (General Staff Officer), the contrast between life at opposite ends of the battlefield, and the view of Charteris and Kiggell, are more understandable. G.S.O. had begun the war at St Omer but had moved with GHQ to Montreuil. He was so well aware that life at GHQ was totally different from life in the trenches that he described life at the base as 'fantastic'. But it was not by any means without its own particular strains. He describes one man

> who had done his work in the line so well as to win a reputation for great courage and administrative ability, and had carried through with quiet skill and simple dutifulness the responsibilities of the 'small family' of a regiment but found, when he was transferred to GHQ that the sense of responsibility was too great for his temperament. The feeling that the motion which his hand started set going so great a series of actions got on his nerves to the extent that he could neither sleep nor eat with comfort nor decide the simplest matter without torturing doubt as to whether it were right or wrong. He 'moved on' within a few days.

Fortunately, decided G.S.O., there were not many like him. G.S.O.'s style, of which the last paragraph is a typically incoherent example, must have produced some mystifying orders. He saw Montreuil as 'the focus of a spider's web of wire, at one end of which were the soldiers in their trenches, at the other the workers of the world at their benches'. He felt that life at GHQ was 'almost indecorous' but 'inevitable in the circumstances'. He continued:

> Such as it was I attempt to record it – a serious life in any sense of the word, monkish in its denial of some plea-sures, rigid in discipline, exacting in work, but neither austere nor anxious – such a life as studious boys might live in a Public School, if there can be imagined a Public School in which sport was reduced to the minimum essential to keep one fit for hard 'swotting'. But a life with some relaxations, and some pleasures, cheerful,

actually light-hearted. . . .

Questions of the conduct of the war must obtrude somewhat in this book, but it will be only in so much as they are a necessary background to the story of the life of GHQ – of GHQ in its later phase when it had moved from St Omer to Montreuil and had become what it was in the final result, a capable Board of Directors of as glorious a company of soldiers as the world has known.

G.S.O. informs us that: 'It was the task of General Headquarters to try to see the War as a whole, to obtain a knowledge not only of the strictly military situation but, to an extent, also of the moral and political situation of the enemy, and our own forces.' He continues with a fact which is often overlooked but explains much of the earlier ineptitude of the Higher Command: 'Before the Great War the British nation did not allow its Army any chance at all of war practice on a big scale. Our Generals, whatever skill they might have won in studying the theory of war, had had no opportunity to practise big movements. They were very much in the position of men trained in the running of a small provincial store who were asked suddenly to undertake the conduct of one of the mammoth "universal providers".'

G.S.O. – who was, no doubt, a very senior and important officer in GHQ – has interesting theories about the war which he is helping to direct. 'Trench warfare,' he considers,

was a German expedient to keep superior allied forces occupied in France while the remainder of the German army won 'cheap victories' elsewhere. But when Field Marshal Haig took over the chief command he adopted the system of frequent 'raids' to give to the 'Trench War' some of the character of moving war, and that proved a highly useful step. Still, the Trench War was not of the genius of our people; and it was very dull. If I were seeking the fit adjective which could be applied to it in the superlative it would certainly not be 'exciting' nor yet 'dangerous'. The life was exciting and it was dangerous – a little. It was, however, neither very exciting nor very dangerous. But it was very, very curious.

'Curious' was one of the few words which were probably never applied to trench warfare by those required to take part in it. But the GHQ view, from some 50 miles away, does help to explain why men were so often asked to do the impossible, at the cost of their lives, for no obvious purpose.

> Behind the parapet it was almost as safe – and on dry days as pleasant – as on a marine parade. A solid fortification of sandbags, proof against any blow except that of a big high-explosive shell, enclosed on each side a walk, drained, paved, lined with dug-outs, in places adorned with little flower beds. . . . But it was tedious, and very clearly impossible to win while it lasted. For victory the Germans had to be turned out of those trenches. So during the tedium of the Trench War we would comfort ourselves with the thought that very soon the Big Push must come.

He went on to explain the advantages and disadvantages of Montreuil as a site for GHQ. It was on a main road, but not on a main railway line 'which would have been an inconvenience. It was not an industrial town and so avoided the implications alike of noise and a possibly troublesome population.'

In fact the population, which was just over 2000, was strongly anti-British. In medieval times it had been at the centre of Anglo–French wars, and had often been besieged. 'Montreuil cherished its dislike of the English and probably had never been so happy for centuries as when in 1804 it was the headquarters of the left wing of Napoleon's army for the invasion of England.' The population was not 'troublesome' in the normal sense of the word. Nevertheless there were signs that the hostility had not entirely disappeared when a few bombs fell on the town late in the war.

> After the first bombing attack, orders were issued that no soldier, except sentries and officers on night duty, was to be allowed to sleep in Montreuil. The whole garrison (5000) was to go into the woods at night or take refuge in the deep dugouts which were tunnelled under the town. It was thought that the Germans had discovered GHQ

172

and had resolved one night to wipe it out. But this nightly march out of the troops did not make a favourable impression on the inhabitants, who mostly had to stay. Some of them openly jeered; others made pointed remarks.

'Where are the English?'

'The English are in the woods of Wailly,' was a favourite street-corner gibe.

However, not all the Montreuillois were hostile during the war and some were very friendly indeed. And after 1919 friendliness seemed to have spread throughout the whole population.

It was, of course, unusual for GHQs to be bombed. A current Army saying had it that there was a mutual agreement that GHQ on each side was to be spared from air raids, but that this was really a wicked German plot:

'The German scores both ways.'

'How is that?'

'Well, his staff is spared, which is valuable to him. And our staff is spared, which is also valuable to him.'

There was, of course, plenty to be done at GHQ, even if the soliders in the Ypres Salient would not have believed it. GHQ was to provide links with the War Cabinet in London and with the Allied armies in the field, and

> had to decide the strategy of the campaign in its relation to the British sector. The Commander-in-Chief, in consultation with the Chief of Staff, his Quartermaster-General[1] and his Adjutant-General,[2] decided when and with what forces we should attack, when adopt a defensive policy. To come to those decisions a close and constant study was necessary by the various branches of GHQ, of the state of the enemy's forces, our own numbers and morale, our possibilities of transport and supply.

The duties and responsibilities of GHQ were, of course, enormous. Undoubtedly those employed there worked very conscientiously:

It did not leave much time for idleness! At GHQ in my time, in my branch, no officer who wished to stay was later than 9 a.m. at his desk; most of the eager men were at work before then. We left at 10.30 p.m., if possible, more often later. On Saturday and Sunday exactly the same hours were kept. I have seen a staff officer faint at the table from sheer pressure of work and dozens of men, come fresh from regimental work, wilt away under the fierce pressure of work at GHQ.

But not, perhaps, as fast as they would have wilted away in the mud at Passchendaele.

The extreme character of the strain at GHQ used to be recognized by a special allowance of leave. A short leave every three months was, for a long time, the rule. With pressure of work, that rule fell in abeyance and a GHQ Staff Officer was lucky to get a leave within six months. Compared with conditions at GHQ regimental work was care-free and pleasant.

How a supposedly intelligent man could write this sort of nonsense is difficult to understand, but at least it shows the apparently unbridgeable gulf in those days between the staff and those in the line. Staff were always suspected of having more leave than was fair, but there was nothing that the regimental soldier could do to prove it.

With his personal staff the Commander-in-Chief was quartered at a château near Montreuil.

One rarely saw 'the Chief'. He seldom had occasion to come to the offices in the École Militaire, and it was only the highest officers who had to go to confer with him. But his presence was always felt. There was no more loyal band of brothers than the Grand Staff of the British Army in 1918, and the humblest member at GHQ expressed the spirit of the Commander-in-Chief, and within his sphere, was trying to do exactly as the Commander-in-Chief would do.

It is clear that whatever regimental soldiers – British, Canadian, Australian, New Zealand – thought of Haig, his own staff almost worshipped him. He was, of course, the ideal British Army senior officer – quiet, impressive in appearance, taciturn to the point of being inarticulate, an excellent horseman and polo player, and a keen student of war. The fact that he did not like the French, and that he was stubborn and remote, were all points in his favour. The tragedy was that he was personally kind, and if he had seen at close hand the miseries his policies were causing he might have thought twice about them. On the other hand, he might not: he was utterly convinced of the need for the Flanders campaign, at whatever cost. But he cannot really be blamed for distancing himself from the Passchendaele battlefield. He felt that he could control the battle only if he remained well back from it. He was not lacking in courage. And even now, in distant retrospect, it is difficult to think of a contemporary general who would have performed differently or better. There was, and is, an Army belief that the concentration of overwhelming force at a single point will eventually lead to a breakthrough and eventual victory. Regrettably, it is not easy to produce and concentrate a force sufficiently powerful to overcome a well-entrenched enemy without losing most of that force in the process.

There was nothing unusual about Haig's distancing himself from his subordinates. Until very recently the concept that a senior commander should remain apart from those beneath him was not questioned. It dated back to the days of feudalism and was unlikely to have changed much in the nineteenth century, when Haig was a young man and when the gulf between officers and other ranks was enormous. There was an equally unbridgeable gulf between officers and civilians. Civilians may have thought officers arrogant, brainless and conceited – as they often were – but no one would presume to challenge the right of the regular officer to hold supreme command in war, even if his policies did mean sending thousands of men to their deaths for no clear strategic gain. Even Lloyd George, whose ability and persuasive powers were outstanding, did not feel he could remove Haig from the position of Commander-in-Chief despite the fact that he, and many others, thought that the policies Haig was pursuing from Montreuil were rapidly bleeding the country to death.[3]

175

The food at GHQ was not as good as might have been expected, although wine was abundant and cheap. 'Montreuil,' writes G.S.O.,

> being practically a seaside town, the fish was naturally not good, authority having transferred to this English colony in France the invariable tradition of British seaside resorts to send all the fresh fish away and consume the refuse. Our fish was always plaice and it was often plaice that had known better days. One wag spoke of it as the 'vintage plaice', professed to know that it had been 'laid down' the year the war started and that the 'bins' would not be exhausted until after the war ended.
>
> After dinner the routine was to go and look at the map before settling down again to work. Military Intelligence, in one of its rooms, kept up to date hour by hour a map of the fighting front, and after dinner we would crowd into the room to see the latest official news put up on the map and to hear the latest unofficial stories which embroidered the news. One evening, as a great advance on our part was marked up on the map, the clerk, moving the flag pins, announced:
>
> 'They say the enemy cleared out so quickly that they left the hospitals behind, and the Australian Corps has captured fifty German nurses. They report that they are looking well after them.'

The remark caused some laughter and a general who was present promptly rebuked the whole group: 'Gentlemen, the Australians are a gallant race. The German – er – ladies will be quite safe with them.'

Subsequently one of the officers said that he (and others) was disconsolate for the loss of this session in the map room. 'I miss,' he said, 'our pleasant daily habit of advancing ten kilometres on a front of fifty kilometres.'

Although there were no women at GHQ, and the town itself was kept clear of French *demi-mondaines* by the gendarmes, lack of female company did not cause problems: 'Perhaps I may dare the explanation of the general absence of "sex interest" in our lives, that here were gathered together a band of men with very exacting and very important work to do, and that they simply had not time nor inclination to bother about what is usually an amusement of idle lives.'

Looked at in retrospect, G.S.O.'s knowledge of the campaign he had helped to plan is disconcertingly inaccurate. If others were as ill-informed as he seems to have been, it is small wonder that the unfortunates who had to fight according to GHQ strategy suffered so badly. But as a source of information about 'the other end' of the war when the fighting was continuing so grimly at Passchendaele he is invaluable, and what he says throws much light on the entire campaign.

The supply of shells, food and all the other multifarious needs of the Army seems to have been well organized. The medical services seem to have been admirable, except when they were overwhelmed. There were, as might be expected, prejudices which caused tensions. The British, being a nation of horse lovers, felt that horses and mules should have the best possible rations even though their subsequent exposure to unpleasant deaths displayed a certain callousness.

GHQ during the last stages of the campaign had a hard task to keep the animals of the British Expeditionary Force properly fed. At the outset of the War the horse ration erred, if anything, on the generous side, and a good deal of it wandered into the mangers of the civilian animals of the country, much to their contentment. As the War dragged its exhausting length along, money became scarce, food supplies scarcer still, and transport facilities scarcest of all. Then the ration of the animals had to be cut to a point which represented just sufficient and nothing more. Even so, it was a much better ration than the French gave to their horses, and there were repeated efforts by the French Authorities to persuade us to come down to their ration.

But our High Command was stubborn in its championship of the animals. There was a very strong representation of the cavalry on the Staff; and, besides, the

British as a race have a sentiment about animals which is not shared to the full by the Latin races. The average British soldier would as soon go short of food himself as see his animals hungry. At one time the British War Cabinet yielded to the strong representations that were being made that the British Army wasted resources and transport in the feeding of the animals, and ordered a heavy reduction in the horse rations. Even then the British Command in the Field did not give up the cause for lost, continued to argue the matter, and, by pointing out that a vast amount of extra work was just then being thrown upon the animals by the reduction of Field Artillery ammunition teams from six horses to four, secured a compromise decision which made a much smaller reduction in the ration.

The British daily ration of food for a horse per day in 1917 was 22.2 pounds a day; the French ration was 16.1 pounds.

G.S.O., naturally enough, has something to say about regulars and temporary officers. Seventy years later it seems almost incredible that, when men were fighting and dying in the conditions of Passchendaele, anyone should have cared what a man's background and accent were if he could do his job and had courage. But plenty did, although perhaps more at GHQ than at Passchendaele, and even more in England than at GHQ. *Punch* often printed jokes making fun of 'temporary' officers who were clearly not gentlemen born. Usually the dialogue revealed the 'temporary' dropping his aitches. The fact that the Chief of the Imperial General Staff, the exceptionally intelligent and able General William Robertson, also dropped his aitches seems to have escaped the notice of the editorial staff of *Punch*. G.S.O. wrote:

The 'Regular' in 1914 and early 1915 was, I suppose, pretty generally convinced that there was not much hope in the 'Temporary'. Especially was this conviction firm in the mind of the very junior Regular who had a blighting scorn for the 'Temporary', whom he called a 'Kitchener', and affected to regard not as an officer at all but some sort of stranger whom you had to admit to the

178

Mess and tolerate in uniform because authority said so, but who obviously was not a 'pukka' military man for he could not talk about his 'year' or exchange stories about wonderful 'rags'. The average senior Regular probably thought very much the same sort of thing, but, having cut his wisdom teeth, did not allow it to show so palpably.

'Kitcheners' were men who had enlisted in response to Kitchener's call: 'Your Country Needs You'. They came in their thousands, and were slaughtered in vast numbers on battlefields like Loos and the Somme. The fact that little of the original snobbish attitude towards them remained at the end of the war was due not so much to the regulars modifying their attitude as to there being fewer of them to express it, and fewer still who were willing to listen. In addition snobbery had turned its attention elsewhere, to colonial troops. The word 'colonial' was out-of-date, but that did not stop people using it, except when some large 'colonial' took exception to it. Canada had ceased to be a colony in 1867 and had become a self-governing dominion. Australia had followed suit in 1900, New Zealand in 1907 and South Africa in 1910. None of them was inclined to put up with old-fashioned snobbery, but they knew that the famous old regiments of the British Army tended to regard Dominion troops as raw, unskilled and unrefined, and this put the average Anzac, Canadian or South African on his mettle and made him determined to show that he could beat the British any day when it came to fighting Germans. This is said to have caused some unnecessary losses, when Dominion troops took on impossible tasks which had already defeated British troops.

By 1917 the Dominions were represented in the Imperial War Cabinet, but although they were self-governing they had originally had no option whether or not to take part in the war. When Britain had declared that the British Empire was at war with Germany, it meant every country within the Empire from Britain to the smallest colony, even though it was left to the Dominions to decide what their actual contribution should be. But the horrific losses of the Somme and Passchendaele made the Dominion Governments decide that, in the event of another World War, they would make their own decisions about participating and not be bundled into it by statements made thousands of miles away in London. There-fore, in 1939, the Dominions came in when the subject had been debated in their own Parliaments, and South Africa would not have come in at all (although it would have supplied thousands of volunteers for British forces) if General Smut's eloquence had not brought the necessary votes.

Other factors besides heavy losses influenced the attitudes of the Dominion troops. One was their view of British generals. Birdwood was popular and Plumer was respected, but Gough was disliked, particularly by the Canadians. The Australians liked Birdwood and thought he should be promoted: Haig and the War Cabinet, on the other hand, thought that Birdwood had already reached his ceiling and perhaps exceeded it. Birdwood had been at Clifton and Sandhurst with Haig, although he was four years younger. That gap made Haig seem to Birdwood almost like a member of another generation. The latter was much stronger intellectually, and passed the examination for Sandhurst which Haig had been able to avoid.

Birdwood was generous in his attitude towards Haig, although this does not seem to have been reciprocated. Birdwood, of course, knew about conditions on the battlefield. As a Corps Commander he need not have spent much time in the trenches, but he did. 'We made great efforts to avoid "trench feet" – a complaint officially regarded as a crime and avoidable, though I must confess I myself succumbed to it,' wrote Birdwood in his autobiography, *Khaki and Gown*. 'Even though I wore good thick boots, laced lightly to encourage the circulation, I found that the many hours I had to spend tramping through icy mud turned my feet into blocks of ice, and gradually a couple of toes gave out and troubled me for years afterwards.' The Australians in Birdwood's Corps felt he had their best interests at heart; they were not so sure about Haig or the British politicians. The fact that the Supreme Commander was not even British at all, but a Frenchman, Foch, was a further source of discontent to the Australians. They had been prepared to travel 10,000 miles to fight on French soil, but their motivating force had been a desire to help the British Empire against German tyranny; they had scant sympathy for the French, whose language and culture few of them understood, and they did not like the thought that Australians were possibly dying for strategic theories which, if successful, would benefit the French more than anyone else.

Although the Australians could produce excellent and successful cavalry, as they would soon demonstrate during Allenby's Palestine campaign, they did not take too kindly to 'cavalry' generals, of whom General Sir Hubert Gough was one. Gough did not lack intelligence but, as he subsequently explained, it took him a long time to come to terms with reality in France. 'We were always looking for the GAP, and trying to make it, hoping that we would pour through it in a glorious exciting rush, and so put an end to any more heavy fighting. But war against an efficient and brave enemy is not so quickly ended as this. Under such conditions, war is a matter of hard blows, heavy loss, long, stern and desperate struggles, and victory will not be gained until the *morale* of one side or the other be broken.'

It seems that the Higher Command could never quite decide precisely what its aim was: the 'Gap' or wearing down the enemy. In his *Official History of Australia in the War of 1914–1918* C.E.W. Bean wrote:

> From early August the question of whether the battle was being fought on the right lines was still deeply concerning the staff at GHQ and Haig circulated to all his army commanders on August 7th a second, admirably lucid appreciation prepared by it, in which the question was again raised whether the objectives set for July 31st were not too extensive. It was pointed out that the object of the present offensive, in the earlier stages was not to break through the Germans but to wear them down. Should not the depth of the objectives be limited by consideration not merely of the range of the artillery, but of the training, discipline and bodily strength of the infantry. Should not the objective be near enough for the troops to reach it in good order and without fatigue, so that they could resist the counter-attack and prepare quickly for the next advance.

On seeing this paper General Rawlinson pointed out that there had never been a systematic attempt to wear down the Germans, and that if ever we adopted one we should soon know if it was successful. Haig pondered Rawlinson's remarks and then decided on the 'step-by-step' approach to wearing down German morale. Bean wrote:

Of the continued local attacks that had been made in August, little is said in the official despatches, the reader of which might almost gather that, apart from the second general attack of August 16th, the operations of August were regarded as being of minor importance. Yet in this maintenance of pressure by the old Somme methods, not in the least adapted for attrition, lay the tragedy of the August offensive.

The harm done had been irreparable. First, these events had convinced the British Prime Minister and some members of the War Cabinet that from the Ypres offensive nothing was to be expected except a series of attainments each acclaimed in the press as a 'victory' but each, except for the first, really insignificant in every result but that of exhausting both sides, certainly the British. Owing to the losses incurred Lloyd George had, by August 23rd, resolved to stop the offensive in ten days' time and divert the Allies' effort into the Italian theatre. He and his colleagues can hardly be blamed for inconsistency – the conditions on which they had always insisted had not been adhered to: the 'step by step' battle for whose success they were waiting had not been fought. Instead there had been continual local fighting and heavy consequent loss. Between August 5th and September 9th the British forces in France suffered 109,000 casualties and during August the II Corps alone suffered 27,300 – that is, more than the total German loss in the 'tragedy' of Messines.

A second result was equally serious. The fighting in August overtaxed and discouraged the British troops to an extent which their stubborn Commander-in-Chief did not realise but which was obvious to everyone in touch with the true feeling on the battlefield. The German troops saw it clearly, as the British infantry staggered through the mud to attack them and it was from statements of German prisoners that some notion of the facts, which gave cause for anxiety, came to the ears of General Gough. The truth was that these strikes, aimed at the morale of the German army, were wearing down the morale of the British. Whether the British commanders were aware of the facts or not, it was the August fighting that gave to the Third Battle of Ypres its baneful reputation. The fighting at Passchendaele two months later merely added to this.

Crown Prince Rupprecht, who had often been impressed by the staunch bearing of British prisoners, was shocked on August 16th by one of them saying they would gladly have shot down the officers who ordered them to attack. On the 22nd he notes that captured soldiers again blamed the officers and the officers the staff. On the 25th he was informed by his infantry that whereas the British would formerly hold out though outflanked, they now surrendered easily. The German infantry, on the other hand, was imbued with confidence in its own superiority.

German historians admit that their own troops were suffering to the limit of their endurance; von Kuhl even believed they suffered more than the attacking British, and in some respects their morale undoubtedly suffered. Yet it is notable that Ludendorff still had sufficient confidence to begin, at this stage, preparations not only for attacking the Russians at Riga, but for crushing the Italians by sending eight or ten divisions to assist the Austrians. If the Russians were forced to peace a vast additional reinforcement would become available to the west.

However, although the Ypres battles were more exhausting to the Allies than to the Germans, they continued almost as if, once begun, it was impossible to stop them. Some areas were fought over again and again: Glencorse Wood changed hands eighteen times.

But Haig's position with the army and the nation was so strong that he fought his offensive through to the end, even in the winter mud of Flanders, securing reinforcements by combing out the troops in France when he could not obtain sufficient drafts from England. The fact that more than half the fighting was in the wet caused this battle to be remembered with more detestation than any in which British troops ever took part. Even General Gough – though after Mouquet Farm and Bullecourt he was credited by the Australians with the initiation of every unpopular action of the Higher Command – was against its continuance. The Prime Minister was seeking to put an end to it. But Haig and Robertson, standing immovable as two grim Covenanters for a stern article of their military faith, persisted and carried the British Empire with them.

The Australian official historian is scrupulously fair. He weighs the cost but concludes that Haig's persistence was justified. Had German attention not been diverted from the French plight, the results could have been catastrophic. Furthermore he feels that Haig's tactics in the Passchendaele battles were fully justified. Previously there had been local attacks on narrow fronts which had resulted in heavy casualties for scanty gains. These had been succeeded by wide attacks using fresh infantry which was protected by heavy artillery barrages. Although these were not invariably successful, as was seen earlier, for the creeping barrages often went ahead and left the infantry floundering in the mud, overall they were infinitely less wasteful than the previous tactics.

General von Kuhl, the German historian, had this to say of the British tactics: 'On this point Field-Marshal Haig was right in his judgement – even if he did not break through the German front, the Flanders battle wore down the German strength to a degree at which damage could not be repaired.' And Ludendorff, although still confident enough to reinforce the Austrian troops on the Italian Front, said: 'The troops had borne the continuous defensive with extreme difficulty. Skulkers were already numerous. They reappeared as soon as the battle was over, and it had become quite common for divisions which came out of action with desperately low effectives[4] to be considerably stronger after only a few days. Against the weight of the enemy's material, the troops no longer displayed their old stubbornness.'

Nevertheless, it was the opinion of French, German, and most of the British leaders that Haig's ambition to reach the Belgian coast was never attainable. Unfortunately Haig was unable to accept this view, although his colleague Robertson did. Haig always believed that a breakthrough from Passchendaele to the coast was possible and that the sooner his armies struggled to the top of the ridge the sooner the grand design could be proved right. But to do so it was necessary to make all possible speed. He could have reached the ridge and exhausted the Germans without sacrificing the cream of the Allied armies if he had not been in such a desperate hurry. The official Australian view was that he should only have attacked when the weather was reasonably good, and there were indeed intervals when the rain was not cascading down. One of them, of course, was in the period between the Messines triumph and the launch of the all-out offensive of 31 July – a gap of some ten weeks.

General Sir James Marshall-Cornwall, who was on Haig's staff in 1917, working in Intelligence, believed tht Haig was too much influenced by his closest advisers, notably Charteris and Kiggell. In his biography *Haig as Military Commander*, Marshall-Cornwall wrote:

> Haig must be blamed for giving too much credence to the exaggerated estimates of German deterioration which were daily instilled into his ear by Charteris, whose counsels certainly warped Haig's judgement and induced the illusion that only one more push was needed to achieve final victory.
>
> Haig's shoulders were broad enough to bear the weight of responsibility which had been laid upon him. He never sought to shift that burden onto the shoulders of others.

A reasonable and loyal defence of Haig's policies. But where does loyalty eventually lie? To Haig, who survived the war and became a field-marshal, eventually to die in surroundings which were as comfortable as they could be made, or to the soldier in the trenches like E.C. Vaughan:

It was then 6.30 p.m. With a grey face the C.O. turned to

185

me saying, 'Go up to the gunpits, Vaughan, and see if you can do anything. Take your instructions from Taylor.' As I saluted, backing out of the low doorway, he added forlornly: 'Good luck.' I called up my HQ staff and told them that we were making for the gunpits, warning them to creep and dodge the whole way. Then I ran across the road and dived into a welter of mud and water, followed by Dunham, and – at intervals – by the eight signallers and runners.

Immediately there came a crackle of bullets and mud was spattered about me as I ran, crawled and dived into shell holes, over bodies, sometimes up to the armpits in water, sometimes crawling on my face along a ridge of slimy mud around some crater. Dunham was close behind me with a sandbag slung over his back. As I neared the gunpits I saw a head rise above a shell-hole, a mouth opened to call something to me, but the tin hat was sent flying and the face fell forward into the mud. Then another head came up and was instantly struck by a bullet. This time the fellow was only grazed and, relieved at receiving a blighty,[5] he jumped out, shaking off a hand that tried to detain him. He ran back a few yards, then I saw him hit in the leg, he fell and started to crawl, but a third bullet got him and he lay still.

I had almost reached the gunpits when I saw Wood looking at me, and actually laughing at my grotesque capers. Exhausted by my efforts, I paused a moment in a shell-hole; in a few seconds I felt myself sinking and, struggle as I might, I was sucked down until I was firmly gripped round the waist and still being dragged in. The leg of a corpse was sticking out of the side, and frantically I grabbed it; it wrenched off. . . . The attack had not even reached the front line and it was impossible to advance over the mud.[6]

But though Haig bears the responsibility for the suicidal attacks on Passchendaele, it must not be forgotten that he too was a subordinate. The German Government and the Kaiser had begun the war and Britain had only come in because the territory of a neutral ally had been invaded. And if Haig's policies were the cause of much British misery, the policies of Crown Prince von Rupprecht also had their victims, as E.C. Vaughan recounted:

It was a strongly built pillbox, almost undamaged; the three defence walls were about ten feet thick, each with a machine-gun position, while the fourth wall, which faced our new line, had one small doorway – about three feet square. Crawling through this I found the interior in a horrible condition: water in which floated indescribable filth reached our knees, two dead Boche sprawled face downwards and another lay across a wire bed. Everywhere was dirt and rubbish and the stench was nauseating.

On one of the machine-gun niches lay an unconscious German officer, wearing two black and white medal ribbons; his left leg was torn away, the bone shattered and only a few shreds of flesh and muscle held it on. A tourniquet had been applied but had slipped and the blood was pouring out. I commenced at once to readjust this and had just stopped the bleeding when he came round and gazed in bewilderment at my British uniform. He tried to struggle up but was unable to do so and reassuring him, I made him comfortable, arranging a pillow out of a Boche pack. He asked me faintly what had happened, and, in troops German, I told him, 'Drei kaput – others Kamerad'[7] at which he dropped back his head with a pitiful air of resignation. I offered him my waterbottle but when he smelled the rum he would not touch it, nor would he take whisky from my flask, but when one of my troops gave him water he gulped it greedily.

Now with a shrieking and crashing, shells began to descend upon us from our own guns, while simultaneously German shells began to shell their own lines. In my haversack all this time I had been carrying a treasure which I now produced – a box of 100 Abdullah Egyptian cigarettes. I had just opened the box when there was a rattle of rifles outside and a voice yelled 'Germans coming over, Sir.' Cigarettes went flying into the water as I hurled myself through the doorway and ran forward into the darkness where my men were firing. I almost ran into a group of Germans and at once shouted 'Ceasefire' for they were unarmed and were 'doing Kamerad'.

The poor devils were terrified; suspicious of a ruse I stared into the darkness while I motioned them back against the wall with my revolver. They thought I was going to shoot them and one little fellow fell on his knees, babbling about his wife and 'Zwei Kindern'. Going forward I found that several of the party were dead and another died as I dragged him in. The prisoners clustered round me, bedraggled and heartbroken, telling me of the terrible time they had been having 'Nichts essen', 'Nichts trinken', always shells, shells, shells. They said all of their company would willingly come over. I could not spare a man to take them back so I put them into shell-holes with my men who made a great fuss of them, sharing their scanty ration with them.

Re-entering the pillbox I found the Boche officer quite talkative. He told me how he had kept his garrison fighting on and he would never have allowed them to surrender. He had seen us advancing and was getting his gun on to us when a shell from the tank behind had come through the doorway, killed two men and blown his leg off. His voice trailed away and he relapsed into a stupor. So I went out again into the open and walked along our line. . . .[8]

If Haig bore a heavy burden of responsibility, so did the German High Command – even the long-dead Count von Schlieffen, who had put them all into that position by his grandiose plan which had not been quite good enough to secure a rapid victory. On each side commanders were poring over their maps in GHQs, while conscientious staffs were working hours which in peacetime would have seemed impossible – all eventually to bring Vaughan and his like into contact with the bellicose German officer and his less than whole-hearted company. No one could be expected to see the tragic absurdity of it all.

The Canadians, who fought the final battles at Passchendaele, had no illusions about the difficulties of the task they were expected to undertake. Their commander, Lieutenant-General Currie, who saw the battlefield on 17 October, thought it so bad that any attack over it was unlikely to be justified by results. But orders were orders. Methodically, but without enthusiasm, he reviewed the situation: much needed to be done before the attack could be launched. He realized that heavy artillery barrages would be needed if the Canadians were to gain their objectives and therefore set in hand an extensive programme of road-building: as soon as roads were made, mostly of planks, he ordered the construction of strong gun platforms. He refused to be fobbed off with a lesser number of guns than he considered necessary. Nothing was going to prevent the Canadians sustaining heavy casualties, but at least they would be for some purpose. The worst experience for troops was to lose heavily in trying to take objectives which they could not reach. If there was an element of success, heavy casualties might seem justified, however much one might deplore them.

GHQ saw the Battle of Passchendaele from one point of view, and a very distant one at that. The Canadians saw it at the other end: they fought over some of the worst portions of the battlefield before they reached the higher ground and clinched the victory. They had been brought in as the only troops fresh enough to capture the position, and when the task was accomplished what was left of them went back to their former position elsewhere in the line. Victory was theirs, but its cost had exceeded its strategic value.

Notes

1 Responsible for overall supplies.
2 Responsible for manpower.
3 There is, of course, a mystique about being a 'regular', whether in the Navy, Army or Air Force. Up till recently it was very rare for a retired Army officer not to stress his former rank when he became a civilian, and the retired captain, colonel or wing commander expected, and received, some deference. However, if

a retired officer took a job in civilian life he could well find that deference replaced by hostility. For that reason in the last two or three decades many ex-regulars have dropped all reference to their former ranks and become plain 'Mr'. Very senior officers retain their rank titles when they become members of boards of directors and never doubt their ability to perform any duties as well as civilians, as indeed some can and do. But the idea that a civilian might go straight into one of the services at the top, particularly in time of war or emergency, is still as unthinkable today as it was in 1914–18.

4 'Effectives' were men fit for combat.

5 A wound which was not too serious but was sufficient to give the recipient a spell in hospital and recuperation in Britain, which was generally known as 'blighty' – a word of unknown origin.

6 E.C. Vaughan, *Some Desperate Glory*.

7 Surrendered.

8 Vaughan, ibid.

10

The Supporters

It is said that for every man in the line there must be eight men behind supporting him. Nobody seems to have suggested exactly how the eight are employed and in what proportions, but it is self-evident that there must be substantial forces building and repairing roads, transporting food, guns and ammunition, maintaining communications, acquiring and assessing intelligence reports and providing many other services. But perhaps the most valuable of all these 'rear' elements are never thought of as being part of the support – the Royal Army Medical Corps, the 'medics'. They may be found on the battlefield itself tending the wounded, at work in the casualty clearing stations close to the front line, in each of the chain of medical stop points all the way to the base hospital, on the hospital ships and, finally, staffing the hospitals at home. They work closely with the stretcher-bearers, and often with the padres too. Casualties are high among the medics, for when there is imminent danger they prefer to try to save the lives of their patients rather than look after their own.

They are not held in high esteem by those who have not seen them at work. Medically, many of them are in a low grade and classed as unfit for combat duty. Among them can be found conscientious objectors who have been directed to this work, although some may have volunteered. Often, when wounded men recover and find they have lost the contents of their pockets, they tend to blame the RAMC and assert that the initials RAMC stand for 'Rob all my comrades'; other soldiers may be excited at the prospect of combat and danger, but the medics, who are not even armed, simply face danger without any opportunity to retaliate. At Passchendaele, the plight of the medics was worse than almost anyone's. Sergeant R. McKay of the 109th Field Ambulance, 36th

Ulster Division recorded his experiences in the form of a diary:

August 6th: Today awful: was obliged to carry some of
the wounded into the graveyard and look on helpless till
they died. Sometimes we could not even obtain a drink of
water for them. Working parties are repairing the road so
that the ambulances will be able to go right up to the
Mine Shaft. Yesterday and today have been the most
fearful couple of days I ever put in. We are waiting every
minute until a shell lights amongst us. We would not
mind so much if there were no wounded. Went up to
Wiltje at night: ambulances now going right up, one at a
time. As a rule, I am not very nervous, but I don't wish
to spend another night at St. Jean corner.

August 7th: Bringing the wounded down from the front
line today. Conditions terrible. The ground between
Wiltje and where the infantry are is simply a quagmire,
and shell holes filled with water. Every place is in full
view of the enemy who are on the ridge. There is neither
the appearance of a road or path and it requires six men
to every stretcher, two of these being constantly employed helping the others out of the holes; the mud in
some cases is up to our waists. A couple of journeys to
and from the Mine Shaft to the line and the strongest
men are ready to collapse. All the Regimental Aid Posts
are in pill-boxes which have been wrested from the
enemy and they are of great strength. Some of them have
had as many as five direct hits from 5.9's and are nothing
the worse. Unfortunately, all of them have a serious
fault, their door being towards the German line. It is a
job getting into them as they are all under enemy
observation, and once in it is worse getting out as he puts
a barrage round them when he sees anyone about.

August 8th: Ground dried up a little today, noticed the
dead lying in every imaginable position in surrounding
shell holes. Carrying wounded from the line. Relieved by
a fresh squad and returned to Red Farm for a rest.
Unfortunately, it rained again to-night.

August 12th: Red Farm. Aeroplanes over every night

on bombing raids. I would just as soon be up on the line as here at the Main Dressing Station as the enemy is shelling all round.

Though unarmed, stretcher parties were still considered fair game by the other side:

August 14th: Bombardment by British heavy, enemy retaliating; many casualties. We can only get up to the First Aid Posts early in the morning (3–4 o'clock a.m.) and at twilight (8–10 p.m.). One party of stretcher bearers was bringing down a wounded man when an airman swooped down and dropped a bomb deliberately on them. The enemy shells the stretcher bearers all the time.

August 15th: Working day and night. Fortunately, plenty of rum can be had as there are jars lying about which ration parties throw from them when they get caught in shell fire at night. Bombardment goes on all the time: numerous cases of gassed men coming in. At night the enemy sends over gas shells and the artillery are suffering badly, especially the gunners and drivers, but for every shell sent over, fifteen to twenty are returned from our guns.

Sometimes the gas does not affect the men until three or four days have elapsed when they suddenly collapse. Some of my stretcher bearers have no fear; one man, Cpl. Service, was taking a wounded man down when a gas shell came over and burst just in front of the party – 'Hold your breath and come on,' Service said, as he covered the wounded man's head with a blanket, and he walked on unconcerned. The same man [Service] was with me one morning when we volunteered to go up at 4 o'clock a.m. and take forty-eight men along to bring six seriously wounded from a pill-box known as Scottish Post. The Germans had a barrage on round the house when we got up but we got in through it and got the wounded out, seven cases altogether. As soon as we managed to get out through the barrage the gunners followed us with shells the whole way down. We were well scattered out, each stretcher party with its patient separated as far as possible from the next one. However, we were all obliged to follow one path along duck-boards and alongside these at one point two tanks were stuck in a hole. I saw the stretcher party in front of mine all blown down by a bursting shell; my five men and I lay down in over twelve inches of mud. None of the party in front appeared to be much injured as one after another they picked themselves up and lifted their patient and ran for it as quickly as possible. My party was next on the list to receive attention. From where we were lying we could hear the gun firing at us, then came the drone of the shell which immediately developed into a wild screech (resembling an express train flying through a station at full speed), all ending up in a deafening explosion. Every time the gun would fire, some one would call out, 'Here she comes again', and we would crouch down closer to the ground. The German gun had fired ten or twelve 5.9's at us when he placed one just to the left of our stretcher. Mud was flying everywhere when we heard the gun go again and I could have sworn the next shell was coming fair down on my back. Luckily it just missed the stretcher and only covered us with more mud. The position was too hot, and was getting on our nerves, so we just grabbed the stretcher and ran for it. . . .

Reinforcements, though welcome, created their own problems in the primitive conditions:

We have been strongly reinforced by additional stretcher bearers. In addition to men from the 108th and 110th Field Ambulance, we have over a hundred infantry of the Liverpool Scottish also. All the cooking for these three hundred odd is done in the mine-shaft, and all cooking is done on two Primus stoves; one is lucky if he gets hot tea once in twenty-four hours. The smell of the place is abominable, as one staggers along the shaft splashing through the water, he is tripping and falling all the time, now it is over an empty petrol can, then over a pack or perhaps one of the bearers who in spite of the discomfort is sleeping soundly, exhausted too much to care about anything.

The 36th (Ulster) Division attacked this morning at 5 o'clock a.m. Owing to the state of the ground tanks were unable to move. The 108th and 109th Brigades only took part in the attack, as the 107th had held the forward positions on up to the morning of this attack and it was too weak to take any part in it. The casualties the 107th suffered holding the line has been something terrible. The infantry took a few pill-boxes and a line or two of trenches from the enemy in this attack but at a fearful cost. It is only murder attempting to advance against these pill-boxes over such ground. Any number of men fall down wounded and are either smothered in the mud or drowned in the holes of water before succour can reach them. We have been working continuously now since the 13th inst. and resulting from the renewal of the attack today, more wounded are coming down than any day since I came up. Wounds are nearly all bad. The stretcher bearers are done up completely. Owing to the constant walking in the mud towards the line and then in the water in the mine shaft, many of the men's feet are all swollen and blistered, and if one takes off his boots he finds it almost impossible to get them on again. Luckily the weather is warm; indeed, down in the mine shaft the heat is oppressive owing to bad ventilation.

The 109th Field Ambulance has suffered many casualties here. Today the enemy put a shell in through the door of a pill-box called Bank Farm, killing practically all inside. Cpl. Greenwood, Private Barrett and Private McCormick were all killed. The enemy have nothing but pill-boxes on this front; as soon as the infantry captures one, they find themselves faced by another.

August 16th: Shelling goes on as bad as ever; wounded being brought down all day. Rat-trap-farm, Plum-farm, Scottish Post and Spree-farm are the names of the First

Aid Posts up the line. All these are in full view of the enemy. We had nine men belonging to the 109th Field Ambulance wounded today.

August 17th: Smell of the Mine Shaft worse then ever. There is a heap of dead lying up at the entrance where they have been thrown out. I was told by Captain Johnston that the Division was being relieved to-night and to warn men of the 109th Field Ambulance that they could make their way down to headquarters. One man, B. Edgar, asked me when I was going down, and I said in the morning between two and three o'clock. Edgar then said he was going to have a sleep and not to go down without calling him. I looked at him and said, 'Where in Heaven's name are you going to sleep here?' and for answer was told that there were two dead men at the entrance with a blanket thrown over them, and I would find him in under the blanket, and here he would not be disturbed, as all three were lying in the open above ground.

August 18th: Came down from Mine-Shaft at 3 o'clock a.m. I have had no sleep since I went up on the 13th, and when I took my boots off my feet looked as if they were par-boiled. Never do I want to be in such a place again. The enemy still keeps throwing shells into Ypres day and night and the thoughts of going through this town of desolation is a continual nightmare to nearly everyone. The oftener one passes to and from the battle line through the town the worse the dread becomes. Why it is so, I cannot say. All the 36th Division have been relieved now. The 109th Field Ambulance alone had over thirty casualties, killed, wounded and gassed – and this out of one hundred men who were going up the line.

August 22nd: Williamson very sick, evacuated . . . with Typhoid Fever. Several men have already gone away with same disease.

Captain H. Dearden also served with a Field Ambulance. He soon found himself in the line:

My billet is priceless: I sometimes lie in my valise and smile at the sheer grotesqueness of it all. Here am I, a ratepayer of the Borough of Westminster, in my bed; and with me in the same room are ten other gentlemen, a quantity of mud-soaked straw for our beds to rest on, guttering candles and a smell like a damp grave. Mud is simply everywhere: there is a terrible draught and still an impression of no air prevails.

It is really impossible to give the least idea of the country here, the desolation and destruction simply beggar description. For at least eight miles round where I am now there is not a stone building of any sort or kind left, and practically not a tree. There are a few gaunt wild armed things here and there, all shell-smashed and chipped, and these just make the country all the more dreary. The hill sides are pocked with great shell holes, and the roads are constantly being renewed as fast as they are shelled to bits.

Dearden was taken by his colonel to see the new ground they had just captured:

Dead bodies everywhere, men and horses lying like sleepy children, side by side and limbs asprawl, and since the enemy only left here two days ago the novelty and realism has not worn off, and they are still men and still horses, and not just bloated heaps of skin and clothes, like those further back. Hands and legs stick out in the most uncanny way from heaps of earth and sandbags, and in the wind which flutters their muddy sleeves, they almost seem to be waving a greeting or calling for help. . . .

We were having our sandwiches in our present front line trench when a man came along to tell us that someone had been sniped around the corner. We took about thirty strides round a heap of sandbags and there he lay in the mud of the fire step, just quietly dying. He was a big strapping fellow about 30 years of age, with a skin like a girl's and fair crisp hair. . . . He had been having his lunch and had stood up to look around and the Boche had got him neatly through the head behind the ear. He died while we stood round with our sandwiches in our hands, and in thirty strides we were round into our own little bay again, and the Regimental M.C., was cutting his disc off and getting him taken away.

A few minutes later, when Dearden was continuing his tour,

. As we walked along there was a queer little noise like a violin string breaking and an officer next to me said: 'There's some devil sniping us.' I said, 'Oh, I wondered what it was,' and also wondered what had happened to my stomach that made me feel as if my lunch had gone wrong.

Soon one of the NCOs located where the firing was coming from, and two men armed with Lewis guns set off to destroy it. There were two snipers and both attempted to run back to a safer place. They did not succeed: the Lewis gunners got them both. Dearden learnt that the Germans often left 'stay-behind' parties to do as much harm as they could in newly taken land. One could not but be pleased at their elimination, but it was also impossible not to admire their courage.

But this sort of suicidal course was not limited to one side. There was an Irish sergeant who, just before dawn, would take four men out and post them in No Man's Land. As soon as it was light he would stroll about in the open. Inevitably, at least one bullet would be aimed at him and when this happened he would slip back into the trench and wait for the return of his outposts. From their reports he would locate exactly where the sniper was. 'He has been doing this every day since I came,' said Dearden, 'and has made many bags, but it implies a recklessness which is to my mind almost insane.'

He noted that men had acquired an almost nonchalant attitude to shells. When two fell in a field, wounding several men,

in two minutes the men were out again walking round and grooming horses, and the whole incident apparently

198

forgotten. An accident like that in England would draw a crowd of three hundred people for half an hour. Here it's over and forgotten in five minutes of its occurrence.

I was fired on deliberately and individually to-day for the first time, and it gives you such a strange cold furious desire to hit back, it was curious to realise it afterwards. I was going up to my advance dressing station with my orderly when a Boche aeroplane came over. The orderly said: 'That's a Boche, sir' and I said 'Oh' and looked up with quite a kindly feeling for the airman, he made such a pretty picture against the blue cloud-flecked sky. All at once he dived down on us and I heard his machine-gun making a noise like a riveter's hammer and bullets started to 'phit, phit' all round us. 'Here's a dug-out, sir' said the orderly and we darted about ten yards up the road and in like a couple of startled rabbits. It seemed almost inconceivable that anyone should go out of his way to fire on two individuals like that, and the thing which made one literally boil was the impotence which forced one to run to earth like a rat. If that Boche had descended then from engine trouble, I should have strangled him gladly, having no other weapons, and the Geneva convention could have gone to hell. How true, as the Bishop of London says, this war is undoubtedly uplifting us!

The Bishop of London, the Right Reverend A.F. Winnington-Ingram, was waging his own personal war at this time. Although he felt that the war was a great moral crusade, he was greatly disturbed at the temptations to which servicemen were exposed when on leave. He found immorality everywhere and campaigned vigorously against it on the London Council for the Promotion of Public Morality. Anyone who was lucky to last long enough in the Passchendaele battles to enjoy a brief period of leave regarded the Bishop as an interfering busybody who had no idea of what he was talking about and still less about conditions in the war zone.

Once in the line Dearden found, like McKay, that most of the time he was desperately tired but could never catch up on sleep.

Had a poorish night. Up all the time with front line casualties. Several died after on the way down or in the aid post. We were heavily shelled all night, and had to wear our respirators for about two hours because of gas shells, I have had no sleep for four days and am pretty well dead beat. . . .

He had plenty to say about the rain:

At one time, during a halt, a party coming out of the line met us on the duckboards and of course gave way to us. As they stood in the mud to their knees, I heard one man say as we passed him. 'Them as made this bloody war ought to be made to come out and do it. We'd soon have —— peace, I know.'

A very popular sentiment.

We reached our jumping off place at about midnight, still in torrents of rain, and then proceeded to take up our stations. We dug trenches and got inside merely as a protection from shell fire, which was heavy, and not with any idea of shelter from the rain for the trenches were full of water up to the knee before you had been in five minutes.

Here under a continuous downpour we remained all night, waiting for Zero which was 5.20. At 5.15 it was just grey in the east. Our guns were keeping up a very heavy fire, and the Boche was plastering us with the stuff, too, when suddenly at 5.20 it seemed as though someone had flung wide the door of hell. I have never heard anything and could never have conceived anything like the volume of sound our guns made. The sides of my trench shook and rocked, for I put my hand on them to feel; and one's head simply reeled with the roar of the heavies, field guns, and 'hows' and the continuous rattle of our machine gun barrage. Over one's head, rising high amidst the deeper roar, was the ripping, tearing noise of our shells passing across, blended into one long continuous scream. The Boche let loose a tremendous barrage too. . . .

Although zero hour was 5.20 the first men did not go over the top till 6.40, though the RAMC soon found plenty of work to do. But,

> That was where I envied the troops. They have at least something to kill with and get excited over, while my bearers and I have to walk slowly along about fifty yards behind, doing nothing for long stretches, and able to see everything that goes on.

The fact that they were in a first aid post, tending wounded Germans as well as British, did not protect them from snipers, as Sergeant McKay had also discovered. Dearden himself had several narrow escapes. And:

> Once when we were wrestling with one stretcher a bearer who was on the end near me suddenly let go and pitched forward into the mud, very nearly bringing us all down. He had been picked off by a sniper, through the back, and he died in the aid post about an hour afterwards, poor lad.

Dearden's experiences on the battlefield, where he was twice wounded, eventually left him in no fit state to serve any more and he was invalided out of the army before Armistice. Subsequently he wrote sixteen books, seven plays and many articles, all of which were notable for shrewd and witty observations on human behaviour. His remarks on medicine in the Army will instantly be recognized by former soldiers as having the unmistakable ring of truth:

> For those who went through the war the three words 'Medicine and Duty' are likely to retain for ever the simple beauty that once was theirs; but to such as were denied that refining influence some explanation may be of interest.
>
> When a soldier presented himself for treatment, espe-

cially in or near the trenches, his physician – by much training – was led to adopt towards him an attitude of mind guaranteed to ruin that same physician in the shortest possible time in any other place on earth. That is to say, he endeavoured to prove, exclusively to his own satisfaction, that there was nothing whatever the matter with his patient, and the fact that the latter rarely accepted his diagnosis did not in the least degree affect the nature of his treatment. Having arrived at this conclusion (and to the sufferer it must have seemed that nothing short of an audible death-rattle could prevent him doing so) he was accustomed to administer a brisk aperient and mark his card 'Medicine and Duty'.

These words seem to me symbolic, for to the private soldier they epitomized the war. He took, during those four years, an astonishing amount of medicine, compounded of wet and cold, and agony and bloody sweat, and of the nobility with which he fulfilled his duty no one who saw it is likely to lose the memory. But of the many who saw it, not a few, alas, lost that memory with their lives, and the others are mostly too busy ensuring their own survival to have much leisure for memories.

Arthur Osburn had begun his military career as a private in the Artists Rifles, but served in the First World War as a doctor in the RAMC; he became a lieutenant-colonel, and was also awarded a DSO. He commented drily: 'Several incidents are, if I may say so with all due respect, described in the official history rather as the English would have had them happen than as they actually occurred.' He was also very much concerned with the way the Army treated the private soldier.

The private soldier, who may be just as sensitive and as well-educated as those above him, must suffer and endure, often without knowing the object or the purpose of his exertions: that alone almost doubles the sense of uncertainty and the hardship of war. He must put up not only with the guile and fury of the enemy but with this constant uncertainty, and with the failures, blunders, impatience and often contradictory orders of his officers. Because it is mainly with the 'vile body' of the rank and file that Generals experiment, it is the rank and file that must always be the *first* to learn just how and why and to what extent each attack or manoeuvre has been a failure, the *last* to learn the extent or significance of a success. Often knowing that their efforts have failed and are merely bringing death or mutilation to themselves, they must yet continue an obviously futile attack until some officer – perhaps a boy only half their age – has convinced some other officer far from the fighting line that success is impossible.

The difference in our Army between the comforts and honours obtained and the hardships that have to be endured by the rank and file and the easier lot of their officers would be grotesque even if we were not all of the same race. The failures and follies of officers are often far more leniently punished than similar failings in the ranks, who not only have less comfort and food but have much less to fight for. Whoever wins or loses the battle which he is ordered to fight, the economic surroundings of the average soldier at home are such that often he could scarcely be worse off than he is already even were his country defeated.

Although he is writing about conditions in the First World War, much of what he said was true also in the Second World War; however, many features had also changed by then, and have continued to change. One may doubt whether the 1914–18 soldier would have been as well off if defeated: this was certainly not the experience of the French in the Franco–Prussian War, nor of the Germans in both World Wars. Osburn felt very strongly that for the extra hardships endured by the man in the ranks he should 'in all justice, receive far greater admiration and respect than the officers and generals who have been "set over" him'.

Undoubtedly the man in the ranks has less comfort than the officer, but this seems to be true of all armies, not merely the British. In fact, in so-called egalitarian states the gap between officer and men is much wider than it is in Britain and in the USA (where it is very small). The theory behind the 'gap' is that the officer has more responsibility, needs more time to think, and cannot do his job properly if he is constantly enduring unrelieved hardships. Bluntly, the life of an officer is more important than that of the average soldier, which is why the enemy will try to find him and kill him. Nevertheless Osburn was undoubtedly right in insisting that the contribution of the ordinary soldier should be accorded the respect and admiration it deserved.

He felt, too, that serving in the RAMC required exceptional quantities of courage, whether as officer or in other ranks, because their job meant that they had to wait *unarmed*. 'Waiting unarmed' is 'the worse penalty to which an imaginative man can be subjected'.

> As more and more of the New Armies arrived, the change in spirit and feeling intensified, and the older Regular Army, in which officers and men had known one another for years, almost disappeared. We began to realise that the war must go on indefinitely, that there would be no glorious and dashing victory for anyone: only demoralizing waits and slow exhaustion.
>
> The hypocrisy and untruthfulness of much of our highly-coloured propaganda about Belgian 'atrocities' were beginning to be realised. The Belgians themselves blurted out certain things which gave the show away. Many of them, it seems, fearing French ambitions and policy in Europe, had at first actually welcomed the German invaders.

If so, they soon learnt their mistake. Certain towns, notably Louvain and Dinant, were virtually sacked; their citizens were shot or bayoneted: a policy of deliberate terror – *Schrecklichkeit* (frightfulness) – was adopted to stun the general population into abject surrender and co-operation. However, the Germans did not boil up corpses to make soap in the First World War, as was thought: that did not occur till the Nazis established their concentration camps some twenty years later.

Osburn mentions that there was often less ill-feeling towards the Germans than towards Britain's allies:

Disgust was felt by many for our Belgian allies: others distrusted the French. The French in turn were showing quite plainly their distrust of English good faith by refusing our army its more obviously convenient position next to the Channel ports. The Italians were evidently bargain hunting – not fighting. As for the famous Russian 'steam roller', it was living up to its primitive prototype, cumbersome, ineffective, blundering and erratic.

He noted, too, that the equality of self-sacrifice was not being practised even in the British Army.

There were many young officers, almost too good-looking and much too young, who apparently had powerful friends at court, mostly lady friends, and who became ADCs to the Corps' Commanders or obtained safe staff billets with the most astonishing rapidity and persistence. There was a profusion of these bright and haughty young men in fur collars, wearing eye-glasses and smelling rather of scent and face powder, who, expensively tailored and safely ensconced in palatial chateaux, five, ten, fifteen miles from the front line, were able to eat, drink, play bridge and gossip, even about 'secret orders', not wisely but much too well. These sleek darlings, without ever having heard the whisper of a passing bullet, scorning mere mention in despatches, became miraculously decorated with foreign orders and Military Crosses, and great was the bitterness and discontent amongst the ordinary fighting soldier, wet to the hips in foul mud and generally living under conditions that no sanitary inspector would consider fit for a pig on an English farm.

Osburn's exposure of these staff dandies had some effect, for during the Second World War generals would rarely accept a man as an ADC unless he had been wounded, or in some other way incapacitated, when on active service. However in Cairo, Alexandria and many other places during the later war there were still plenty of 'smooth operators' who had no intention of going anywhere within range of a rifle bullet.

Others, too, incurred Osburn's disapproval. There were 'horsey men in uniform' who bought horses for the Army and passed them on at a profit, there were those whose patriotic exhortations were in direct proportion to their distance from the front line which others were manning, and there were those who wasted valuable materials in building elaborate and unnecessary structures miles to the rear.

The duties of the RAMC were onerous and varied:

> A Field Ambulance had nearly everything on its charge from a hypodermic syringe to a horseshoe, from horses and motor cars to the kukris of the wounded Ghurkas. We must take care of the wounded and their kits of every unit and nationality: Hindus, Portuguese, German, Chinese coolies or Australian gunners. We must test well-water for poison and 'short-sighted' men for funk; we must keep oats for our horses and champagne for our invalids, vaccinate French babies in distant villages, and build shell-proof dug-outs for wounded in the reserve trenches. We must parade alongside crack regiments with our pile chains shining and our wagons freshly painted. We must record, check and enumerate *everything*. An old torn pocket-book records a list of our 'returns', – death, desertion, drunkenness, diphtheria, self-inflicted wounds, shell-shock and shell dressings. We must know all about mumps and mange, horseflies and hot-water bottles, trench boots and trench foot, vermorel sprayers, vaccine, venereal disease, and vermin, chilblains, colic, constipation and chaplains.

> It was soon evident that it was almost as important to restore the morale of the sick and wounded as to cure their ailments. They must go back to their Regiment in the front line not flabby and 'hospitalized' but still soldiers, their rifles clean as well as their teeth. But often the limit of endurance was reached for all of us.

> The weight of the patient with his kit and rifle, the whole of it clogged with mud and soaked with rain, the stretcher and the sodden and frequently blood-soaked

blankets that covered it, could be tremendous; the stretcher-bearers' hands growing numb with exposure to rain and bitter wind. When they got their patient through these miles of perilous mud to the Advanced Dressing Station, it would be perhaps only to find that he was already dead.

Osburn bitterly resented the fact that his stretcher-bearers were disparagingly referred to farther down the line as 'non-combatants'. He noted sardonically that the RAMC as a whole, including the officers, were regarded as social inferiors by officers of certain regiments; he was not impressed when his former contempories at Eton expressed surprise at finding him doing such work, even though it was often more essential than the job they were doing themselves.

Nor had he much time for bellicose chaplains who seemed to have forgotten that the Germans were also human beings. He had even less for generals who insisted that there was no such illness as shell-shock and that the patient was only shamming. But he had enormous respect for the men, whether officers or soldiers, who endured the unendurable, as he had seen with his own eyes so many times.

His comments on the injustice of war must have given much encouragement to the Pacifist Movement when he voiced them in the early 1930s. In criticizing the Belgians so freely he appeared to forget that it was the Germans who had invaded and occupied most of their country. The invaders had committed various atrocities on the way, and even if a few extra ones were subsequently added on by the Belgians there was plenty of independent testimony for what had actually been perpetrated. With his experience of German snipers aiming at first aid parties, it seems surprising that Osburn can regard them as benevolently as he did. The Germans were fighting to win, and since the aim of the rescuers of wounded men was to repair the damage and return the soldiers to the line it is not surprising that they regarded both wounded and rescuers as legitimate targets. The British soldier who would have done the same was a rare bird, for when a man was wounded he was, in the eyes of a British soldier, a target for compassion rather than bullets.

There are, of course, millions of kind, compassionate Germans.

The problem is that in the past they have too often been led by men like Schlieffen, Bismarck, Moltke, Hitler, Goering and Goebbels. When that happens there is nothing to be gained by saying that most Germans are nice and some of them compose delightful music. Instead, any country which happens to be in their way – Belgium, France, Poland and Britain, to name but a few – needs to make a fight of it, however many scented staff officers may be created in the process. Passchendaele was so appalling that in the 1930s strong Pacifist movements made much ground in Britain and France. Disarmament was seen as a suitable way to avoid wars. Unfortunately the heyday of pacifism was also the heyday of German rearmament, first surreptitiously, then openly. Poland was the first victim, but there were soon others and many harmless people died or suffered years of misery in concentration camps. Passchendaele lasted for four months; the Second World War lasted six years. Perhaps the worst feature of Passchendaele was that it made many members of the public think that war could and should be avoided at all costs, and that this would happen if a few sensible people set their minds to it. Loos had been an appalling battle, and the Somme had been worse, but in those two there had seemed to be some point and intelligent generalship (though little enough in fact). Passchendaele seemed the classic example of half a million men being sacrificed for a low ridge, possession of which could not confer victory on either side. That was the final tragedy of Passchendaele; it disheartened the democracies and, as they became less willing to preserve peace by preparing for war, so were the militarist regimes of Germany, Italy and Japan encouraged to think they would be easy victims.

Osburn would no doubt have been horrified if he had known that his account of his experiences had served to encourage the attitudes he most deplored. But indirectly it probably did. One of the most notorious events of the 1930s was the Oxford Union debate on the motion 'That this House will not fight for King and Country'. The aim of the original motion had been partly to sound undergraduate opinion on whether they would be prepared to face another Passchendaele for merely patriotic reasons, and partly to shock. The undergraduates said they would not, which caused a staged uproar in the press. It was decided to put the motion to the test once more and Randolph Churchill, an ex-member about whom it might be said no cause was truly lost till he had made it his own, came down to oppose the motion. Once again it was carried.

Unfortunately Hitler and Mussolini, unaware that the Union represented but a fraction of Oxford opinion, decided that Britain had lost her will to fight and that any future war would be a walkover. The Oxford Union, as well as not being representative of student opinion in Oxford, let alone elsewhere, is not an entirely serious society. It managed to strike a serious note on this occasion, though inadvertently.

A different type of supporter from the medical one, but of great value nevertheless, was the humorist. One might think that little enough would be found to laugh at in trench warfare, but Bruce Bairnsfather and many others did.

Bairnsfather's best-known cartoon had appeared as early as 1915 and showed his famous 'Old Bill', a plump, middle-aged cockney, crouching in a shell hole with a fellow soldier. It had a single-line caption which clearly answered the other's complaint about the inadequate nature of their shelter: 'Well, if you knows of a better 'ole go to it!' Old Bill's walrus moustache made him seem a very benign and long-suffering soldier. Bairnsfather knew his subject, and had seen his like in the trenches in 1914 and 1915 before he himself was wounded in action. By 1916 he was so well known that he was posted to the Intelligence Department at the War Office as an official cartoonist. It was no desk-bound job, for he was sent to various battlefields on which it was thought he would find further inspiration. In the Second World War he was official cartoonist to the US Army in Europe. Bairnsfather was particularly skilled at observing situations about which soldiers (not only cockneys) could make pointed and witty remarks. He himself was steeped in military tradition for he had been born in India, the son of an Army officer, and had been educated at Rudyard Kipling's old school, the United Services College in Devon. But even Bairnsfather was hard put to find much that was potentially humorous at Passchendaele.

The Wipers Times was published between February 1916 and December 1918. 'Wipers' was the British soldier's pronunciation of the word Ypres. The Editor was Lieutenant-Colonel F.J. Roberts, MC, and the sub-Editor Major J.H. Pearson, DSO, MC. When a collected edition was published, Roberts was informed that he had to write a history of the paper. Part of it ran:

Our paper was started as the result of the discovery of an old printing-house just off the Square at Ypres. Some printing-house and some square. There were parts of the building remaining, the rest was on top of the press. The type was all over the country-side; in fact the most perfect picture of the effects of Kultur as interpreted by 5.9s ever seen.

One of our sergeants, by nature an optimist and in a previous existence a printer, said he could make the press print if he had a brace of light-duty men to help him. He got them, and was as good as his word, as within three or four days, he brought me a specimen of his handiwork.

Paper was there, ink in plenty, everything in fact except 'copy'. As none of us were writing men, we just wrote down any old thing that came into our heads. Little incidents of daily life in the Salient were turned into adverts or small paragraphs.

To get an idea of the birth of the paper one has to try to visualize Wipers in those early days of 1916. We lived in rat-infested, water-logged cellars by day and Hooge by night. As an existence it had little to recommend it. The editorial den was in a casemate under the old ramparts built by Vauban – heaven knows when. However God rest his soul! He gave us the only moments of security we had for three long months, and often we drank to his shadow.

Our casemate will always be vividly remembered by those who knew it. We had a piano – loot from a neighbouring cellar where it had been propping up the remnants of a house – a gramophone, a printing press and a lot of subalterns. When Fritz's love tokens arrived with greater frequency and precision than we altogether relished we would turn our whole outfit on together. The effect of 'Pantomime Hits' on the piano, 'Dance with Me' on the gramophone, a number of subalterns, and 5.9s and 4.2s on the roof, has to be heard to be realised.

At dusk, donning boots, gum, thigh, we would set off

to Hooge to work till dawn in feet of liquid mud composed of – various things better left unsaid – trying to make a little cover for the lads who were holding on to the remains of Belgium in the teeth of every disadvantage, discomfort and peril.

Yet always at the most inconvenient moment came a persistent demand from an ink-covered sergeant, 'Copy wanted, Sir.'

Numbers 1 and 2 of 'The Wipers Times' will always be our particular pets because of the circumstances under which they were done. They were produced on the original press up by the Cloth Hall in the days when the air was usually full of shells. One page only could be done at a time, and we had no 'y's and 'e's to spare when one page was in the 'chaser'. So that when the page was put up in our casemate the sergeant and his 'devils' would go to the door and look at the atmosphere. If all was moderately quiet then they would make a dash for the 'works' and stay till Fritz got too near to be pleasant. Also there were days of wild alarms and excursions, and often one had to stop writing an article in order to 'stand-to'.

There is no more disruptive order in the Army than 'stand-to'. It is issued when an emergency may be imminent – often at dusk or dawn – and it requires everyone, with very rare exceptions, to cease whatever work he is doing and make himself available for battle, usually with his personal weapon which in 1917 would be a .303 Lee-Enfield Rifle, possibly supplemented by a .38 revolver. 'Stand-to' would last until the immediate emergency was over. Almost invariably 'stand-to's cut into time badly needed for sleep. Roberts was a member of the 12th Battalion, Sherwood Foresters, a pioneer battalion in 24th Division, whose job was to supervise the construction of trenches and dugouts at Hooge. It involved travelling along the notorious Menin Road up to Hooge at least twice in every twenty-four hours. When he was not travelling to and from Hooge he would be working, when he was meant to be resting he would be editing *The Wipers Times*, and if not 'standing to' would be able to occupy what was left of the rest of the day with trying to get some sleep.

The first edition ran to one hundred copies, but soon that number had to be doubled.

> All our numbers were printed in the district of the name they bear, and the last five are called the 'B.E.F.[1] Times', for reasons not unconnected with the censor.
>
> Have you ever sat in a trench in the middle of a battle and corrected proofs? Try it. The paper has never yet been printed out of the front area, and once our works were within 700 yards of the front line and *above ground*.

By 1917 *The Wipers Times* had become *The BEF Times* for security reasons, although it is difficult to imagine that the Germans would either find breaches of security in its pages or even be ignorant of its former title and present circulation. Publication of *The Wipers Times* was, not surprisingly, erratic. It was not invariably humorous. The editor made the point: 'Remember that the hilarity was more often hysterical than natural, and that these are our first efforts at journalism, so your criticisms may be kind.' He thanked many people who had helped with copy and in particular mentioned Gilbert Frankau. Frankau had been commissioned into the East Surrey Regiment in 1914, fought at Ypres, Loos and the Somme and in Italy. In the Second World War he became a squadron leader in the RAF. He was a prolific and very successful novelist.

On 15 August 1917 the issue cost one franc. It began with an editorial which apologised for the delay since the previous issue, was saddened at the loss of so many old friends but was glad to welcome new ones, and mentioned that on his last leave in London the editor was 'filled with wonder at the bare-faced robbery which is rife. We should imagine there are many people who will be sorry when the war is over and they don't all keep restaurants.'

Next came two poems, followed by a satirical article entitled 'We Attack at Dawn'. This began with a somewhat fanciful version of the barrage.

> The disgruntled bosom of mother earth heaved with spasmodic writhings as the terrible tornado tore the trees. I was picking wallflowers in Glencorse Wood when all this happened. . . . I stood on that historic spot and

212

put my watch right by the barrage. It came and the
world wilted. Then on came the gallant Esquimaux and
Peruvians (I mustn't mention anything English, it isn't
'done') and with a wild rush scattered Germany's grey-
clad hosts. . . .

This was signed 'By our Special Correspondent' and grew ever
more farcical until it concluded with the sentence, 'In fact we
attacked at dawn.' Although the article is gently guying those war
correspondents who rarely used a simple expression if they could
think of an elaborate one, it also touches on the resentment felt by
British regiments when their achievements received less credit than
they deserved, even to the point that some of their victories were
attributed to others.

Then another poem, 'Roads'.

> *Belgium, rain and a sea of mud*
> *The first seven years are, they say, the worst;*
> *The pavé roads when you're spitting blood*
> *And all you have is a priceless thirst.*

There were five more verses, the last of which ran:

> *Maybe one day we'll forget the rain*
> *The mud and filth of a Belgian scene*
> *But always in mem'ry I'll see again*
> *Those roads with the stumps where the trees had been.*

Next came: 'Great Labour Meet at Dickebush. Flamsey Mac-
Bonald in the Chair.' It seems that Ramsey MacDonald was far
from popular, and that his integrity as well as his courage were
doubted.[2] Then followed a skit on a race meeting, 'The Bois de
Riaumont Stakes', and two poems, one ending with the verse:

> *The way to get on in the Army is to*
> *Wangle a place on the Staff:*
> *For that's where they say things and DO*
> *Them – and though the incredulous laugh*
> *I'm inclined to believe it myself; their*
> *Pay's not enough by a half.*

A somewhat complicated piece, purporting to be by an American dancer, was called 'Curly Shellog at the Front' after Shirley Kellog, a well-known music-hall actress. Curly's piece took the form of a letter to an American friend and was presumably written by someone who knew the correct idiom – perhaps Gilbert Frankau. Then there were more poems, a series of misleading definitions of Army terms, a sale or exchange column – 'Pleasant country estate, has been shot over. Owner desirous of leaving', a description of a cricket match in exaggerated journalese, more poems, an alleged serial, a correspondence column carrying indignant letters. ('As ratepayers we must protest against the increasing noisiness of a set of hooligans who operate chiefly during the night hours, and who seem to rely chiefly on fireworks to make a disturbance in an otherwise peaceful village'), a 'Late News' column, and finally implausible advertisements – 'Has it ever struck you that water is a necessity, not only for the radiators of the Staff's cars, but for a lot of other things. Therefore ECONOMISE in it. There is no need for you to drink it.' It was very much a front-line paper. The jokes may not have been very subtle or very funny but they were written by people who were in the line too, and that made all the difference.

Other supporters of soldiers' morale, though not perhaps morals, came remarkably close to the front line. Poperinghe was almost entirely devoted to 'entertaining the troops' and was often under shellfire. Before the war it had been a small cloth manufacturing town, specializing in what became known as 'poplin'. Troops retiring to Poperinghe for a brief spell out of the line were interested in food, drink and women, though not necessarily in that order. Several of the cafés which served innumerable meals of egg and chips are still to be seen today, though serving slightly less basic fare. The women, who were much condemned by the moralists but probably did more than the latter to cheer many a soldier's last few hours, are no longer there. Many of them had been forced into prostitution by sheer necessity. Their homes and former livelihood had been destroyed by the war, and were probably now in the centre of a battlefield. Husbands and fathers were either dead, wounded or serving on a distant part of the Front. The French took a very practical attitude towards morality in those days. Arthur Osburn recalled that he had seen a 'remarkable' letter which was found on the body of a dead Frenchman. It was from his wife, who said that she was worried about his being deprived of women and had therefore given herself to soldiers in a billet in order to earn money, so that in the area in which her husband was serving he would be able to buy himself a 'good class of woman'. She enclosed 100 francs and hoped he would choose women who reminded him of her. Osburn felt that no Englishman could possibly understand such a sentiment, but felt that the woman's motivation was much more creditable than that of many women in Britain who 'morally seemed suddenly to have sunk below men', for no particularly altruistic reason.

One of the most famous wartime cafés in Poperinghe was Ginger's.[3] The establishment was run by one Madame Cossey who had three red-haired daughters, but it was 'out of bounds to troops' – in other words limited to officers only. It was always packed, and the consumption of champagne was said to be prodigious. A few yards away was Talbot House, mentioned earlier.

Another popular establishment in Poperinghe was Skindles (again officers only). This was not, of course, the original name, which was rather long and unwieldy, but a nickname given to it by one of its patrons: the original Skindles is a hotel with a famous restaurant on the Thames at Maidenhead in Berkshire. The proprietress of Skindles in Poperinghe also had three daughters, with the racy names of Maria, Zoe and Lea.[4]

The Army chaplains, of whatever denomination, were of course more concerned with the troops' spiritual welfare than with their physical needs. But the best of them, like the Reverend Mervyn Evers, MC and bar, knew that their Christian message must be expressed in practical terms that related to the horrors the men were enduring in the trenches, and the reality of sudden death. Hard-working, with a strong sense of responsibility to the fighting men and willing to share their experiences, Evers was noted for his courage and sympathy. After the war he wrote his memoirs, of which the following is an excerpt:

> Le Bizet was a small Belgian village with an estaminet and also a room in one house that I was able to make into a recreation room for the troops when they were relieved

by whichever was the reserve company. If I remember rightly I had a bunk in the M.O.'s First Aid Dug-out and we both messed at the H.Q. Mess. So at last after one year at home with the troops I found myself in the trenches with the same troops. The first day or two I was horribly afraid, rather like a rabbit mesmerised by a stoat, my form of mesmerism was what we called a German 'minnie' – minnenwerfer – or trench mortar which was capable of blowing one to smithereens. However it did not take me long to find the antidote. This was on two levels. On the lower level one's job was not to stand about but to move about helping and cheering up the troops. But much more importantly on the higher level to commit oneself wholly to Jesus Christ so that it was His sole responsibility to see whether you lived or died. Or to put it in a lower key it is said of Truman when he was President of the U.S.A. that he had on his desk at the White House a framed card with the caption on it: 'The buck stops here!' The question had been asked of the highest authority who alone could give the answer. And after that I was never again troubled by fear.

And this was the gist of my message to the troops. Their courage was beyond praise, but it was largely based on fatalism. By and large their philosophy was very much that you were all right until the bullet with your regimental number on it came along and then your 'number was up'. Together with this committal to Jesus Christ the heeding to His injunction 'Be not anxious for the morrow' or in other words 'live one day at a time'.

During our year at home I had started a Christian Union both in the Lancashire Fusiliers and also in the Loyal North Lancs with a membership card with the regimental crest on it which each member was to sign and keep giving his allegiance to Jesus Christ promising to carry out His commands and wherever possible to win others for His cause and kingdom. And as far as I possibly could I kept these meetings going at the front as well as at home. In addition to this I prepared a large number of men for Confirmation again both at home and when we were out in France and Belgium.

My Sundays involved a large number of Services at places some distance apart. To cover the ground we chaplains had each been issued with a horse. And when I set off in the morning to take my Services I was more like a travelling Christmas Tree than anything else!! My luggage was a portable Communion Set, a haversack of Parade Service books and a haversack containing my silk Cassock (which I still have, though in rather a tattered condition) and silk surplice, hood, scarf and stole. . . . The busiest Sunday I can remember was at Vimy Ridge when I started at the Transport Lines at 7.30 a.m. and ended up in reserve trench dug-out at 8.30 having taken Services throughout the day.

For the first month or so our casualties were very light and due mostly to enemy snipers. And I made it a practice from the outset always to write a personal letter to the bereaved parents of the men who had been killed. Imagine my confusion when one of my favourite young Christians who was an absolute first-classer named Sam Rowlandson had been killed by a sniper's bullet and I had buried him in the Cemetery behind the lines and written to his wife a very personal letter to be told by his friends in his company what a beautiful letter it was as it had been sent to be printed in their local paper!

Our first real baptism of fire occurred when the Germans, who out-gunned us very heavily, opened up on our reserve battalion and Headquarters in the village of Le Bizet and I made it my business to move in and out of the billets rescuing the wounded, and it may be this that the C.O. – J.D. Crosbie – referred to in his letter congratulating me on my first M.C. on the Somme.

And as always in the winter life in the trenches was far from comfortable with the trenches a sea of mud and the dug-outs very little better. . . .

Although in the line the officer and his men were in such close proximity that they seemed almost indistinguishable, distinction began very quickly once they came out again. Even in the support trenches there was a marked difference in the degree of what few comforts there were, and in the rear areas officers and men were so separate militarily and socially that they might have belonged to different species. However, this did not prevent an 'other rank' from becoming an officer, if his record seemed to merit the promotion. Officers were killed at such an alarming rate during the earlier battles, particularly on the Somme, that the authorities were forced to look in the ranks for replacements. Some of these were experienced NCOs of some years' service who had been lucky enough to survive, but the majority were young men of intelligence and undistinguished though adequate education. They were not at all the sort of people who would have been considered – or even wished to be – for Sandhurst or Woolwich, but they became thoroughly competent and reliable officers none the less. Promotion within a regiment serving in the front line was likely to be swift – although the War Office would usually tag 'Acting' on to any rank held – but behind the lines it was inevitably a much slower process.

In the First World War there were very few counter-attractions to draw an officer away from his regiment. He might perhaps be given a staff posting or posted to instruct in a training camp, or he might volunteer to join the comparatively small Tank Corps. There were no Commandos, SOE, SAS or the like, but there was a very considerable attraction in the Royal Flying Corps.

The RFC had been formed in 1912 and by the time of Passchendaele had given clear evidence of the growing importance of air power. Reconnaissance, bombing and strafing of German troops on and beyond the Passchendaele Ridge have already been mentioned. Names of aircraft were now well known: the British DH2 and Sopwith Strutter, the French Spad and Voisin, the German Fokker and Albatross. Equally familiar were the names of the war aces: the Canadian Billy Bishop (seventy-two victories); the Germans Baron von Richthofen and Ernst Udet; the French Fonck and Guynemer; the British Albert Ball, VC, and Raymond Collishaw. The public knew the names of the air aces even though they did not know the names of the Army commanders.

Up until the end of the First World War the airmen were always thought of as a useful supporting element. It did not occur to anyone that one day this new arm might be expected to win wars on its own; yet the German air Blitzkrieg and the Allies' Strategic Air Offensive were only a generation away. Nevertheless the First World War aviator was rightly thought of as a dashing and heroic figure. He would be a romantic one too, if his life lasted long enough. Although some of the air battles over the salient were between upwards of sixty aircraft, the aviator was seen as pitting his lone skills against the oppressive enemy. The enemy, of course, was not merely the German pilot, with his cunning tricks such as the Immelmann turn which enabled the pursued to become the pursuer, but also the weather, anti-aircraft fire, the unreliability of the aircraft itself and, not least, the Higher Command which so badly misused air power. Theirs was usually a short life but not necessarily a merry one.

Notes

1 British Expeditionary Force.
2 Mainly because in July 1917 he had attended a secret meeting in Paris of the Stockholm Peace Conference, which consisted of international socialists, among whom were German delegates.
3 It survives today, renamed the Café de Ranke.
4 The present Skindles is no longer on the former site, nor even a café, although when it was moved after 1918 to its present site it took the Skindles sign with it, and therefore can easily be found.

11

The Other Side of the Hill

Although the war looked depressing enough from the Allied point of view in mid-1917, to the Germans it looked even worse. Theobald von Bethmann-Hollweg, the German Chancellor, a liberal by inclination, was convinced that the war should be ended as soon as possible by using President Woodrow Wilson as a peace negotiator. Unfortunately for all, Bethmann-Hollweg was both tactless and liable to be dominated by the military elite. In July 1917 he was forced to resign and was replaced by Georg Michaelis.

Woodrow Wilson was a genuine idealist, with many admirable qualities, but he lacked the ability to handle negotiations skilfully. The fact that the Passchendaele campaign was being fought in a welter of blood and mud in late 1917 was due in no small measure to Britain's endeavours since the beginning of the war to blockade Germany, and Germany's attempts to break that blockade by a vigorous U-boat campaign partly based on Belgium and Dutch ports. A breakthrough from Passchendaele to the U-boat bases was an important issue for both sides. Meanwhile the Americans, who wanted to trade with all the belligerents, were angry to find that the blockade interfered with their very considerable seaborne trade with Germany; Britain therefore began to be the object of some ill-feeling. However, when Germany announced that any Allied merchantman in the vicinity of France or Britain was likely to be sunk without warning, and neutrals could easily find themselves sunk by mistake, American thought became hostile to Germany. The issue came to a head when the *Lusitania*, a Cunard liner, was torpedoed off the coast of Ireland with the loss of 1200 lives, of which 128 were American. Indignation ran high, and there was a call in the United States for immediate war with Germany, but, after Wilson had made a formal protest and the Germans had

220

partially restricted their U-boat campaign, the atmosphere became calmer. However, this state of affairs did not last long.

The Allied blockade of Germany had been so successful that the civilian population was being reduced to near starvation. The winter of 1916–17 was the severest for twenty years, and when the potato crop failed turnips became the staple diet. At this time the word *ersatz* (substitute) began to be widely known: the situation offered considerable scope for ingenuity in the sophisticated German chemical industry. In Germany, therefore, 1917 began with the grim prospect that if the war did not end soon the result would be the collapse of the Army from lack of supplies, and starvation for the civilian population. The quickest way to end the war was clearly by breaking the blockade, and to this end the Kaiser signed an order decreeing that all ships within a wide range of Britain, France and Italy would be sunk on sight.

The decree, which was signed on 1 February, almost precipitated America into the war, but was not quite the last straw. Twenty-four days later British Intelligence handed the American Government a telegram which they had intercepted and decoded. It was from the German Foreign Minister, Zimmermann, to the Mexican Government. It proposed that if America joined in the war against Germany, Germany, Mexico and perhaps Japan should form an alliance as a result of which Mexico's former territories would be restored to her; these were now the states of New Mexico, Texas and Arizona. It was thought that the Zimmermann telegram was almost too good to be true and must have been 'invented' by British Intelligence, but it was perfectly genuine. Six weeks later America declared war on Germany. It was April 1917.

The situation was not quite as bad for Germany as it might seem. The collapse of Russia was clearly imminent and the German Army still held important strategic areas, not least the Passchendaele Ridge. If they could pre-empt any proposed British offensive in that area and by a lucky stroke break through and reach Calais, and even Boulogne, their submarine campaign, aided by these new bases, would turn the blockade tables on Britain itself. But whatever happened must happen before America was able to get her armies into France.

The chances of victory before America could mobilize and deploy her forces were considerable. America had decided to take no chances and therefore had introduced conscription immediately. This would be overwhelmingly effective in the long run – if there were a long run – but was an encouragement for Germany in the short term because drafting huge numbers of Americans into the Army meant that most of their small regular Army would need to be used in training, rather than in going overseas to fight.

The American Navy was a different story, and the German Higher Command soon noted that its use in the Allies' newly adopted convoy system was robbing the U-boats of much of their effectiveness. However, even if the sea battle was not going entirely to Germany's liking, the land battle was. Nivelle's costly venture had restored complete confidence in the German Army and its defensive lines. Surprisingly, the Germans did not realize just how much damage had been done to French morale and, when they were told the French Army was on the verge of mutiny, if not actually engaged in it, they simply refused to believe the news until it was too late to exploit it.

There were, however, political clashes on the Home Front which did not augur well for a united, all-out German effort. General Erich von Falkenhayn, who had succeeded Moltke as Chief of the General Staff, was considered more of a politician than a soldier and did not get on well with General Erich Ludendorff, Hindenburg's second in command. Ludendorff believed that the best and quickest way to win the war was by defeating the Russians decisively and finally and then turning to the West. Falkenhayn decided that the war would be won at Ypres and had sent Ludendorff fewer troops than he had requested for the Eastern Campaign. Ludendorff therefore blamed Falkenhayn for subsequent failure to make much progress before the Russian Revolution and also for the German failure at Verdun; he was not alone in doing so. In August 1916 the Kaiser had decided that Falkenhayn no longer enjoyed the Army's confidence (a fact which should have been clear to him long before), accepted his resignation and established a form of military dictatorship with Hindenburg as the First Chief of Staff of the Armies in the Field and Ludendorff as the Second Chief.

Ludendorff now decided to prove the correctness of his elevated appointment and, as a first move, issued orders for new tactics to be used on the Western Front. Flexibility, rather than rigidity of defence, would be the new method and, as was seen earlier, flexible defence became extremely effective in the front line. He approved of Bethmann-Hollweg's proposal to Woodrow Wilson that he should begin negotiations for peace, seeing that when these inevitably collapsed the Allies would be blamed and a propaganda victory scored. He realised that whether America was offended or not, all-out submarine warfare was essential if the war was to be brought to a successful conclusion. But he regarded Bethmann-Hollweg as a danger, both to the unity of Germany and to his own plans.

Eventually the pressures on Bethmann-Hollweg told and he resigned on 13 July 1917. His successor, Michaelis, was an ex-civil servant and a nonentity, as well as being old and very deaf. Hindenburg was little more than a figurehead. Supreme power now lay with Ludendorff, but he was sitting on an insecure pinnacle and he knew it. Plumer's victory at Messines had come as an unpleasant surprise in more ways than one: a vital part of the ridge had been lost to the enemy, but more disturbing were the reports that the attack and subsequent bombardment had revealed the German infantry to be less stalwart than they had been previously. Ludendorff had every confidence in General Sixt von Arnim, who commanded 4th Army, but if morale was crumbling even Arnim would be hard put to hold back the Allies.

Furthermore, the defences around the Ypres Salient were not yet completed. A defensive strategy, similar to that which had devastated Nivelle's offensive, had been planned for the area. It was to consist of three strong lines: Flandern 1, Flandern 2 and Flandern 3. Flandern 1 ran through Gheluvelt, Broodseinde and just to the west of Passchendaele, and was complete by 31 July. Flandern 2 was not complete but ran through Passchendaele itself; Flandern 3 ran on average two miles behind Flandern 2 and was not complete but had some formidable defences. There was also a series of strong constructions between Staden and Roulers.

Conditions in Flanders seemed to worry Ludendorff more than they worried Haig; he was greatly concerned about the effect of the weather and mud on the military efficiency of the troops who had to fight there. Conditions were, of course, as bad for both sides, but at least the British were not receiving heart-rending letters from their families at home:

You wouldn't believe how things are at present, hundreds of people stand in front of the butchers, cheese mongers, and egg shops. Each person gets one egg a week, sometimes none at all. We don't get sugar any longer. It is high time the war ended.

There is really nothing, not even when one has the money to get anything. No sugar, fat, not an egg, no milk, no meat, nothing at all.

That particular letter, found on the body of a dead German, was read by British and not by German Intelligence, but Ludendorff knew very well that such letters were being sent. There was no way of stopping them. Letters from soldiers in the line could be, and were, censored on the grounds of military security, but censorship of letters travelling in the opposite direction would have been impossible.

Food shortages were not, of course, exclusive to Germany in 1917: Britain also had her share. E.S. Turner reports that 4000 people queued outside Smithfield meat market from 2 a.m. onwards in the snow. There were queues elsewhere for horseflesh. Staple foods, like bread, were rationed. Coal was not merely severely rationed but also had to be collected by the user as so many coalmen had been called up. Hoarding food – if you could obtain it – was a crime. Nevertheless, there was enough food in the country to provide for fairly luxurious meals in restaurants – for those with the money to buy them. Daylight saving by the introduction of Summer Time had been introduced in 1916, although opposed on the grounds that it was already in use in Germany and Austria. But whatever the hardships on what was called the Home Front, they were as nothing to those experienced in Flanders.

Of the opening day of Haig's offensive, Ludendorff recorded:

On 31 July the English, assisted by a few French divisions on their left, had attacked on a front of about 31 kilometres. They had employed such quantities of artillery and ammunition as had been rare, even in the West. At many points along the whole front the enemy had penetrated with tanks. Cavalry divisions were in readiness to push through. With the assistance of counter-attack divisions, the 4th Army, whose Chief of Staff was now Colonel von Lossberg, succeeded in checking the hostile success and localizing its effect. But, besides a loss of from two to four kilometres of ground along the whole front, it caused us very considerable losses in prisoners and stores, and a heavy expenditure of reserves.

The official account was rather more factual and omits the reference to the mythical cavalry divisions:

The results of the first heavy blow, which the enemy with his massive superiority in men and equipment had prepared and carried out, were a gap about 16 kilometres wide and up to three kilometres deep between Poesele and Hollebeke as well as smaller gains between Hollebeke and the Lys. The losses were heavy. From 21 to 31 July, the 4th Army had lost 30,000 men, of whom about 9000 were missing, together with 35 guns.

Kuhl expressed it even more dramatically:

In the early morning of 31 July a storm of fire broke out the like of which had never been experienced before. The whole Flanders earth moved and appeared to be in flames. It was no drum fire any longer; it was as if Hell itself had opened. What were the horrors of Verdun and the Somme in comparison with this great expenditure of power? Deep into the farthest corners of Belgium one could hear the mighty thundering of battle. It was as if the enemy wanted to announce to the whole world, 'We are coming and we shall overcome.' At 6.30 in the morning the British and French troops rose from their trenches, following the heaviest drum fire, and moved into the attack.

He was taking an equally despondent view towards the end of August:

About 25 August, the first part of the great struggle was ended. The British target was quite clear. It was their intention to obtain the high land east and north of Ypres as a springboard for a breakthrough into the Flanders plain. So far their efforts had been contained. But the fighting strength of numerous German divisions was being used up and the prompt replacement by fresh divisions from the whole area of Crown Prince Rupprecht's Army Group was already difficult.

While Kuhl was concerned at the number of casualties, Ludendorff was yet more worried about what he called 'firmness':

The costly August battles in Flanders and Verdun imposed a heavy strain on the western troops. In spite of all the concrete protection they seemed more or less powerless under the enormous weight of the enemy's artillery. At some points they no longer displayed that firmness which I, in common with local commanders, had hoped for.

The enemy managed to adapt himself to our method of employing counter-attack divisions. There were now more attacks with unlimited objectives such as General Nivelle had made in the Aisne–Champagne battle. He was ready for our counter-attacks and prepared for them by exercising restraint in the exploitation of success. In other directions of course this suited us very well.

I myself was being put to a terrible strain. The state of affairs in the West appeared to prevent the execution of our plans elsewhere. Our wastage had been so high as to cause grave misgivings, and had exceeded all expectations.

Ludendorff touches on the dilemma which faces all successful attackers. Should they continue and hope to turn victory into rout – or should they pause, consolidate and allow those on their flanks to catch up and straighten the line? The Germans' ability to deliver a swift counter-attack by reserve troops on to attackers who had broken through but not yet had time to consolidate had paid rich dividends, but now the attackers were well aware of the dangers and cautiously prepared for counter-attacks rather than attempting to gain more ground.

Although the British troops would have been surprised if they had known it, the Germans were extremely worried about what appeared to them to be a constant stream of disasters in Flanders. Ludendorff wrote:

> After a period of profound quiet in the West, which led some to hope that the Battle of Flanders was over, another terrific assault was made on our lines on 20 September. The third bloody act of the battle had begun. The main force of the attack was directed against the Passchendaele–Gheluvelt line. Obviously the English were trying to gain the high ground between Ypres and the Roulers–Menin line, which affords an extensive view in both directions. These heights were also exceptionally important for us, as they afforded us ground observation posts and a certain amount of cover from hostile view.
>
> The enemy's onslaught on the 20th was successful, which proved the superiority of the attack over the defence. Its strength did not consist in tanks: we found them inconvenient but put them out of action all the same. The power of the attack lay in the artillery, and in the fact that ours did not do enough damage to the hostile infantry as they were assembling, and, above all, at the actual time of the assault.

The battle was indeed far from over and would not be until Allied troops were in Passchendaele or had all died in the attempt to capture it. Ludendorff continued:

> Another English attack on the 21st was repulsed, but the 26th proved a day of heavy fighting, accompanied by every circumstance that could cause us loss. We might be able to stand the loss of ground, but the reduction of our fighting strength was again all the heavier. Once more we were involved in a terrific struggle in the West, and had to prepare for a continuation of attacks on many parts of the Front.

August and September had been bad months for Germany but there was worse to come. However, Ludendorff's account gives insufficient credit to the way the German infantry was fighting back. The attacks were not, overall, as successful as he would have hoped but they did display the resolution and 'firmness' which he felt was declining at this stage in the war:

> After each attack I discussed the tactical experience with General von Kuhl and Colonel von Lossberg, sometimes at the Front, sometimes on the telephone. Our defensive tactics had to be developed further, somehow or other. We were all agreed on that. The only thing was, it was so infinitely difficult to hit on the right remedy. We could only proceed by careful experiment. The proposals of the officers on the spot tended rather in the direction of our former tactics. They amounted to a slight, but only a slight, reinforcement of our front lines, and the abandon-ment of the counter-attack by the counter-attack divisions: local counter-attacks being substituted for this. These local counter-attacks were to be made by a division in the second line, to be brought up close and spread over a wide front, before the enemy's attack began. So, while the Front was to be held rather more densely once more, in order to gain power, the whole battlefield was to be given more depth than ever. GHQ would thus, generally speaking, have to provide a second division for every fighting division in the front line, an unheard of expenditure of force.

But the new tactics did not work: the German Official History contains this entry:

> Once again the losses had been extraordinarily severe. The new combat methods had not proved themselves successful on 4 October. The more heavily manned front line which had suffered heavy loss from artillery fire had been over-run by enemy infantry, who had attacked in superior numbers with tank support. All the counter-attack divisions behind the Ypres Group and the Wyts-

chaete Group[1] had to be used. The Army High Command came to the conclusion that there was no means by which the positions could be held against the overpowering enemy superiority in artillery and infantry. Loss of ground to these heavy enemy attacks was unavoidable. Up to now the High Command had tried to cover the heavy losses suffered in these giant battles but it would not be possible to do this for very long.

In connection with the new regulations regarding the fighting method, the Supreme Command is asking for opinions regarding the amount of ground which could be given up without prejudicing the safety of the U-boat bases, in particular also how to retain its fighting strength in Flanders through the winter. The Army Group stressed that it was less concerned with a determined retention of the marked fighting zones than with a more elastic defence – where necessary, a limited yielding at the main points of pressure, and counter-attacks against the flanks of an attack.

With this in mind an offensive had been suggested for 5 October in the area of Gheluvelt against the right flank of the British. Every major enemy attack had won from one to one and a half kilometres of ground by virtue of his overwhelming arms and ammunition. One could not hope to do any better than this oneself. Such a success would constrict the British, would compel them to regroup and would bring their offensive to a halt. It would be of great significance if we could win just eight days till [before] the onset of winter.[2] But as the Army Group could not supply the necessary forces the offensive plan had to be cancelled.

That manoeuvre, if implemented, might well have been a disastrous setback for the British troops. A slow advance was difficult enough: a hasty retreat would have been totally chaotic.

The lack of reinforcements was explained in the German official account:

In a report prepared on 11 October Crown Prince

Rupprecht laid down that the consumption of strength in Flanders on 4 and 9 October had grown so much that technical difficulties had arisen on the railway during the relief of divisions. Such demands on the strength could no longer be made good. The bringing up of reinforcements for other Army groups would become quite impossible as soon as the French returned to the attack. Bringing the divisions up to strength was becoming more difficult. The 4th Army must adapt itself to manage with less strength. The necessity of saving strength and men was more necessary than that of retaining ground. If it became absolutely necessary the Front would have to be withdrawn so far from the enemy that he would be compelled to undertake a new artillery deployment. In addition the Supreme Command suggested on 13 October that, in order to relieve the railway problem, divisions which had not lost more than 1500–1800 men should be kept in Flanders and given a three- to four-week rest for retraining and refitting.

Ludendorff's comment was:

There were further severe engagements on 9 and 12 October. The line held better than on the 4th, although in some places the enemy penetrated to a considerable distance. The wastage in the big action of the fourth Battle of Flanders was extraordinarily high. In the West we began to be short of troops. The two divisions that had been held in readiness in the East, and were already on their way to Italy, were diverted to Flanders.

By 20 October the Germans, according to their official account, had lost 159,000 men out of the 63 divisions which had been in action on this Front. In addition the effect of fighting on the retreat, under heavy fire in appalling ground and atrocious weather conditions, was having a serious effect on morale. But this slowly yielding defence could never bring victory; that could only be gained by attack.

Ludendorff expressed this even more dramatically:

The fifth act of the great drama of Flanders opened on 22 October. Enormous masses of ammunition, such as the human mind had never imagined before the war, were hurled upon the bodies of men who passed a miserable existence scattered about in mud-filled shell-holes. The horror of the shell-hole area of Verdun was surpassed. It was no longer life at all. It was mere unspeakable suffering. And through this world of mud the attackers dragged slowly, but steadily, and in dense masses. Caught in the advanced zone by our hail of fire they often collapsed, and the lonely man in the shell-hole breathed again. Then the mass came on again. Rifle and machine-gun jammed with the mud. Man fought against man, and only too often the mass was successful.

What the German soldier experienced, achieved, and suffered in the Flanders battle will be his everlasting monument of bronze, erected by himself in the enemy's land.

The enemy's losses were also heavy. When we occupied the battlefield again in the spring of 1918 we encountered the horrible spectacle of many unburied corpses. They lay there in thousands. Two-thirds of them were enemies, one-third Germans who had found a hero's grave there.

And yet it must be admitted that certain units no longer triumphed over the demoralising effects of the defensive battle as they had done formerly.

On 4 October the German official account reported:

On the northern wing of the Front under attack the French threw back the German division holding the line, which had suffered in a gas attack, about a kilometre and reached their objective without severe losses. Counter-attacks were unsuccessful in breaking into the main defence line, but during the course of the day they were thrown back and in part driven out of the outpost area. Only on the boundary between the Staden and Ypres Groups were they able to make a salient about a

231

kilometre wide.... South of the Ypres–Menin road about 500 dead British were counted in one regimental sector alone and the numbers of the fallen were said to be many more in the area north of the road. The number of British prisoners was more than 300. It seems that once again the outpost system had proved itself.

But with the Canadians now making an all-out effort, the Germans were still very much on the defensive. The official account for the beginning of November runs:

The capture of Passchendaele was once again denied to the British. However, there was a salient in the German lines. Contact was lost between the Staden and Ypres groups.[3]

On the morning of 31 October the left wing of the Staden Group threw the British back some way and closed the gap. On the same day and on 2 November the right wing of the Ypres Group[4] tried to capture the heights west and south west of Passchendaele. The first attempt was not carried out because of strong enemy defensive fire, the second gained some ground but did not reach the desired objective. Other than this there were only small operations on both sides until 5 November. The numerous enemy attempts to press forward into the outpost area showed that a big new attack was imminent.

The 'big new attack' was, of course, the Canadian advance on 6 November. As was seen earlier, the village of Passchendaele was not very strongly defended and the Germans now concentrated on limiting further advances. Their official account summarized the position:

The intention of mounting a counter-attack on the next morning met with the objection of the Army High Command. The location and state of available troops – so said General von Lossberg in conversation during the night with the Ypres Group – was unknown. Whether the orders would come through at the right time was questionable. The British would have established themselves by the next morning and without strong artillery preparation an attack would be hopeless.

Losses around Passchendaele were once again considerable. The British took over 400 prisoners, but they also, according to German troops' reports, seem to have suffered heavily. They had succeeded in taking the bitterly fought-for Passchendaele, which Field-Marshal Haig had wanted to take before the end of July and which had been his immediate objective since 12 October. The success was meaningful inasmuch as the rise in the ground gave good observation into the German artillery positions. The British had a favourable base for further attacks against the inner wings of the Ypres and Staden Groups. A speedy renewal of their offensive had to be reckoned with.

Ludendorff used less restrained language in his description:

On 26 and 30 October and 6 and 10 November, the fighting was again of the severest description. The enemy charged like a wild bull against the iron wall which kept him from our submarine bases. He threw his weight against Houthulst Forest, Poelcappelle, Passchendaele, Becelaere, Gheluvelt, and Zandervoorde. He dented it in many places, and it seemed as if he must knock it down. But it held, although a faint tremor ran through its foundations.

The impressions I continuously received were very terrible. In a tactical sense everything possible had been done. The advanced zone was good. The effectiveness of our artillery had considerably improved. Behind every division in the front line there was another in support, and we still had reserves in the third line. We knew that the enemy suffered heavily. But we also knew he was amazingly strong and, what was equally important, had an extraordinarily stubborn will. Only one thing we did not know: how long the battle would continue. The enemy must tire some time.

But to the Germans on the ridge the enemy showed little sign of tiring. Even after 10 November, Ludendorff wrote:

> Artillery fire remained lively. The enemy's conduct was no different to that in the earlier pauses in the major assaults. The conclusion that the battle was at an end could not be drawn. Although the Supreme Command as well as the High Command of the Army Group and Army had long been of the opinion that Field-Marshal Haig was not capable of continuing the offensive through the winter it was, however, quite uncertain when he would finally stop.

However, after 20 November the Germans realized that Haig had now issued orders that there should be no more offensives in the immediate future. Ludendorff assessed the situation as follows:

> The battle had lasted over four months and had led to enormous consumption of strength. A total of 73 German divisions had taken part in it from 15 July to 10 November. The German 4th Army lost from 21 July to 31 December 1917 about 217,000 men, of which 35,000 were killed and 48,000 more missing.

The breakdown of casualty figures tends to be misleading. At Passchendaele large numbers described as 'missing' had probably been killed; 'wounded' included many who would die later, some even before they left the battlefield. Very few of those who had been wounded badly enough to be listed as such in German records would ever be fit for active service again.

Crown Prince Rupprecht of Bavaria, Commander Northern Army Group, maintained that to have limited British gains to the middle of the ridge was actually a German victory, for the bitter fighting had prevented a breakthrough which could have had disastrous consequences. To this end, he considered that the German losses were justified:

> Sons from all parts of Germany had shown heroic bravery and powers of endurance and brought to nought

the attempt by the British and French to achieve the breakthrough which, had it succeeded, would have brought about a decision because it would have meant the capture of Flanders and our U-boat bases. Despite the use of unheard-of masses of men and material the enemy has not achieved this. A narrow strip of completely destroyed crater land is his only gain. He has bought this gain with extremely high losses while our own casualties have been less than in any previous defensive battle.

Thus the battle of Flanders is a severe defeat to the enemy and is for us a great victory. He who was present can be proud to have been a Flanders warrior.

The German official account took a more pessimistic view of the extent of the losses and their justification:

Above everything else the battle had led to a vast consumption of German strength. Losses had been so high that they could not be replaced and the fighting strength of battalions, already reduced was further reduced. That the enemy, despite the most thorough preparation, numerical superiority, bravery and perseverance, had been able to achieve so little was partly due to the adverse weather conditions which made movement in the Flanders soil extremely difficult. But water and mud were no less a disadvantage to the defenders. These conditions, more than the bloody fighting, led to a rapid wearing out of the troops and were, along with the lower numerical strength of the German divisions and the serious inferiority in guns and ammunition, among the reasons why the German defence required a more rapid relief of divisions than during the enemy's attacks.

The 73 German divisions which had fought in Flanders within the space of four months could only be brought together by replacing the fought-out divisions of the 4th Army by fresh troops from all other armies.

All these German accounts freely acknowledge that their troops had been outgunned and fairly beaten. They had, of course, fought extremely bravely and skilfully and there is much in Crown Prince Rupprecht's opinion that their dour resistance had prevented Haig's wished-for breakthrough. A true assessment of the battle would be certain to say that the Germans had fought extremely well but that the British, Australian and Canadian troops had fought slightly better.

Hindenburg, writing in 1919, considered that: 'From the point of view, not of scale, but of the obstinacy which the English displayed and the difficulties of the ground, the battles in Flanders put all our battles on the Somme in 1916 completely in the shade. . . . It was with a feeling of absolute longing that we waited for the beginning of the wet season.' By the 'wet season' Hindenburg presumably meant a time when it could be expected to rain all the time, not merely most of the time. Those who fought in the Passchendaele battles might well have thought that nothing could be wetter than the conditions which they were enduring.

The German reports do, however, slightly restore the reputation of Charteris, who has always been blamed for encouraging Haig by giving him over-optimistic accounts. Clearly there was some truth in his frequent assertions of deterioration in German morale, but unfortunately this was not as great as he constantly affirmed. Furthermore, it seemed that the morale of the German Higher Command was affected more than that of the troops on the ground. British, Canadian and Australian troops found little enough evidence of fading morale among the soldiers opposing them.

At the end of *The Unreturning Army* Huntly Gordon, who was in A Battery, 112 Brigade, Royal Field Artillery, included the following:

> It was the practice of G.H.Q. to circulate periodically to all commanding officers a summary of extracts from German documents and correspondence obtained from prisoners and other sources. To us this series of circulars was known as 'Comic Cuts', the title of a weekly comic paper of those times.
>
> The following extracts refer to life on the German side of Ypres Salient during August and September 1917. I

am not sure that we derived much positive pleasure from reading these testimonials, but it was encouraging to hear that the efforts we made under such difficult conditions were not without effect.

1. 'We were under intense bombardment from 27th July until 12th August, and could not be relieved. We had colossal losses; the company was originally 140 strong and on 12th August when we paraded we were only 18 men. It was the same with the whole regiment.'

2. 'One looks out from the front line on shell-holes which are half-full of water. In front and behind, the whole place is a lake. Most of the dugouts are water logged and derelict. Out of those that are occupied one has to pump the water every hour. One daren't show oneself outside by day.'

3. 'Well, I won't write any more; you can imagine what it was like. One Company had 17 killed, the Sergeant-Major went mad, you can imagine the rest. Who knows whether we shall come out? Last year I was at Verdun; it was bad there, too, but here there is no trench – nothing; one has to lie out on the open ground, and wait for death in the drum-fire. If this goes on, and we go to the front-line tomorrow, I shall soon fall out and not go up again.'

4. 'I am the only one who withstood the maddening bombardment of three days, and still survives. You cannot imagine the frightful mental torments I have undergone in those few hours. After crawling out through the bleeding remnants of my comrades and the smoke and debris, and wandering and fleeing in the midst of the raging artillery fire in search of a refuge, I am now awaiting death at any moment. You do not know what Flanders means. Flanders means endless endurance. Flanders means blood and scraps of human bodies. Flanders means heroic courage and faithfulness, even until death.'

5. 'Here we are back at the front, and again in that terrible corner in front of Ypres. We came into the line this morning, or rather into a waste of craters. Out with

our spades, and quickly dig a hole, and I am sitting in it as I write this. One can neither lie down nor stand up. We must stay several days in this hole – there is no other shelter besides these craters. In a word, this is our front line, not the slightest trace of bomb-proof shelters – there are none in the whole of our sector. So I am sitting here for Germany's glory and honour, waiting till a merciful shell or bullet sends me to a better land, because there is as little prospect of my coming out of this alive, as there is of a victorious peace for our country, and that is the general opinion among the men. This can't go on for ever, there must be an end some time.'

6. (From a German civilian). 'My brother at the front tells me that, in his opinion, the only end there can be to this awful war is for Germany to be defeated. The English will hang on for ever. Oh! I hope it isn't as bad as all that, but for my part I'm indifferent; all I know is that it's got to end one way or another – we can't stick it another winter.'

Notes

1 German Area Commands.
2 The military winter began when campaigning was no longer possible because of the deteriorating weather.
3 These two German Army Groups covered and flanked Passchendaele.
4 The Group to the south of the village.

12

The View from the Trenches

The names of the battles of the First World War, all of them fought some seventy years ago, are perhaps better known to the general public than those of the more recent Second World War. It is generally felt that nothing has ever matched those appalling years which brought Loos, Festubert, Arras, the Somme, and especially Passchendaele. In comparison the great conflicts of the Second World War, so glamorized by film and television, seem almost social occasions. In films about the North African Campaign it is easy to forget that men did not merely race around in tanks – they also died in them, and particularly unpleasantly. The battles of the desert and the jungle, of the Italian Campaign, of D-Day and the North-west Europe Campaign are marked by their cemeteries just as surely as the battles of the First World War; they are smaller, of course, but, like the older cemeteries, they all represent lives brought to an end when the fullness of life should have been just beginning.

But the acres of white crosses are by no means the whole story. Many a man survived the battlefield with his physical – and often mental – health so damaged that his life could no longer be enjoyed and perhaps ended prematurely. The terrific toll taken on the bodies of soldiers, whether in the trenches of the First World War or on the more open terrain of the Second, was impossible to assess. In 1987 two questions are often asked: One is, 'Why did they do it?'; the other, 'How did they do it?' To these is often added the statement: 'They'd never do it nowadays.'

Why did they do it? Why did they join the Army in the First World War, many of them as 'Kitcheners', and then continue to put up with unbelievable hardship, living in mud, surrounded by decaying corpses, knowing that all too easily they could share the same fate; why did they do this and not mutiny? The French Army mutinied, although it was pulled back from the brink of total dissolution. The German Army mutinied. The Russians simply stopped fighting. But the British Empire troops carried on fighting to the end and won.

Why? There seems to have been a combination of influences. One of them was pride – the feeling that if you were British you carried on whatever the cost until the job was finished. That was an internal motive. Secondly, there was the external motive: you kept going because that was what your relatives, your friends and your closest companions in the Army expected you to do. Thirdly came the desire to be revenged on the Germans for all the damage they had inflicted on your fellow soldiers and were still trying to inflict on you. Fourthly, and perhaps the most compelling, was that there was no visible way out. There *could not be* a way out if the officers died as quickly as, and sometimes even more quickly than, the NCOs and lower ranks. If there was an alternative they, the officers, with their better education and opportunities, would surely have taken it. But they did not. And there were no other leaders who might show the way. Once you were in, you were in, and that was all there was to it.

The answer to 'How?' is simple enough. You endure what you have to, as long as you can last. This is also the answer to the glib. remark, 'They'd never do it nowadays.' In 1940, in France, certain parts of both the French and British Armies put up a less stalwart fight than they were expected to do if the worst came to the worst. They were outmanoeuvred and outclassed. Dunkirk was not an 'epic', as it was sometimes described: it was the evacuation of a beaten, demoralized, weaponless Army. But after Dunkirk and the Channel there was nowhere else to go. The German Air Force was defeated in its attempt to obtain air superiority prior to an invasion, but it pounded the people of Britain relentlessly night after night, killing and wounding over 10,000 people each month. How and why did people – men, women and children – endure it? They did so because there was no alternative. It was the same for the citizens of Hamburg, Berlin and Düsseldorf when their turn came. It was the same for the Russians at Stalingrad and at Leningrad; it was the same for the people of Malta. They endured because the alternative was death in a concentration camp or perhaps by

240

massacre. There comes a time when there is no place to hide, and when death while fighting is infinitely better than any alternative. The conquered in the twentieth century may be in a happier position than those defeated by the Romans or their successors, but they may on the other hand find themselves liable to death by genocide. And even if they escape a violent death, starvation or disease may well achieve the same end.

The lessons are all there for us to learn. If a ruthless conqueror like Hitler, Mussolini or Tojo launches war on people whom he thinks incapable of much resistance those in his way will find little mercy whether they fight or try passive resistance. It is best to fight: paradoxically it is your best chance of survival. There are still potential Jenghiz Khans in the world.

Unfortunately for those enrolled in armies – of whatever nation – it has long since been agreed that once a man is in uniform the best way of preparing him for battle is to make him lose his sense of personal identity. In certain modern armies men are not even known by names; they are just one of a number. When three are killed, three more anonymous figures are pushed forward to replace them. It makes for a very good army.

In the First World War the British soldier who eventually found himself fighting and dying at Passchendaele received many rude shocks on his way there. He was welcomed into the Army but the smiles on faces were soon replaced by scowls. His training was hard: by 1917 the ludicrous situation of men still in civilian clothes practising drill with wooden rifles, under the instruction of men who hardly knew the movements themselves, had long since disappeared. Now he drilled with the .303 Lee-Enfield rifle which he would carry into battle with him. He was told it was his best friend. It had a bolt action which replaced each round as it was fired – the movement required to reload might well be spotted by an alert sniper who would then mark him as a victim. His rifle carried five rounds in a clip; the magazine would hold fifteen rounds but was less likely to jam if loaded with ten. This rifle was very effective, and accurate up to 500 yards, but it was heavy and cumbersome, especially when it had a bayonet fixed.

Gradually he became accustomed to being kept waiting for no apparent reason, to lying on hard beds, to boredom, to being with companions he would rather not have known, and to some bullying and sadism by NCOs who were only too well aware that this was the first, and probably the last, chance they would have to exercise the power to make others miserable. Often the more senseless sadism occurred because it was an Army tradition; men would be kept waiting in the rain because it would teach them that 'they were in the Army now'.

Norman Gladden was called up in May 1916 at the age of 18¾. At his medical examination he was considered fit for home service only, but the heavy losses on the Somme caused him to be upgraded medically and soon he was posted to a different regiment. This time it was the Northumberland Fusiliers, whom he joined in September 1916.

> The situation in France was then unspeakably depressing. Even our arrival at the base camp had been welcomed by a group of jeering nondescript Tommies, no doubt down from the line, as 'more for the slaughterhouse'. . . .
>
> To add to our discomforts the new draft was received by the battalion without ceremony or any sort of induction. We were absorbed by our company like bodies being sucked down into a morass and made to feel we were without rights of any sort. We had difficulty in obtaining our just rations, poor as they were, were put on all working parties – from which the old hands honestly thought they had earned exemption – and even in the trenches found ourselves without shelter because we had not yet learned the ropes. The N.C.O.s and officers never appeared unless there was some mission to perform, and for once in my life I learned what it would be like in a society without authority in which the ordinary man delivered his own privileges according to his own scale of values.
>
> This was my worst period in the army, a time when depression effectually completed the task which the enemy had legitimately in hand. As if by a miracle I escaped death or even wounding, but the lackadaisical conditions eventually led to my temporary release when the prevailing wetness brought on the peculiar army

complaint known as trench feet.

Although his illness was diagnosed, he was not evacuated for treatment until it developed into septic ulcers. A period in hospital in Rouen and Cardiff followed by convalescent leave cured his feet, and in May 1917 he was once more en route to the Front. Ypres, he found, was a much better organized Front than the Somme had been. They were met by the colonel and inspected by the medical officer.

> The afternoon found us in Poperinghe on a visit to the army baths. I came to this historic place as to an old friend whom I found sadly aged even in the few brief months since my first visit. There were more jagged gaps in the architecture, more military traffic in the streets and many fewer civilians anywhere. The war was rapidly getting the upper hand.

Then Ypres itself:

> It was with no little awe that I came to the grim ruins of that City of the Dead. As we assembled in the main square, surrounded by spectral shapes, we seemed to be almost encircled by the enemy lights that rose and fell above the low ridges commanding the town. It was a comparatively quiet night for our début. There was only the murmur of laden limbers streaming through the town and of burdened men flowing amidst the empty frames of former dwellings. At frequent intervals lights gleamed up from sandbagged cellars showing that the place had its dwellers even in day-time when every square foot was under enemy observation.
>
> We left the city on foot through the ancient ramparts, whose substantial construction continued to defy the enemy shells. Here the lights seemed to be so close as to deny the possibility that all our field defences lay between the town and the ridge occupied by the Germans. In fact there was more space than appeared in the deceptive darkness between us at the time, but it was one of the outstanding miracles of the war that our armies

had been able to hold such a closely invested place. The price, of course, was high but this was a key position, as the enemy recognised.

We soon discovered the deceptiveness of those distances as we traversed the broken ground to the dump at Zillebeke, which was the night's rendezvous. Occasionally we halted without apparent reason as night-moving troops often did. The atmosphere seemed electrified and I was filled with an almost tangible expectancy of evil. Shortly something was bound to happen. I experienced that all-embracing fear I had so often felt on the Somme. I was literally consumed by a fatalistic desire to do something to pierce the shroud by which we seemed to be divided from some awful truth.

While halting at a spot by Jackson's Dump, a member of the Group, to soothe his nerves – of course against the strictest orders – lit a cigarette. So great was his desire – and so obscured his judgement – that he was prepared, in that place of all places, to risk not only his own but all our lives! Though the match was shielded in his cupped hands the flame glowed through his fingers like a beacon in the darkness of the night. A howl of indignation went up, as the file hurriedly moved off. The riposte was not long delayed. An enemy machine-gun began to traverse accurately across the track, scattering us like rabbits to the shelter of a ditch, but not before two of our company lay writhing in agony with bullets in the lower parts of their bodies. The firing ceased and, after the wounded had been tended, we moved forward again in an advanced state of nerves. Every shadow in the near distance seemed to harbour the threat of death. Needless to say, the thoughtless one was not hurt! Not that his action was at all exceptional. Under the stresses of the battlefield a smoker could become desperate enough to be willing to risk anything for his normal means of relief from tension. I formed the view that the habit of smoking had merely increased the capacity for such tension and that the smoker's nerves in war were not any steadier than those of the rest of us.

It would appear that Gladden was a non-smoker; he must, however, have been well aware that in the Army, then and later, it was the *ritual* of cigarette smoking that made it a craving, rather than the actual satisfaction of tasting the smoke. From the beginning of Army training all intervals were announced as a 'break off for a smoke'. Periods of waiting were made less tedious by smoking. Soldiers were experts at lighting a cigarette, taking two or three deep draws and then, after pinching out the lighted head, tucking the rest inside the band of a cap or beret. The mere possession of any sort of cigarette gave a feeling of security: when both cigarettes and money had run out all was gloom. Overseas, the Army issued a weekly cigarette ration. Non-smokers often hoarded these and drove hard bargains when smokers' cigarettes had run out. This – and stealing the hoard – often produced serious trouble in barrack rooms. Non-smokers were often disliked and resented; smokers, like the one above, might put lives at risk by smoking near explosives. The smell of smoke sometimes gave away positions with fatal consequences, but in the catalogue of soldiers' basic needs – cigarettes, drink, women – cigarettes were an unchallenged first.

Gladden continued:

> This particular incident made it abundantly clear to me what great advantages the enemy derived from occupying the high ground above the town. His fire, both machine-gun and artillery, could be accurately directed upon selected map references with the practical certainty of finding a target. All around us in stacks covered with flimsy camouflage were accumulations of trench-mortar shells, boxes of rifle grenades and other types of ammunition looming up like humps out of the darkness. They seemed to invite enemy firing, but must have been so situated to be masked from observation.

Although all the company was made up of basically trained riflemen it also included specialists. Some had developed an expertise with grenades, which could be launched either by hand or rifle, some had become part of trench mortar teams, others had become machine gunners. Trench mortars had originally been very crude devices by which a bomb could be launched upwards and outwards via a piece of piping, but by 1917 these were properly manufactured weapons which gave more than a hint of their deadly successes in the Second World War. By 1917 machine gunners had been formed into a specialist Corps, but there was a need for Lewis gunners within companies and Gladden became one. The Lewis gun was a light automatic weapon which used up ammunition at an alarming rate, and was liable to overheat or jam from a variety of causes. The Germans, of course, had a similar range of weapons.

Gladden found that Ypres, although appalling, was better organized than the Somme in that troops were taken out of the line and rested or retrained more frequently. Except at the worst moments rations were delivered regularly and now had more variety than in the past. Some of the new additions were popular but some soldiers had become so accustomed to the corned beef, McConochie's meat and vegetable stew and Tickler's plum and apple jam that these were now preferred to variations. Similarly, when out of the line, egg and chips was preferred to any more exotic dishes which might be on offer. These preferences should not be misunderstood. The soldier knew what suited him and what he liked. He would have been unwise to spend his small amount of pay on something which might leave him hungry or, at the worst, with indigestion.

Gladden went into action once more on 18 September in what would become known as the Battle of Menin Road. As his company waited behind their start line during the cold night, they were given a swig of rum:

> I gulped down my share thankfully and felt warmer, but only for a short while. There were still too many hours of cold waiting ahead of us to render this medicine effective but we were grateful for the gesture.

The night was suprisingly silent. Then:

> An officer coming forward from the group behind us, snapped his watch into his pocket, and signalled us forward. We were moving: a few minutes silence – intensified, eternal. Then the guns cracked out from behind us and we were running forward in the reflected

light of the artillery. I could feel and see crowds of men moving on all sides, spreading waves of humanity directing their puny flesh towards the enemy positions. The air above us seemed to be roofed in with rushing shells, while some way ahead a curtain of flame and smoke completely blotted out the landscape. . . .

Though my feet were moving with all the energy needed to carry me with my burden across the ground I felt that they were in fact rooted to the earth and it was all my surroundings that were moving of their own accord. For a brief moment I was detached from the awful present. . . .

Our barrage – a wave of inconceivable confusion – began to creep away from the edge of the wood, whose trees stood out even more clearly as the fumes gradually cleared. Now the whole situation changed as if by magic, evil magic for us. . . . Snipers bullets began their deadly work. Machine guns, opening out ahead, began to traverse methodically across our front, like flails of death crossing and recrossing as they sprayed the advancing line. I felt a tearing stream of lead swishing across as the muzzle slewed and I could scarcely believe I had not been hit. The defenders were resisting with deadly effect. I heard screams around me. From the edge of the wood, now much closer, flashes from rifles and machine-guns filled the air like venomous darts. Terror now ruled my dying world.

I could not distinguish our front wave clearly, for daylight was fully upon us. And if I had further capacity for fear, such fear gripped me now. . . .

In the general confusion of the advance, Gladden was cut off from the rest of his company. After searching for it for some time he found some members of another company. All their officers had been killed and they were trying to decide what to do next. He was saddened to learn that his own company commander, who would have joined the Royal Flying Corps after this battle, was now dead:

I felt a stab of painful sorrow at the senseless elimination of a good, brave, and truly gentle man. . . .

The gently sloping ground in front leading to the Tower Hamlets Ridge was a churned mass of shell-holes, jagged timber and other debris. It was from this shelter of rubbish that the German snipers began their deadly work after the advancing groups had passed. During the day mopping-up parties, especially assigned to the task, crossed out into the waste and disposed of those Germans who persisted in offensive action after the ground had been lost. We both admired and hated these brave men. Admired them for their persistence and bravery, hated them, illogically to some extent, for what we considered was unsportsmanlike action. Possibly they were more desperate than brave, having been taught they would get no quarter in any case. Of course, their persistence meant that it often worked out this way, for the moppers-up would have been foolish to take chances.

In spite of being in action for several days, Gladden was miraculously lucky in sustaining only a very minor wound. At the end of it, with his company reduced to half its original strength, he was marched back to a camp at the rear. On the way they were halted and a few made a dash into a nearby canteen. For this they were all punished by being made to sit in the roadway for the entire halt. They had done no harm, but the officer who had been put in charge of the party, 'immaculate in his clean uniform, for he had been one of those detailed to stay behind', thought that this breach of discipline should not be overlooked.

Private Gladden, though perhaps more articulate than some of his contemporaries, was a good example of the average soldier. Although a survivor of many battles, he never became indifferent to danger: on the other hand he never gave way to the abject terror he often felt. He liked and admired some officers, but hated others. He began his war on the Somme, continued it at Passchendaele and finished it in Italy in 1918. Most of the time he kept a diary, which was strictly illegal and particularly difficult for a ranker. To him, as to so many others, the war became like weather – something over which one had no control but which could make one reasonably happy or utterly miserable at will.

Edwin Vaughan went to the war with the boyish attitude of many young officers of the time. He became a captain, won an MC and survived. Subsequently he found he could never settle to civilian life and, after returning to the Army for a while, joined the RAF and became a pilot. But his health had been undermined by his wartime experiences: he was invalided out and died at the age of thirty-four. He was nineteen at Passchendaele, where he spoke of a day behind the lines:

> This was a glorious day. We were working on a road by Courcelles so, having drawn rations for the troops, Hammond and I marched them off in beautiful sunshine, tunics open and lively songs pouring out in chorus. We got them started and then we wandered off to investigate a small house nearby. It was a sad little place for, although all the families had gone, the floors were littered with kiddies clothing, dolls, and toys.
>
> We went out again to the troops and as all the shell-holes were now filled, we started them digging to drain the water into the ditch. While they were doing this Hammond and I played at being engineers, I building a reservoir in a puddle and he constructing an elaborate system of locks and channels and waterfalls to drain it off into a puddle of his own.
>
> We had just commenced to fight about it when Dunham came along with our lunch – two packets of sandwiches, a bottle of real *English* beer for me, and one of lemonade for Hammond, who was TT.
>
> A little farther on we saw another larger house, which we approached. It had evidently been a staff HQ. We decided to lunch there and passed the word along to the troops to knock off. They were all very happy working in their shirt sleeves, singing gaily and chaffing each other – pouring sweat under the sun's hot rays.
>
> Against a high red wall thirty yards away stood a greenhouse, with a little glass left, and inside a tangled mass of vines, tomatoes and weeds. At one end a dugout had been made, lower down a long rustic bridge crossed a rapid brook on the banks of which stood a miniature

rustic hut and occasional willow tree. Lying here on the soft grass we ate our lunch, basking in the hot rays of the sun and finding life sweet. Then smoking and talking we made brooches and bows out of sedgegrass and tiny flowers. In order not to desecrate the happy little ruin we buried our sandwich paper and replaced the turf (though there were dozens of empty tins lying round). Then we threw our empty bottles into the stream and raced beside them, each cheering his own craft, TT versus Toper – until after about half a mile they were caught in the weeds.

Strolling quietly back in silence, we found a dead pigeon and buried him, railing in his grave with little sticks and chains of plaited sedgegrass, and in his coverlet of pimpernels we erected a tiny white cross.

Then we went out on to the hot, white road where our troops lay under the hedge, some smoking, some asleep. Most of them had pulled bunches of may and dogroses which bedecked their caps and all were very lazy and happy when we went along to distribute the chocolate which Dunham had brought. Then we continued our work until 4 p.m. when we marched back feeling that life was worth living and war worth fighting.

Less than four months later he was taking a muster parade of the company. It was the day after the Battle of Langemarck:

Poor old Pepper had gone – hit in the back by a chunk of shell; twice buried as he lay dying in a hole, his dead body blown up and lost after Willie had carried it back to Venheute Farm. Ewing, hit by machine-gun bullets, had laid beside him for a while and taken messages for his girl at home.

Chalk, our little treasure, had been seen to fall riddled with bullets, then too he had been hit by a shell. Sergeant Wheeldon, D.C.M. and bar, M.M. and bar, was killed, and Foster. Also Corporals Harrison, Oldham, Mucklow and the imperturbable McKay. My black sheep – Dawson and Taylor – had died together, and out of our happy little band of 90 men, only 15 remained.

So this was the end of D Company. Feeling sick and lonely I returned to my tent to write out my casualty report, but instead I sat on the floor and drank whisky after whisky as I gazed into a black and empty future.

13

Hindsight

Passchendaele was such a murderous battle, quite apart from the conditions of mud and weather in which it was fought, that one question will always be put: did the result justify the cost? The answer, sadly, seems to be 'No.' The Allies had held the Ypres Salient for three years and both sides had attempted to break through. By mid-1917, when Haig began his offensive with the capture of Messines, this had not been an exceptional battle area in terms of the Western Front. It seemed to have settled into a form of stalemate, with the Germans unable to break through to the Channel ports and the British apparently unlikely ever to force a way through Belgium.

Two factors changed this situation. One was the mutiny of the French Army, the other Haig's belief that if he could reach the Passchendaele Ridge the way into Belgium and subsequently Germany would be clear. Haig therefore felt that these two factors were combined. Pressure must be taken off the French, and the best and quickest way to do it was to drive forward through the German line in the northern sector. If a breakthrough near Ypres could be achieved fairly quickly, there would be no need to worry about French morale. That would be restored fast enough if final victory appeared to be in sight, and especially quickly if the British seemed likely to achieve it without French help. French pride could not possibly let that happen.

This was all very reasonable. Nevertheless it still left a question unanswered. Was the Ypres Salient the best point to choose to make a breakthrough into Germany? In view of the immensely strong position of the Germans in that area, the answer again seems to be 'No.' A drive further north from the French and Belgian sectors might be easier, although an obvious disadvantage was that necessary troop movements and exchange of sectors – to which the French might not have agreed – would have demonstrated very clearly to the Germans what was in Haig's mind, and they would no doubt have taken appropriate defensive measures. Subsequent events proved that Cambrai offered the greatest possibilities.

Other areas had been tried before. The Somme had ended in stalemate, and after the previous carnage in that area it would hardly be tried again. Names like Aubers, Neuve Chapelle, Festubert, Givenchy, Loos, Arras and Bapaume all carried an aura of heavy losses and ultimate failure to make larger-scale gains – and nothing short of a large-scale gain would win this war. Vimy had been a victory but it had cost dearly; areas further south seemed to have little to commend them. But Ypres, on the other hand, was conveniently placed for supplies and reinforcements, and a tactical gain here would have enormous strategic benefits, one of which would be to curb the U-boat campaign.

But whatever justification there might be for the Ypres offensive of 1917, three enormous tactical blunders were made at the outset. The first was to misuse the massive artillery firepower by pounding the salient into a swamp, the second was to use 5th Army for the main advance instead of pushing 2nd Army northwards along the ridge after the capture of Messines, and the third was to delay the offensive until 31 July. There were excellent excuses for making all these blunders: it was eventually artillery more than infantry which settled the outcome of the battle; advancing along the ridge would have been extremely difficult; and the delay in the offensive was based on a combination of the need to recover from the Arras battle and an over-optimistic view of the weather prospects.

There remained, of course, the possibility of doing nothing. Questions of whether the war should have been fought at all were now totally irrelevant: it had been going on for three years; peace initiatives had failed; it was unlikely to be settled either by starvation of Britain by the U-boat campaign, or by starvation of Germany through the blockade; it could only be determined by victorious offensives. And it was well known that the best defence is attack. If the Allies did not attack, doubtless Germany would. Indeed, in the following spring it did and swept all before it until stopped more by its own exhaustion than by effective Allied resistance.

Haig's obsession with the idea of a cavalry-style breakthrough and pursuit has already been discussed. He was certainly not discouraged by his closest advisers, almost all of them cavalrymen too. Charteris's breezy optimism probably has much to answer for in that it probably encouraged Haig to take a less than realistic view of his prospects, but the facts are that in spite of everything being against the 1917 offensive it did succeed, and it did capture the ridge. Owing to the weather, victory came too late, and even if it had occurred earlier there is good reason to suppose that the cavalry, far from being able to make an exhilarating dash for Bruges, would have encountered yet another formidable German defence system.

To Haig and his staff the British troops must have seemed invincible. They did all they were expected to do, and more. They fought and beat the Germans who were in positions which they had had three years to prepare, and who, when they fell back, merely retreated to higher and better positions.

In terms of human casualties, and the appalling conditions in which it was fought, Passchendaele must rank as one of the most gruelling battles in the history of warfare. The tragedy of that battle, as with so many others on the Western Front, was that it resulted in death and misery for hundreds of thousands without achieving a decisive result. All the gains arising from the capture of the Passchendaele Ridge were lost again early in the following year. But Passchendaele, like many other battles between 1914 and 1918, seems to have been an unavoidable conflict in the conditions of the time: neither the Allies nor the Germans could see any productive alternative.

Seventy years later, the fact that Passchendaele could have been fought at all seems almost inconceivable. But fought it was, and perhaps the best way to remember it is as an occasion when the men of both sides displayed almost superhuman courage and tenacity.

14

Visiting the Battlefield Today

The visitor to Ypres today will have little difficulty in seeing all the places mentioned in this book. Many of the old names have gone, of course, but it is easy enough to find the places they marked if you use the Michelin 213 map and the excellent battlefield guides which are on sale.

One extremely useful guide is *Before Endeavours Fade* by Rose E.B. Coombs, MBE. Rose Coombs, previously a radar operator with the RAF, worked in the Imperial War Museum from 1946 to 1983 and in the latter part of that time was Special Collections Officer. She has visited the battlefields literally hundreds of times. Although her book covers all the French battlefields, it manages to give a comprehensive account of each.

For the Ypres battles she gives five separate tourist routes, each of which is fully illustrated with photographs, some of them taken from the air. The poignant and impressive photographs include the grave of Rifleman V.L. Strudwick of the Rifle Brigade, who was killed at the age of fifteen, the grave of Gilbert Talbot in Sanctuary Wood Cemetery, an aerial view of Hill 60 showing its many craters, and a number of German bunkers which still look so formidable that one wonders how they were ever captured. Ploegsteert Wood is shown, then and now. Although 'Plugstreet', as the soldiers knew it, was on the fringe of the battlefield in 1917, it had already acquired an awesome reputation for mud and ferocious fighting. Among those who fought here were Bruce Bairnsfather and Winston Churchill. After Gallipoli, Churchill commanded the 6th Battalion of the Royal Scots Fusiliers in this sector before being taken back into the government to become Minister of Munitions. He was a very active and daring officer who spent much more time in forward, very exposed outposts than was wise for a CO.

Spanbroekmolen, the Pool of Peace, is the enormous Lone Tree Crater made by 91,000 pounds of ammonal in June 1917. A photograph taken at Bois Quarante, near Wytschaete, shows the edge of an extensive German trench system in which, the owner of the interesting nearby museum will inform you, Corporal Hitler fought in 1917 and to which he returned, with a somewhat higher rank, in 1940. All around are large numbers of what appear to be unexploded shells and other ammunition from the period. These trenches, which have been partly renovated, give a better idea of the original trenches than many in other sectors which have now largely fallen in and filled up. The book also contains a photograph of the casemate in the Ypres ramparts, near the Lille Gate, where *The Wipers Times* was printed.

But before visiting the battlefield itself the visitor will be likely to spend some time in Ypres, which on Belgian maps and signposts is called Ieper. The town is full of relics of the First World War. The Cloth Hall has been rebuilt in its original (external) form, a task which took forty-two years to complete. The interior is now filled with modern offices but there is also a comprehensive Salient 1914–18 Museum. From this a stairway leads past the belfry up on to the roof, where it is possible to observe the battlefield up to the ridge. It is not surprising that the Germans shelled both this and the neighbouring St Martin's Cathedral to rubble.

Also nearby is St George's Memorial Church, of which the foundation stone was laid by Field-Marshal Lord Plumer in 1927. The idea of building a church here originated with Earl Haig, who envisaged it as a religious centre for the large number of Britons who came to the area in the post-war years. Although every part of the church is a memorial, it is neither sombre nor depressing: it is a memorial to sacrifices almost beyond comprehension, but they are too great for emotion to have a place here.

The other great memorial in Ypres – although the town seems a memorial in itself – is the Menin Gate, on whose archway are carved the names of 54,986 dead 'who have no known grave'. Standing on the site of the former Antwerp Gate, it was designed by Sir Reginald Blomfield, who was also the architect of St George's Memorial Church. The gate, too, dates from 1927 and was inaugurated by Field-Marshal Lord Plumer. During the First World War there was no actual gate here, but the gap in the

Vauban ramparts was marked by two stone lions, one on each side. Very rightly these have now been transported to Australia, where they may be seen in Canberra. There is, however, a British lion cut in stone above the gate, and below it an inscription. Every night at eight the Last Post is sounded by members of the Ypres Fire Brigade, using silver bugles presented for this purpose by the British Legion and the Old Contemptibles Association. Usually two firemen perform this duty, but on special occasions, such as anniversaries, the number is increased to six.

The Lille Gate, although less well known nowadays, was as important as the Menin Gate in its day, when it was known as the Messines Gate. Because it was less exposed than the Menin Gate it was probably used even more in 1917; but thousands went out through both, never to return.

Poperinge (as it is now spelt) is still a busy, lively town, though no doubt less so than when the Germans periodically sent a few shells into it. It was occupied again by the Germans between 1940 and 1944, but before they arrived the prudent Poperingians had removed all the prized possessions of Toc H and hidden them. They were all put back after the war.

Another very useful guide is that produced by Tonie and Valmai Holt, who have also conducted numerous tours of the battlefields. This includes a necessary warning against picking up souvenirs, of which a number have been turned up by ploughs and put in dumps to await disposal by Belgian Army explosives experts. Many of the souvenirs look interesting and harmless: they are not. Apart from the danger of an explosion, all are contaminated by the polluted ground and a cut from a jagged edge could easily be fatal.

The Holts have examined various casualty figures and come up with surprising statistics. In the first battle (in 1914), the Germans lost 130,000 against the Allies 108,000; in the second battle the Germans lost 35,000 while the British and French lost 70,000 (of which 60,000 were British); in the third battle the British lost 300,000, and the French 8500, while the Germans lost an estimated 260,000. But, as was said earlier, no one knows exactly: what is clear is that over half a million from both sides were killed or wounded in the Passchendaele campaign.

This guide also contains details about the German cemeteries, which are tended by the German War Graves Welfare Organization. The only German cemetery in the salient is at Langemarck, and it contains 44,294 bodies, including 25,000 in a communal grave. Other cemeteries nearby are at Hooglede (8247), Menin (47,864) and Vladslo (25,664).

At Tyne Cot is the largest British war cemetery in the world, with 11,871 graves. The names of another 35,000 soldiers who have no known grave are recorded on a wall at the back of the cemetery: these would have been on the Menin Gate, but when the records were assembled it was found that there were too many for inclusion on the panels of the Gate. Tyne Cot is said to have derived its unusual name from the fact that a battalion of Northumberland Fusiliers were reminded by a nearby barn of Tyneside cottages. Inside the cemetery the visitor will find formidable German pillboxes, one of which was used as an advanced dressing station after it had been captured by the Canadians.

One of the most interesting places to visit is the Sanctuary Wood Museum, which is privately owned by Monsieur Jacques Schier. Behind the museum is a complex of the original trenches, and a few blackened tree trunks in the newly grown wood. But the most powerful memory will be that of looking into the remarkable collection of 3D pictures, mounted in wooden viewing boxes. These photographs were taken at the time, and many of them might turn even a strong stomach. But as you look, almost in disbelief, it should be remembered that such sights were commonplace to those whose fate took them to the salient in 1917.

Eventually the visitor will enter Passchendaele itself which, for no particular reason, has now become Passendale. It has all been rebuilt since 1918, but its strategic importance is still obvious. In the centre of the village is the church; the north windows are a memorial to the 66th Division.

Another useful booklet, *Ypres 1914–18*, has been produced by Mr L. Coate, head of humanities in a Sussex comprehensive school, who took parties of pupils on study visits to the battlefield and designed this guide to explain the sites they were visiting.

The area between Steenstraat and Ploegsteert, between Poperinghe and Passchendaele, is so small that all the main parts of it can be seen within a week. But few of those who go there will be content with one short visit. This small area is not merely a single battlefield: almost every few yards of it seem different from the rest.

Perhaps this is because so much is known of the events which took place here seventy years ago, or perhaps it is because, in spite of its apparent peacefulness today, the land has never recovered from the agonies men inflicted on each other here. One does not need to be particularly sensitive to feel that there is something intangible about places such as Hooge, the Menin Road, Gheluvelt, Sanctuary Wood and Messines.

The history of the world is full of war, and a visitor to battlefields needs little imagination to visualize the scenes on them during and after the battle. But in the area of the Ypres Salient no imagination at all is needed. One is simply aware of the fear, the courage, the misery, the hope, the determination and endurance which enabled men – British, Canadian, Australian, New Zealanders, French and German – to fight to the death here.

> *Death will stand grieving in that field of war*
> *Since your unvanquished hardihood is spent.*
> *And through some mooned Valhalla there will pass*
> *Battalions and battalions, scarred from hell;*
> *The unreturning army that was youth;*
> *The legions who have suffered and are dust.*[1]

Notes

1 Siegfried Sassoon, 'The Troops'.

SELECT BIBLIOGRAPHY

ARTHUR, Sir George, *Lord Haig*, Heinemann, 1928.

BARNETT, Correlli, *Britain and Her Army 1909–1970*, Allen Lane, 1970.

BARRIE, A., *War Underground*, Muller, 1962.

BATH, H., *Frankreichs schwerste Stunde. Die Meuterei der Armee 1917*, Potsdam, Protte, n.d.

BAVARIAN OFFICIAL ACCOUNT, *Die Bayern im grossen Kreige, 1914–1918*, Munich, Kreigsarchiv, n.d.

BEAN, C.E.W., *Official History of Australia in the War of 1914–1918*, Vol. IV, Angus and Robertson, 1933.

BEUMELBERG, W., *Flandern 1917*, Oldenburg, Stalling, 1928.

BINDING, R., *A Fatalist at War*, Allen and Unwin, 1929.

BLAKE, Robert, *The Private Papers of Douglas Haig 1914–1919*, Eyre and Spottiswoode, 1952.

BORASTON, Lt-Col. J.H., *Sir Douglas Haig's Despatches 1915–1919*, Vols I and II, Dent, 1919.

BRITISH OFFICIAL HISTORY, *Military Operations in France and Belgium 1917*, HMSO, 1948.

CAMPBELL, P.J., *In the Cannon's Mouth*, Hamish Hamilton, 1977.

CHARTERIS, Brig.-Gen. John, *Field Marshal Earl Haig*, Cassell, 1929.

COOPER, Duff, *Haig*, Vols I and II, Faber, 1935.

DEARDEN, H., *Medicine and Duty*, Heinemann, 1929.

DEWAR, G.A.B. and Lt-Col. J.H. Boraston, *Sir Douglas Haig's Command*, Vols I and II, Constable, 1922.

FRENCH OFFICIAL HISTORY, *Les Armées Françaises dans la Grande Guerre*, Paris, Imprimerie Nationale, n.d.

GERMAN OFFICIAL HISTORY, *Der Weltkrieg 1914 bis 1918*, Vols I–IV, Mitler und Sohn, Berlin, 1929–1936.

GLADDEN, N., *Ypres 1917*, Kimber, 1967.

GOUGH, General Sir H., *The Fifth Army*, Hodder and Stoughton, 1931.

'G.S.O.', *G.H.Q.*, P. Allan, 1920.

HAIG, Maj.-Gen. Douglas, *Cavalry Studies*, Hugh Rees, 1907.

HICKEY, D.E., *Rolling into Action*, Hutchinson, n.d.

HINDENBURG, Field-Marshal Paul von, *Out of My Life*, Hutchinson, 1920.

JONES, H.A., *War in the Air*, Oxford University Press, 1938.

KUHL, H. von, *Der Weltkrieg 1914–1918*, Berlin, Weller, n.d.

LIDDELL HART, B.H., *Reputations*, John Murray, 1928.

LIDDELL HART, B.H., *History of the First World War*, Cassell, 1970.

LLOYD GEORGE, David, *War Memoirs*, Vols I–VI, Nicholson and Watson, 1936.

LOSSBERG, F. von, *Meine Tätigkeit im Weltkriege 1914–1918*, Berlin, Mittler.

LUDENDORFF, General Erich, *My War Memories*, Vols I and II, Hutchinson, 1919.

LUSHINGTON, F. (writing as Mark Severn), *The Gambardier*, Benn, 1930.

MARSHALL-CORNWALL, Gen. Sir James, *Haig as a Military Commander*, Batsford, 1973.

OSBURN, A. *Unwilling Passenger*, Faber, 1932.

QUIGLEY, H., *Passchendaele and the Somme*, Methuen, 1928.

REPINGTON, Lt-Col. C. à Court, *The First World War 1914–1918*, Vols I and II, Constable, 1920.

ROBERTS, F.J., *The Wipers Times* (facsimile), Everleigh Nash and Grayson, 1930.

ROBERTSON, Field-Marshal Sir William, *Soldiers and Statesmen 1914–1918*, Vols I and II, Cassell, 1926.

RUPPRECHT, Crown Prince of Bavaria, *In Treue fest. Mein Kriegstagebuch*, Munich, Deutscher Nationalverlag, 1922.

SEVERN, Mark, see Lushington.

STEELE, Captain H., *The Canadians in France 1915–1918*, T. Fisher Unwin, 1920.

TERRAINE, John, *Douglas Haig: The Educated Soldier*, Hutchinson, 1963.

TERRAINE, John, *The Western Front 1914–1918*, Hutchinson, 1964.

TERRAINE, John, *The Smoke and the Fire*, Sidgwick & Jackson, 1980.

TERRAINE, John, *The Road to Passchendaele*, Leo Cooper, 1977.
WILSON, C.M., *Fighting Tanks*, Seeley Service, 1929.

A large collection of unpublished letters and papers in addition to
the above is deposited at the Imperial War Museum in London.
They include contributions from holders of many different ranks
serving in a variety of regiments.

INDEX

Abraham Heights, 122
Allenby, General, 21, 22
Allhusen, Desmond, 109-19, 126,
    128-9
Anthoine, General, 44, 119
Anzac House Spur, 79-80
Armagh Wood, 29
Arnim, General Sixt von, 44, 223
Asquith, Herbert Henry, 1st Earl of
    Oxford and, 65
Aviatik Farm, 100

Bairnsfather, Bruce, 209, 255
Barrett, Private (109th Field
    Ambulance), 195
Barron, Corporal C., VC (Canadian
    Corps), 164
Battle Wood, 45
Bean, C.E.W., 181-3
Becelaere, 100, 163, 233
Bellevue, 153, 156, 162
Bellewaard, 20, 47, 50
Bent, Lieutenant-Colonel P.E., VC
    (Leicestershire Regiment), 108
Berry Farm, 80
Best-Dunkley, Lieutenant-Colonel B.,
    VC (Lancashire Fusiliers), 48
Bethmann-Hollweg, Theobald von,
    220, 223
Birdwood, General, 108, 145, 180
Birks, Second Lieutenant F., VC
    (Anzac Corps), 79
Birr Crossroads, 27, 157, 158
Bismarck, Otto Edward Leopold von,
    2-3, 8
Bixschoote, 45

Black Watch Corner, 80
Blomfield, Sir Reginald, 256
Boy's Own Paper, The, 90
Bremen Redoubt, 81
Brigades
    1st Canadian Brigade, 164-6
    9th Brigade, 153
    10th Brigade, 123, 153
    11th Brigade, 123, 146
    12th Brigade, 142, 153
    13th Brigade, 30, 125
    27th Brigade, 92
    43rd Brigade, 56
    46th Brigade, 160
    55th Brigade, 152
    62nd Brigade, 125
    98th Brigade, 99
    197th Brigade, 140-1
    198th Brigade, 140-1
    South African Brigade, 80, 81
Broodseinde, 60, 79, 96, 105-6, 108,
    120, 121, 126, 135, 223
Bugden, Private P., VC (Anzac
    Corps), 99
Bülow, General, 10
Burman, Sergeant W.F., VC (Rifle
    Brigade), 80
Butte, the, 99
Bye, Sergeant R., VC (Welsh Guards),
    48

Cameron Covert, 125, 126
Campbell, Lieutenant P.J., 90, 95
Carton de Wiart, Brigadier-General,
    VC, 142, 153
Celtic Wood, 122, 141

Charteris, Brigadier-General John
misplaced optimism, 60, 102-3;
105, 126, 154, 169, 185, 236
Château Wood, 46
Chavasse, Captain N.G., MC, VC and
bar (RAMC), 50
Churchill, Winston, 64, 255
Clapham Junction, 47, 54, 57, 156,
157, 158
Clayton, Rev. Philip ('Tubby'), 28
Clonmel Copse, 85
Coate, Mr L., 258
Cockroft, the, 56
Colvin, Lieutenant H., VC (Cheshire
Regiment), 80
Colyer-Ferguson, Lieutenant T.R., VC
(Northamptonshire Regiment), 47
Companies
1st Australian Tunnelling
Company, 31, 68
Balloon Companies, 76
3rd Canadian Tunnelling
Company, 31
171 Tunnelling Company, Royal
Engineers, 30
175 Tunnelling Company, Royal
Engineers, 31
Coombs, Rose, MBE, 255-6
Cooper, Sergeant, VC (60th Rifles), 55
Corps
I Corps, 21
II Corps, 46, 47, 54, 56, 161, 182
III Corps, 21
IV Corps, 21
V Corps, 96
IX Corps, 60, 105
X Corps, 60, 85, 96, 105, 123-4, 125,
156
XIV Corps, 46, 57, 123, 142, 152-3,
161
XVIII Corps, 57, 82, 142, 144,
161-4
XIX Corps, 57, 119
I Anzac Corps, 35, 60, 85, 96, 121,
135
II Anzac Corps, 45, 60, 96, 119,
122, 135, 138
Canadian Corps, 106, 145, 155, 156,
160-6, 189, 232

Coverdale, Sergeant H., VC
(Manchester Regiment), 123
Crest Farm, 162
Currie, Lieutenant-General, 155, 189
Curzon, Lord, 63, 133

Dairy Wood, 122, 141
Daisy Wood, 122, 141
Davidson, General, 102, 154, 169
Davies, Corporal, VC (Royal Welsh
Fusiliers), 48
Dead Mule Corner, 115
Dearden, Captain, H. (RAMC), 196-
202
Dickebusch, 20
Divisions
1st Division, 21, 22
2nd Division, 22
5th Division, 105, 125
7th Division, 21, 60, 105
8th Division, 54
9th Division, 80, 86, 152-3
11th Division, 57
15th Division, 57
18th Division, 152
19th Division, 60
20th Division, 92
21st Division, 60, 105, 124
23rd Division, 60, 78
27th Division, 24
28th Division, 24
33rd Division, 60, 99
36th Division, 192-6
37th Division, 105
39th Division, 60, 80
41st Division, 60, 78, 92
48th Division, 57
49th Division, 60, 139-40, 145
51st Division, 48
55th Division, 81-2, 91
59th Division, 100
61st Division, 57
66th Division, 139-41, 145, 153
Anzac Divisions
1st Australian Division, 60, 78, 145
2nd Australian Division, 60, 78,
144, 145
3rd Australian Division, 60, 153
4th Australian Division, 60, 98-9,
145

5th Australian Division, 60, 98-9, 145

New Zealand Division, 122, 153

Canadian
1st Division, 164-6
2nd Division, 1, 165
3rd Division, 160-1

German
121st Division, 78

Dumbarton Wood, 79

Dwyer, Sergeant J.J., VC (Australian Machine Gun Corps), 99

Eagle Trench, 92

Edmonds, Brigadier-General Sir James E., CB, CMG, 119, 137-8

Edwards, Sergeant A., VC (Seaforth Highlanders), 48

Edwards, Private E., VC (King's Own Yorkshire Light Infantry), 55

Egerton, Corporal E.A., VC (Sherwood Foresters), 80

Elton Point, 159

Evans, Lieutenant-Colonel L.P., VC (Lincolnshire Regiment), 125

Evers, Rev. Mervyn, MC and bar, 215-17

Falkenhayn, General Erich von, 11, 40, 222

Fitzclarence, Brigadier-General, VC, 22

Foch, General Ferdinand, 12, 26, 27, 63, 180

Fowke, Brigadier-General G.H., 33, 37

Francis-Ferdinand, Archduke of Austria, 4

Frankau, Gilbert 212, 214

French, General Sir John, 26, 41, 64

Freyberg, Brigadier-General B.C., VC, 82

Gapaard, 45

Garter Point, 80

gas, 24-6, 30, 55, 78, 96, 114, 118, 128, 155

George V, King of England, 134

Gheluvelt, 21-2, 46-50, 53-8, 66-7, 78, 85, 93, 96, 123-6, 145, 156, 223

Givenchy, 39

Gladden, Norman, 242-8

Glencorse Wood, 21, 54, 56-7, 58, 79, 85

Godley, General, 144

Gordon, Huntly *(The Unreturning Army)*, 236-8

Goudberg, 153, 162, 165

Gough, General Sir Hubert, 38-9, 65, 102, 105-6, 119, 126, 136, 143, 144, 147, 154, 180-1, 183, 184

Gravenstafel, 82, 96, 100, 122

Greaves, Corporal F., VC (Sherwood Foresters), 123

Greenwood, Corporal (109th Field Ambulance), 195

Grey, Sir Edward, 6

Gribaldston, Sergeant W.H., VC (King's Own Scottish Borderers), 55

Haig, Field-Marshal Sir Douglas
early life, 40
military career, 41-2
character, 59-60, 175
diary, 45-6, 63-5, 97, 102-4, 104-5, 119, 135, 143-4, 147, 154, 162, 165, 169
letters to Robertson, 62, 130-2
motives and tactics, 13, 32, 38, 43, 131-2, 135, 184-5, 252
relations with Lloyd George, 39-40, 62, 103, 133-4, 169, 184
criticisms of, 167, 181-2, 184-5, 253, 254

Haldane, Professor John Scott, 97

Halton, Private A., VC (King's Own), 153

Hamilton, Corporal J.B., VC (Highland Light Infantry), 98

Hancock, Private F.G., VC 142-3

Hanebeek Wood, 80

Harington, General, 144

Hellfire Corner, 27, 88

Herenthage Wood, 21

Herschel, Lord, 103

Hewitt, Second Lieutenant D.G.W., VC (Hampshire Regiment), 48

Hewitt, Lance Corporal W.H., VC (South African Brigade), 81

Hibou, Maison de, 56

Hickey, Captain D.E., 124
Hill 37, 91
Hill 40, 96, 100, 122
Hill 60, 21, 29-31, 32, 37, 255
Hill 61, 29
Hill 62, 29, 31
Hillock Farm, 56
Hindenburg, Paul von Beneckendorff und von, 222, 236
Hollebeke, 22, 45, 60, 65, 225
Holmes, Private, VC (Canadian Corps), 160
Holt, Tonie and Valmai, 257-8
Hooge, 22, 27, 28, 29, 32, 47, 100, 156, 158, 210, 211
Hooglede Cemetery, 258
Houthulst Forest, 21, 142, 144, 153, 233
Hutt, Private A., VC (Royal Warwickshire Regiment), 123

Inverness Copse, 54, 56-7, 58, 79, 126, 157, 158
Inwood, Private R.R., VC (Australian Corps), 79

Jacob, Lieutenant-General Sir Claude, 163, 168
Joffre, Marshal, 10, 12, 26

Keiberg, 145
Kiggell, General, 2, 58-60, 62, 102, 119
Kitchener, Field-Marshal Earl, 36, 64, 179
Kluck, General Alexander von, 10
Knight, Sergeant A.S., VC (Post Office Rifles), 85
Kuhl, General H. von, 1-2, 183, 184, 225-6, 228

La Basse Ville, 45
Laird, Lance Corporal A., 92-3
Langemarck, 21, 65, 92, 250, 258
Law, Andrew Bonar, 63
Lekkerboterbeek, 161, 162, 163
Lister, Sergeant J., VC (Lancashire Fusiliers), 143
Lloyd George, David, 1st Earl, 39, 62-3, 94, 97, 103, 104, 132-4, 143, 161, 169, 182
Lone Tree Cemetery, 51
Lossberg, General von, 225, 228, 232
Ludendorff, General Eric, 40, 183, 184, 222-5, 226-8, 230-1, 233-4
Lushington, Franklin *see* Mark Severn
Lusitania, 220

McCormick, Private (109th Field Ambulance), 195
McGee, Sergeant L., VC (Anzac Corps), 122
McIntosh, Private G., VC (Gordon Highlanders), 48
McKay, Sergeant R. (109th Field Ambulance), 191-6
Magermeirie, 145
Maple Cross, 29
Marshall-Cornwall, General Sir James, 185
Maurice, General, 169
Maxse, Lieutenant-General Sir Ivor, 119, 163
Maxwell, Brigadier-General F.A., VC, 92-3
Mayson, Corporal T.F., VC (King's Own), 48
Menin Cemetery, 258
Menin Gate, 119, 256-7
Menin Road, 27, 45, 54, 67, 78, 96, 98, 105, 115-16, 118, 124, 126-7, 136, 156-60, 211, 246-8
Messines, 22, 32-8, 44, 51, 67, 112-15, 223
Michaelis, Georg, 220, 223
Milner, Alfred, 1st Viscount, 63
Moltke, Helmuth, 10
Molyneux, Sergeant J., VC (Royal Fusiliers), 143
Montreuil (GHQ), 56, 58, 170-9
Moorslede, 145
Mosselmarkt, 165
Mount Sorrel, 29
Museum of Peace, Croonaert, Wytschaete, 51

Nash, General, 102, 154
Nivelle, General Robert, 12, 63, 131, 134, 222, 226

Nonnen Boschen, 56, 58, 79
Norton Griffiths, Major J., MP, 32-3, 36-7, 51

Observatory Ridge, 29
Ockenden, Sergeant J., VC (Dublin Fusiliers), 123
O'Kelly, Captain C.P.J., VC (Canadian Corps), 160
Osburn, Lieutenant-Colonel Arthur, DSO, 202-7

Painlevé, Paul, 103, 133
Passchendaele village, 96, 107, 122, 126, 135, 140, 145, 153, 154, 156, 160-4, 223, 232-3, 258
Pearson, Major J.H., DSO, MC, 209
Peeler, Lance Corporal W., VC (Anzac Corps), 122
Pétain, Marshal Henri Phillippe Omer, 12-13, 61, 62, 63, 103, 137
Pilckem Ridge, 45, 50, 146
Ploegsteert, 36, 38, 65, 113, 255
Plumer, General, 35, 56, 65-7, 78, 102, 105-6, 119, 126, 136, 145-7, 154, 163, 180, 223, 256
Poelcapelle, 56, 82, 122-3, 128, 233
Poesele, 225
Polderhoek, 60, 125, 126, 141, 156
Polygon Wood, 21, 44, 54, 79, 96, 98-101, 123, 158
Pool of Peace, Spanbroekmolen, 51, 256
Poperinghe, 28, 214-5, 243, 257
Potsdown House, 80
Price, Captain T., DSO MC, 120-1, 124-5

Quadrilateral, the, 99-100, 156
Quigley, Hugh, 86-90, 95, 147-52

Ravebeek, 145, 147
Rawlinson, General R., 12, 181-2
Rees, Sergeant, VC (South Wales Borderers), 48

Regiments
    Artists Rifles, 162-3, 168, 202
    Bedfordshire Regiment, 116, 117

Black Watch, 99
Cambridgeshire Regiment, 99
Canadian Mounted Rifles, 160
Cheshire Regiment, 80
Cornwall Light Infantry, 56, 125
Devonshire Regiment, 109-10
Dublin Fusiliers, 123
Durham Light Infantry, 115
Gordon Highlanders, 48
Green Howards, 79, 108
Greenjackets, 92
Grenadier Guards, 90-1
Hampshire Regiment, 48
King Edward's Horse, 36
King's Own Regiment, 48
King's Own Scottish Borderers, 55, 80, 125
King's Own Yorkshire Light Infantry, 55, 125
King's Royal Rifle Corps, 28, 55, 111-18
Lancashire Fusiliers, 48, 216
Leicestershire Regiment, 108
Leinster Regiment, 27
Lincolnshire Regiment, 125
Liverpool Scottish Regiment, 194
Manchester Regiment, 123
New Zealand Engineers, 147
Northamptonshire Regiment, 47
Northumberland Fusiliers, 79, 125, 258
Post Office Rifles, 85
Princess Patricia's Canadian Light Infantry, 29
Queen's Regiment, 124
Queen Victoria Rifles, 30
Rifle Brigade, 28, 80, 85, 92, 255
Royal Army Medical Corps, 50, 191-207
Royal Artillery, 69, 71-6, 138-9, 141, 236-8
Royal Engineers, 114, 171, 175
Royal Irish Fusiliers, 55
Royal Scots Fusiliers, 65, 81, 86, 255
Royal Sussex Regiment, 48
Royal Warwickshire Regiment, 58, 123, 141, 156
Royal Welsh Fusiliers, 48, 108

Seaforth Highlanders, 48
Sherwood Foresters, 80, 108, 123, 211
Somerset Light Infantry, 56, 125
South Wales Borderers, 48
Tank Corps, 46, 82-4, 107, 120-1
Welsh Guards, 48
Worcestershire Regiment, 22
German
16th, 17th and 20th Bavarian Regiments, 46
Reutel, 100, 126
Reynolds, Captain, VC (Royal Scots), 81
Rhodes, Lance-Sergeant J.H., VC (Grenadier Guards), 143
Roberts, Lieutenant-Colonel F.J., MC, 209-14
Robertson, Captain Clement, VC (Tank Corps), 124-5
Robertson, Private J.P., VC (Canadian Corps), 164
Robertson, General William, 63, 103-4, 130-4, 143, 161, 178
Roulers, 39, 96, 223
Royal Flying Corps, 34, 44, 49, 76, 91, 162, 218-9
Rupprecht, Crown Prince of Bavaria, 44, 103, 183, 187, 226, 229-30, 234-5

Sage, Private T.H. (Somerset Light Infantry), 125
St George's Memorial Church, Ypres, 256
St Janshoek, 135
St Julien, 44, 48, 49, 56
St Martin's Cathedral, Ypres, 256
Sanctuary Wood, 21, 28, 29, 46, 115, 255
Sanctuary Wood Museum, 258
Sans Souci valley, 79
Sarajevo, 4
Schlieffen Plan, 7-10, 24, 188
Schuler Farm, 100
Service, Corporal (109th Field Ambulance), 193
Severn, Mark, 68-76, 94
Shankland, Lieutenant R., VC (Canadian Corps), 160

Shrapnel Corner, 115
Shrewsbury Forest, 46
Simon, Sir John, 147
Smith, Sir F.E., 64
Smuts, General Jan Christiaan, 63, 169, 180
Somme, battle of the, 11, 12, 13, 49, 138, 139, 179
Springfield Farm, 57
Staden, 96, 223
Steenbeek, 45, 48, 79, 138, 146
Stroembeek valley, 122
Strudwick, Rifleman V.L. (Rifle Brigade), 255

Talbot House, 28, 215
Talbot, Lieutenant Gilbert, 28, 255
Toc H, 28, 51, 257
Tower Hamlets, 60, 79, 92, 93, 99-101, 125, 248
Treaty of London, 6, 19
Triangle Farm, 56
Tyne Cot Cemetery, 50, 258

Vancouver Farm, 57
Vaughan, E.C. (*Some Desperate Glory*), 185-8, 249-51
Verdun, battle of, 1, 11
Vladslo Cemetery, 258

Warneton, 113
Waterend, 81, 100
Westbroeke, 136
Westroosbeke, 135, 143, 154
Wheeldon, Sergeant, DCM and bar, MM and bar, 250
Whitham, Private T., VC, 48
Wilhelm II, Kaiser, 8, 19, 21-2, 221
Winnington-Ingram, Right Rev. A.F., 199
Wipers Times, The, 209-14, 256
Wolverghen, 113
Woodrow Wilson, President T., 220
Woodward, Captain O.H. (1st Australian Tunnelling Company), 68, 108
Woolley, Lieutenant G.H., VC (Queen Victoria Rifles), 30
Wytschaete, 22, 51, 256

Yoxall, Captain, OBE, MC, 167-8
Ypres city, 6, 11, 15-17, 20-6, 210,
    243-4, 256-7

Zillebeke, 20, 115, 244
Zimmermann telegram, 221
Zondervoorde, 21, 233
Zonnebeke, 21, 96, 99, 100, 101, 121,
    122